Space, Time, and Deity

The Gifford Lectures at Glasgow 1916-1918

By

Samuel Alexander

Published by Forgotten Books 2012

Originally Published 1929

PIBN 1000341356

SPACE, TIME, AND DEITY

MACMILLAN AND CO., LIMITED
LONDON · BOMBAY · CALCUTTA · MADRAS
MELBOURNE

THE MACMILLAN COMPANY
NEW YORK · BOSTON · CHICAGO
DALLAS · SAN FRANCISCO

THE MACMILLAN CO. OF CANADA, LTD.
TORONTO

SPACE TIME AND DEITY

THE GIFFORD LECTURES AT GLASGOW
1916–1918

BY

S. ALEXANDER

M.A., LL.D., F.B.A.

HON. FELLOW OF LINCOLN COLLEGE, OXFORD

PROFESSOR OF PHILOSOPHY IN THE UNIVERSITY OF MANCHESTER

IN TWO VOLUMES

VOL. I

MACMILLAN AND CO., LIMITED

ST. MARTIN'S STREET, LONDON

1920

PREFACE

THE following work was written, and, except for some revision, in its present form, for the Gifford Lectures delivered at the University of Glasgow in the sessions 1916–18. The spoken lectures were based upon the book, but for reasons of time did not follow the text closely. I have accordingly omitted all reference to them in the division of the subject. I take this opportunity of expressing my thanks to the University of Glasgow for the honour they did me in entrusting me with the office of Gifford Lecturer ; and to my audience for the attention with which they listened to me.

The substance of various published papers has been incorporated into the book, and in several places, notably in the chapters on Freedom and Value, passages have been repeated verbally with the kind permission of the editors of *Mind* and the *Proceedings of the Aristotelian Society*.

The first volume and the first two chapters of the second were in pages before the summer of last year, and accordingly I have made no reference to Mr. A. N. Whitehead's work on *The Principles of Natural Knowledge*, nor to Mr. Einstein's generalised form of the Theory of Relativity (the earlier restricted form I have ventured to refer to) which has lately become generally known in this country through Mr. Eddington and other exponents. The original papers of Mr. Einstein appeared in 1915 and 1916, and I saw the later one, but felt unequal to it without interpretation. In any case the physical theory is beyond my province, and the metaphysical theory developed in this book, which deals with the same topic but from a different approach, is best left to tell its own tale. But, as Bk. II. ch. iii. contains an apparent contradiction to one part of the new relativity doctrine, I have added a postscript to remove misapprehension, which the reader will find on p. vii.

Some suspicion is entertained of system in philosophy, though I can see no good reason for it. This book is at any rate an attempt at system, but its fault in my own eyes is not that it is systematic, but that it is not systematic enough. Parts of it I may hope to fill out with better knowledge and reflection, in which process I have no doubt that many things in it will need to be revised or abandoned. I am most concerned for the general outline.

Criticism does not occupy a large proportion of the whole, but I have not been able to dispense with it altogether, as I should have preferred. It is, at any rate, not introduced for the sake of criticism, for which I have no taste, but in order to make my own statement clearer. Naturally enough, most of it is directed against those writers from whom I have learned most, and may, I trust, be taken by them as a mark of respect and gratitude. My general obligations will be fairly clear. Apart from these, I have, I hope, indicated where I know myself to have borrowed from others ; but there will be many places where I do not know whether I have done so unconsciously or arrived independently at similar conclusions. My work is part of the widely-spread movement towards some form of realism in philosophy, which began in this country with Messrs. Moore and Russell, and in America with the authors of *The New Realism*. It is, I think, matter for congratulation that there should be such marked differences amongst the independent workers ; because there is better hope that something permanent may be reached amongst them.

My warm thanks are due to Mr. J. S. Mackenzie, who undertook the labour of reading the whole of my proofs, and gave me valuable comments ; and to my colleague the Rev. S. H. Mellone, who read the book for me in pages. Several other friends have allowed me to consult them on special points, in particular Mr. T. P. Nunn, who did me a great service (not the first he has done me, by his writings or privately) by criticising certain chapters of the book, for which I can hardly thank him enough. I add that neither he nor my other friends are to be held accountable for anything I have written.

S. ALEXANDER.

MANCHESTER,
February 1920.

POSTSCRIPT (to Book II. chapter iii.)

In the above chapter I have attempted to refer the category of universality to the empirical uniformity of Space-Time, and have expressed this feature by saying that Space is of constant curvature. This seems at first sight to be directly contradictory to Mr. Einstein's doctrine (in his generalised form of the Theory of Relativity) that Space is warped wherever there is matter, and the more so the nearer to matter, or in other words that Space has a variable curvature. The contradiction is, however, only apparent. When I say that bodies do not change their configuration by displacement in Space-Time, I mean this only so far as Space-Time itself is concerned. On the relativity theory too, Space-Time in which there is no gravitational field is uniform (Euclidean). A body may on the view of the text undergo distortion through its relation to other bodies, as in the familiar instance of the street-urchin who, eager for a cake in a confectioner's window, finds his nose flattened against the pane. And I assume that the presence of matter in Space-Time is properly represented mathematically by the idea of warping.

On Mr. Einstein's view, as I gather, bare Space-Time is merely a limiting conception, and there is no Space without matter. It is of course of profound importance for philosophy which of the two, material events or Space-Time itself, is regarded as primary. A similar topic has been touched upon in chapter vi. of Book I.

CONTENTS

INTRODUCTION

ix

BOOK I

SPACE-TIME

CHAPTER I

PHYSICAL SPACE-TIME

CHAPTER II

PERSPECTIVES AND SECTIONS OF PHYSICAL SPACE-TIME

CHAPTER III

MENTAL SPACE AND TIME

CHAPTER IV

MENTAL SPACE-TIME

CHAPTER V

MATHEMATICAL SPACE AND TIME

CHAPTER VI

RELATIONS IN SPACE AND TIME

BOOK II

THE CATEGORIES

CHAPTER I

NATURE OF THE CATEGORIES

CHAPTER II

IDENTITY, DIVERSITY, AND EXISTENCE

CHAPTER III

UNIVERSAL, PARTICULAR, AND INDIVIDUAL

CHAPTER IV

Relation

CHAPTER V

Order

CHAPTER VI

Substance, Causality, Reciprocity

A. Substance

CONTENTS

CHAPTER VII

Quantity and Intensity

CHAPTER VIII

Whole and Parts ; and Number

CHAPTER IX

MOTION ; AND THE CATEGORIES IN GENERAL

CHAPTER X

THE ONE AND THE MANY

INTRODUCTION

THE title of this book names what is simplest in the universe, and what is, for us, most complex in it. A very large part of the book will be occupied with the mind; but I shall endeavour to exhibit minds in the order of realities which begins with mere events in space and time and ends with God. No explanation is needed for leaving the notion of deity to the end. However immediately we may be aware of God in the religious sentiment, in philosophy there is no short road to deity. But I propose in this introductory chapter to explain the reasons why I begin with Space and Time and not with mind; and by a preliminary and provisional description of the relation of mind to its objects, to show how an inquiry into this secondary topic leads on to the more fundamental one.

Philosophy, by which I mean metaphysics, differs *Philosophy and science.* from the special sciences, not so much in its method as in the nature of the subjects with which it deals. They are of a peculiarly comprehensive kind, and are revealed to the most superficial glance cast at the things or existences in the world. These things fall into groups distinguished from one another by specific characters which some have and others have not. Thus there are material bodies, ranging from ordinary things like stones down to molecules and ions, if these may be called material; there are living things; and there are beings with minds. What is the relation of these different orders of existence to one another? Is there any fundamental nature which they have in common,

B

of which they are specific examples, and what meaning can we attach to such specification? What is the primary form of being, and how are different orders of being born of it? In the next place, alongside of the diversity of kind amongst things, there are certain pervasive features, which, if they are not found in all things alike, have at least an extraordinary universality of range. Such are the permanence in change by virtue of which things are described as substances, quantity, spatial and temporal character, causality. Individuality is a pervasive character of things, but so also it would seem that there is nothing individual which has not in it a character recognisable by thought, and known as a universal. Metaphysics is thus an attempt to study these very comprehensive topics, to describe the ultimate nature of existence if it has any, and these pervasive characters of things, or categories. If we may neglect too nice particulars of interpretation we may use the definition of Aristotle, the science of being as such and its essential attributes.

But comprehensiveness within its subject-matter is the very essence of every science. What else does a science do but bring system and connection into the haphazard facts which fall within its view, elevating (to use a phrase of Lotze's) coincidences into coherences by the discovery of laws, simplifying under conceptions, unifying what is at first multiplicity? Philosophy does but carry the same enterprise to its furthest limits, and its spirit is one with the spirit of science. Two things attest this community of spirit. The more comprehensive a science becomes the closer it comes to philosophy, so that it may become difficult to say where the science leaves off and philosophy begins. In history the chronicle or newspaper is replaced by the scientific discovery, based in turn on scientific criticism of documents, of the underlying movements in men's minds. When, going a stage further, the science undertakes to exhibit the growth and change of the conception of the State in universal history, as Hegel did, it may claim to be a philosophy of history, not because it is philosophy but because it is so comprehensive. The highest generalisations in biology, in chemistry and physics are different illustrations of the same thing. Philosophy, if it is well advised, does not count these doctrines as philosophy ; it learns from the sciences what is life or matter or mental action, and its problem with regard to them is to ask how these orders of fact are related to one another and to the fundamental nature of things. But it is just because philosophy is concerned, amongst other matters, with these comprehensive ideas that the sciences at their upper limit border on philosophy.

The other witness to the unity of spirit, which makes philosophy only one though the most comprehensive of the sciences, is the historical truth that the special sciences are, at least in our Western world, outgrowths from philosophy. It is the vaguer, simpler, and more comprehensive problems which excite men's minds first, when special knowledge is more limited. Gradually specific bodies of facts are separated from the general body of knowledge which is called philosophy. In our own day we are witnessing the separation of psychology from its parent stem.

Common usage corroborates the description that philosophy like science is the habit of seeing things together. A person is said to take things philosophically who sees and feels things in their proper proportion to one another—a habit of conduct which is not always possessed by the professional philosopher. On a certain occasion Boswell had invited Johnson with some others to supper at his lodgings. But, the landlord having proved disagreeable, Boswell was obliged to change the place of meeting from his house to the Mitre, and waited on Johnson to explain the "serious distress." "Consider, Sir," said Johnson, "how insignificant this will appear a twelvemonth hence." [1] That was a philosophic answer, and Johnson had in practical conduct, though certainly not in specula-

[1] Boswell, *Life of Johnson*, July 6, 1763, vol. i. p. 422 (Oxford, 1887, ed. G. B. Hill).

tion, the philosophic mind. So true it is that, as Plato puts it, the metaphysician is a "synoptical" man.

The method of philosophy empirical.

Since, then, philosophy differs from the sciences nowise in its spirit but only in its boundaries, in dealing with certain comprehensive features of experience which lie outside the purview of the special sciences, its method will be like theirs empirical. It will proceed like them by reflective description and analysis of its special subject-matter. It will like them use hypotheses by which to bring its data into verifiable connection. Its certainty like theirs will extend no further than its efficiency in providing a reasoned exhibition of such system as can be discovered in these data. But the word empirical must not be too closely pressed. It is intended to mean nothing more than the method used in the special sciences. It is a description of method and not of the subject-matter, and is equivalent to experiential. On the contrary, the subject-matter of philosophy is, in a special and more valuable sense of the word, non-empirical. Taking it as self-evident that whatever we know is apprehended in some form of experience, we can distinguish in experienced things, as has been indicated above, the variable from the pervasive characters. I shall call this the distinction of the empirical from the non-empirical or a priori or categorial. These a priori elements of things are, however, experienced just as much as the empirical ones : all alike are parts of the experienced world. Philosophy may therefore be described as the experiential or empirical study of the non-empirical or a priori, and of such questions as arise out of the relation of the empirical to the a priori. It is thus itself one of the sciences delimited from the others by its special subject-matter.

Still less do I mean that an empirical philosophy is in some prerogative manner concerned with sense-experience. The senses have no privilege in experience, but that they are the means by which our minds through our bodies are affected by external objects.

Sensations though integral parts of experience are not the only ones. Thoughts are experienced as much as sensations, and are as vital to experience. It may even appear that there are experiences simpler and of a lower order than sensation itself; and it may be possible to indicate the precise relation of these various forms of our experience in the economy of things. A philosophy which pursues an empirical method is not necessarily a sensationalistic one. It deals with the actual world, but the parts of it with which it deals empirically are non-empirical parts of that actual world. The contrast of thought and sense is from this point of view irrelevant.

One of the most important problems, some think the most important problem, of philosophy, the problem of knowledge or of experience itself, is dictated at once by the general nature of the task which philosophy undertakes. The most striking classification of finite things is into minds on the one side and external things on the other. The relation between any member of the one group and those of the other is the relation of cognition or, in general, of experience. Mind knows or experiences; external things are known or experienced. The one is the experiencer, the other the experienced. What is this relation? Is it singular and unlike any other relation between other groups, between, for instance, any two material things, or between a living and a material thing? What is implied in the very fact of experience, in virtue of which we know all that we can know? Some have answered that experience is something unique, and have assigned a privileged position to mind. They have not claimed that privilege in its full extent for the individual minds of you and me, but they have claimed it for mind in some shape or form, whether it be the mind of God, or mind as such, the so-called universal mind. They have been impressed by the inseparability of mind and things within experience. No object, no mind: the mind cannot exercise itself in the void, but only upon some object. That proposition is accepted by all parties. But they have added ; no mind, no object : in the absence of mind there would be not only no experience in the sense that there would be no experiencer, but nothing to be experienced. Not all forms of so-called ' idealism have been so thoroughgoing as the Berkeleyan. Some have been content to insist that what is experienced is dependent on mind and to treat the experienced objects as appearances of an assumed ulterior reality. Even for Kant the world of empirical reality is a world of ideas, unthinkable therefore apart from mind. In this respect, great as was his advance upon his predecessors, he was of their family ; and the value of his achievement can only properly be realised when his doctrine has been purged of its disproportionate respect for mind and regenerated by that purgation.

Attitude t tne empirical method.

. Now the effect of the empirical method in metaphysics is seriously and persistently to treat finite minds as one among the many forms of finite existence, having no privilege above them except such as it derives from its greater perfection of development. Should inquiry prove that the cognitive relation is unique, improbable as such a result might seem, it would have to be accepted faithfully and harmonised with the remainder of the scheme. But *prima facie* there is no warrant for the assumption, still less for the dogma that, because all experience implies a mind, that which is experienced owes its being and its qualities to mind. Minds are but the most gifted members known to us in a democracy of things. In respect of being or reality all existences are on an equal footing. They vary in eminence ; as in a democracy, where talent has an open career, the most gifted rise to influence and authority. This attitude of mind imposed by the empirical method is and may rightly be called in philosophy the attitude of realism, if a name which has borne so many meanings may be so used. By whatever name the method may be called, it does not deprive mind of its greatness in questioning its pretensions. Rather it leaves these pretensions to be examined in their place ; and there is no rashness in predicting that the real greatness and value of mind is more likely to be established on a firm and permanent basis by a method which allows to other existences than mind an equally real place in the scheme of being.

It follows that for the empirical method the problem of knowledge, the subject-matter of epistemology, is nothing but a chapter, though an important one, in the wider science of metaphysics, and not its indispensable foundation.

Let me hasten to add that the contrast of the empirical method with the forms of idealism hinted at above is not in all respects, perhaps not in the gravest respects, valid of the form of idealism which, under the usual name of absolute idealism, has been and is so influential on thinking in this country. That doctrine does indeed maintain that reality is experience and penetrated with mind, lives in a medium of mind, and, whatever it is ultimately, is at any rate spirit. But it would accept with qualifications the empirical principle that minds are existences in a world of existences and alongside of them. One of its tenets is in fact that minds are no more ultimately real than material things. In truth the essence of this creed consists not so much in its idealism as in its faith that the truth is the whole, in comparison with which all finites are incomplete and therefore false. With the omission of the concluding phrase, 'and therefore false,' the proposition might be accepted by other doctrines than idealism. At least the grounds of the proposition are quite other than the grounds of ordinary idealism. I have come to believe that the foundation of it as conceived by absolute idealism is erroneous, for reasons which will, I hope, be clear as I proceed. But if I may for a moment touch a personal note I am all the more anxious not to overestimate differences from a school of thought in which I was myself bred, and to whose leaders, Mr. Bradley and Mr. Bosanquet, I owe so much of whatever capacity I may have attained, however unable I may have proved myself to see things with their eyes.

As to the terms idealism and realism, I should be heartily glad if we might get rid of them altogether:

Idealism and realism

they have such shifting senses and carry with them so much prejudice. They serve, however, to describe a difference of philosophical method or spirit. If idealism meant only that philosophy is concerned with experience as a whole, it has no exclusive title to be considered the true philosophic method ; for all philosophies are concerned with experience as a whole. The real difference between idealism and realism lies in their starting-point or the spirit of their method. For the one, in some form or other, however much disguised, mind is the measure of things and the starting-point of inquiry. The sting of absolute idealism lies in its assertion that the parts or the world are not ultimately real or *true* but only the whole is *true*. For realism, mind has no privileged place except in its perfection. The real issue is between these two spirits of inquiry ; and it is in this sense that the following inquiry is realistic. But no sane philosophy has ever been exclusively the one or the other, and where the modern antithesis has hardly arisen, as with Plato, it is extraordinarily difficult to say under which head the philosophy should be classed.

The study of mind in metaphysics.

But though we do not assume in mind any prerogative being or reality which should make other reality in some way dependent for its existence upon mind, it by no means follows that the study of mind may not be of special importance and value for philosophy. The reason is that our minds are so directly open to our own inspection, and we may become by attention so intimate with their working, that what escapes us in the external world may be observed more easily in our own minds. An illustration is found in the notion of causality. After naïvely describing how the behaviour of the sun towards a piece of wax enables us to collect the idea of a power in the sun to melt the wax, Locke says that this power may be most easily discovered in the operations of our wills, or in the power of our mind over its ideas. Locke's instinct guided him right. If you wish to discover the nature of causality, look first to your mind. You are conscious of your own power in willing in so far as you experience the continuous transition of an idea of some end into the consciousness of taking the final steps to its attainment ; for example, are aware that you have dismissed a troublesome imagination, or that an idea of some object to be attained by your action has been replaced continuously by an act which ends in the perception of the end as attained ; that experience is the experience of power or activity. You do not, as some suppose (including even Hume in a famous passage which misunderstands the argument), you do not compare your action with a notion of power or activity, and find it to be a case which falls under that designation. It is itself the experience of ← exerting power. With this analysis in our mind we may ask ourselves whether causality in the physical world is not in turn the continuous transition of one physical event into another. To do so is not to impute minds to physical things, as if the only things which could be active must, on the strength of the experience referred to, be minds. It is merely to verify under obscurer conditions what is manifest in the working of our mind. It is likely therefore that in respect of the other categorial features of things which may be shared by the mind with things, our readiest approach is through the mind, and the help may extend beyond such cases to those questions which arise out of the relations of various grades of existence to one another.

All such inquiry into the operation of mind must be borrowing a page from psychology. But we need not be deterred by the objections of metaphysical purists from gathering material from every relevant source. The problems of metaphysics are anxious enough without allowing ourselves to be disturbed by punctilios.

There are two ways of procedure which seem open to me to pursue. One is that which I have elsewhere followed hitherto,[1] to begin by examining in detail the relation of mind to its objects, always on the empirical

Alternative courses.

[1] See various papers in *Proc. Arist. Soc.* N.S. vols. viii. to xi. (1908-11) ; *Mind*, N.S. vols. xxi.-ii. (1912-13); *Proc. British Academy*, vol. vi. ('The Basis of Realism,' 1914) ; *Brit. Journ. of Psych.* iv., 1911.

method of analysing that relation in our experience of it ; and to draw from thence what indications are legitimate as to the general nature of things, and of their categorial features. The other way is the one which I propose to follow here : to examine in their order the various categorial features of existence and to exhibit the relation of mind to its objects in its proper place in the system of finite empirical existences. The first way leads ultimately, as will be explained, to this. Only by such an enterprise can the difficulties which present themselves in the problem of knowledge be satisfactorily cleared away.

I propose, however, in the remainder of this introductory chapter briefly to pursue the earlier method and to study the problem of knowledge. I do so partly because it is by that road that I have come myself to consider the larger task, and I cannot help thinking that a man is likely to be more persuasive if he follows the course of his own mental history ; but secondly, and mainly, in order to do something to meet an objection which will inevitably be taken to the other procedure. You are about, it will be said, to examine empirically Space and Time and the various categories of experience. How can you treat these as objects for the mind to examine as it were *ab extra*, when they are unintelligible except in relation to mind ? Has not Kant declared them to be forms of sensibility or understanding, supplied therefore by mind ? Nay, is not your empirical method based upon a sheer mistake ? For in the first place you are treating the objects of experience as if they could be without mind, and yet maintain they are to be open to the mind's inspection. And, as if that were not enough, you are including amongst the things to be examined not merely physical objects but minds themselves. You propose to treat the mind both as an instrument of knowledge and as its object. Before you examine the contents of knowledge you must examine knowing itself.

Now it would be a legitimate reply to these remonstrances, that the existence distinct from mind of the various groups of physical things and the existence of minds as one group among the existences of the world, as thus postulated by the empirical method, may be taken as a hypothesis for investigating reality. Without troubling our minds as to how things are related to our minds, or how we are ourselves related to our minds, let us make the assumption mentioned and see what comes of it. This is of the essence of the empirical method as a scientific method. You do not raise these questions in science. You assume the existence of life or matter and you ask what it is. Let us in philosophy make the same assumption and see whether in the end we do not get illumination as to our minds and knowledge.

This is all I need, and on which I fall back in the last resort if the hearer remains unconvinced by my version of the fact of experience itself. But in the first place I should wish to incline him from the beginning to the initial soundness of the hypothesis as expressing the nature of our experience. In the next place, it will, I believe, serve us usefully by suggestion, and in particular it will throw light on the sense in which it can be maintained that our mind is an experience for us alongside of the other existences in the world, though it is experienced differently from them.

Any experience whatever may be analysed into two distinct elements and their relation to one another. The two elements which are the terms of the relation are, on the one hand the act of mind or the awareness, and on the other the object of which it is aware[1] ; the relation between them is that they are together or compresent in the world which is thus so far experienced. As an example which presents the least difficulty take the perception of a tree or a table. This situation consists of the act of mind which is the perceiving ; the object which is so much of the thing called tree as is perceived, the aspect of it which is peculiar to that perception, let us say the appearance of the tree under these circumstances of the perception ; and the togetherness or compresence

Mind and its objects.

[1] The distinctness of these two elements was made clear in Mr. G. E. Moore's paper on 'The Refutation of Idealism' in *Mind*, N.S. vol. xii., 1903.

which connects these two distinct existences (the act of mind and the object) into the total situation called the experience. But the two terms are differently experienced. The one is experienced, that is, is present in the experience, as the act of experiencing, the other as that which is experienced. To use Mr. Lloyd Morgan's happy notation, the one is an -*ing*, the other an -*ed*.[1] The act of mind is the experiencing, the appearance, tree, is that upon which it is directed, that of which it is aware. The word 'of' indicates the relation between these two relatively distinct existences. The difference between the two ways in which the terms are experienced is expressed in language by the difference between the cognate and the objective accusative. I am aware of my awareness as I strike a stroke or wave a farewell. My awareness and my being aware of it are identical. I experience the tree as I strike a man or wave a flag.[2] I am my mind and am conscious *of* the object. Consciousness is another general name for acts of mind, which, in their relation to other existences, are said to be conscious of them as objects of consciousness.

'Enjoyed' and 'con templat

For convenience of description I am accustomed to say the mind enjoys itself and contemplates its objects. The act of mind is an enjoyment ; the object is contemplated. If the object is sometimes called a contemplation, that is by the same sort of usage by which 'a perception' is used for a perceived object or percept as well as for an act of perceiving. The contemplation of a contemplated object is, of course, the enjoyment which is together with that object or is aware of it. The choice of the word enjoyment or enjoy must be admitted not to be particularly felicitous. It has to include suffering, or any state or process in so far as the mind lives through it. It is undoubtedly at variance with ordinary usage, in which, though we are said indeed to enjoy peace of

[1] See his *Instinct and Experience* (London, 1912).
[2] The distinction is borrowed from some remarks of Mr. Stout, *Proc. Arist. Soc.* N.S., vol. ix. p. 243. See also vol. viii. p. 254, where the 'of' in 'aware of myself' is described after him as the 'of' of apposition.

mind, we are also said to enjoy the things we eat, or, in Wordsworth's words, a flower enjoys the air it breathes, where I should be obliged to say with the same personification of the flower that it contemplates the air it breathes, but enjoys the breathing. Still less do I use the word in antithesis to understanding, as in another famous passage of the same poet, "contented if he might enjoy the things which others understand." Both the feeling and the understanding are in my language enjoyed. I should gladly accept a better word if it is offered. What is of importance is the recognition that in any experience the mind enjoys itself and contemplates its object or its object is contemplated, and that these two existences, the act of mind and the object as they are in the experience, are distinct existences united by the relation of compresence. The experience is a piece of the world consisting of these two existences in their togetherness. The one existence, the enjoyed, enjoys itself, or experiences itself as an enjoyment ; the other existence, the contemplated, is experienced by the enjoyed. The enjoyed and the contemplated are together.

We have called the two elements united in an experience an act of *mind* and the appearance of a *thing*. In strictness they are but an act or event with a mental character and a non-mental object of just such character as it bears upon its face. But it is hard to speak of the perceived table except as being the thing table as it looks from a particular point of view under particular circumstances ; or of the mental act except as an act of the mind.

The anticipatory language was justified, for, in fact, no mental act is ever found by itself in the limited and precisely defined form above described ; and the like is true of the object. A mental act is only a salient and interesting act which stands out in the whole mental condition. At any one moment a special mental act or state is continuously united with other mental acts or states within the one total or unitary condition ; *e.g.* the perceiving of the tree with the sight of adjacent objects,

[margin note: Acts of mind and appearances of things.]

the sensation of the cold air, the feeling of bodily comfort and the like ; not juxtaposed with them, but all of them merely elements which can be discriminated, according to the trend of interest, within the whole mass.   Moreover, not only is the mental act continuous with others at the same moment, but each moment of mind is continuous with preceding, remembered, moments and with expected ones.   This continuum of mental acts, continuous at each moment, and continuous from moment to moment, is the mind as we experience it.   It is in this sense that we have to describe any limited element of mental action as an act of mind.   In the same way the object of the mental act does not exist by itself disconnected from other such objects.   It is not relevant for our immediate purpose that a single thing is itself but selected from a vast background.   What is relevant is that the limited object is found to cohere with other such objects, and this intimately blended continuum is called the thing, the table or tree, which appears partially on various occasions.   Even the single percept of the table or tree betrays this continuity of different separate objects with one another.   For a percept is only partially presented in sense.   Part of it is suggested by what may loosely be called memory.   The tree is only seen from one side by actual sight ; its other side is presented only in idea, in virtue of a past sensory experience of that side.

Thus, immediately, or by a union of many experiences, we are aware not merely of a mental act but of a mind to which that act belongs, which we experience in an enjoyed synthesis of many mental acts, a synthesis we do not create but find.   In like manner we become aware of a thing as the synthesis of its appearances to mind on different occasions, where again the synthesis must not be supposed to be made by the mind, but to be in the actual objects themselves ; it is made manifest to us in the tendency of the separate appearances to link themselves together.   The ultimate basis of this continuity or synthesis we shall examine in the sequel.[1]   Meantime, let us observe that once we have realised this unity of mind or

[1] Bk. III. ch. vii.

of thinghood, we can express the fundamental analysis of experience thus : that in experience things are revealed to mind under various aspects, or in various respects, and that the mind in any experience is compresent with the revelation of the world of things so far forth as it is contained in the experience.   The name object may be retained conveniently as a general name for all that is contemplated, whether it be the partial appearance of a thing, or the thing itself.

Always, however, the object is a distinct existence from *The object* the mind which contemplates it, and in that sense independ- *from the* ent of the mind.   At the same time every object implies a *mind.* selection from the world of being.   The selection may be a passive one ; only those features of the world can be revealed to a mind for which the mind possesses the appropriate capacities.   The colour-blind man may be unable to distinguish red and green, the tone-deaf man to distinguish a tone from its octave.   In part the selection is determined actively by the interests of the mind.   In the one case the objects force themselves upon the mind as a bright light upon an open eye.   In the other case the chief determinant in the selection is the direction of a man's thoughts or feelings, so that, for instance, he will not hear suspicions of a person whom he loves, and forgets the risk of death in the pursuit of duty. This selectiveness of the mind induces the belief that the objects of mind are made by it, so that they would not be except for the mind.   But the inference is erroneous.   If I stand in a certain position I see only the corner of the table.   It is certainly true that I am responsible for seeing only that corner.   Yet the corner of the table belongs to the table.   It belongs to me only in virtue of my confining myself to that aspect of the table.   The shilling in my pocket owes it to me that it is mine, but not that it is a piece of silver.   In the same way it is the engine-maker who combines iron and steel upon a certain plan of selection, but the steam-engine only depends on him for this selection and not for its characters or for its existence as a steam-engine.   On the contrary, if he is to use it, he must learn its ways and adapt himself to them for fear of disaster.

Object is, in fact, a question-begging word. It implies a subject. A table cannot be an object to my mind unless there is a mind, to which it is an object. It must be selected for contemplation. It cannot be known without a mind to know. But how much does it owe to that mind? Merely that it is known, but neither its qualities as known nor its existence. We cannot therefore conclude legitimately from the obvious truth that an object would not be perceived without a percipient, that it owes its being and character to that percipient. Berkeley saw the truth that there is no idea to act as middleman between the mind and external things, no veil betwixt the mind and reality. He found the reality therefore in the ideas themselves. The other alternative is not to discard the supposed world of reality behind the ideas but to discard the ideas, regarded as objects dependent on the mind. Either way ideas and reality are one. But for Berkeley reality is ideas. For us ideas are reality. In so far as that reality enters into relation with the mind, it is ideas.

When the prejudice is removed that an object, because it owes its existence as an object to a subject, owes to that subject its qualities of white or green and its existence ; the appeal lies from Berkeley to experience itself. So appealed to, my experience declares the distinct existence of the object as something non-mental. I will not yet say physical, for so much is not implied in every experience, for example the experience of universals or of number, but only where the object is physical.[1] But the distinct existence of my object from my mind is attested by experience itself. This is a truth which a man need only open his eyes to see.

The mind n ,- templated object to itself,   I do not underestimate the difficulty of that operation. Some of the difficulties of a minor sort will perhaps be met by the exposition itself. But the first condition of

[1] For our apprehension of the minds of others, see later, Bk. III. ch. i. B.

success is to distinguish between the different experiences which the mind has of itself and of the object. Only so can we realise that experience declares mind and things to be fellow members of one world though of unequal rank ; and this was the purpose of our reference to knowledge. To be an experiencer of the experienced is the very fact of co-membership in the same world. We miss this truth only because we regard the mind as contemplating itself. If we do so the acts of mind are placed on the level of external things, become ideas of reflection in the phrase of Locke ; and thus we think of mind as something over and above the continuum of enjoyments, and invent an entity superior both to things and to passing mental states. Such a mind is never experienced and does not enter, therefore, into the view of an empirical metaphysics. Nor is it of any avail to answer that, although not experienced, it must be postulated to account for certain experiences. The empirical method approves such postulation, which is habitual in science. But the unseen entities, atoms or ions which physics, for instance, postulates, or the molecules of the chemist, are all of them conceived on the analogy of something else which is known to experience. The mind, however, which is postulated in our case, is a mere name for something, we know not what, which claims all the advantages of the mind which we do experience, but accepts none of the restrictions of that mind, the most important of which that it shall not go beyond what is found or suggested by experience. Whatever else the evidence entitles us to say of the mind, its connection with mental acts must be as intimate as the connection of any substance with its functions, and it cannot be such as to allow the mind to look on, as it were, from the outside and contemplate its own passing states.

The possibility of introspection might seem to falsify this statement. It might be thought that in observing our own minds we were turning our mind upon itself and making itself an object of contemplation. But though looking into one's mind is sometimes described, with our

Introspec contempl. tion.

objectifying tendency, as looking into one's breast, which is a contemplative act, it is very different. Introspection is in fact merely experiencing our mental state, just as in observation of external things the object is contemplated. The accompanying expression in words is extorted from us, in the one case by the object, in the other case by our own mental condition. Now except in refinement and in purpose there is no difference of kind between the feeling expressed in the ejaculation of disgust and the reflective psychological analysis of that emotion. Replace the interjection Ugh ! by a whole apparatus of elaborated speech ; instead of the vague experience of disgust let us have the elements of the emotion standing out distinct in enjoyment, and we have the full-blown introspection of disgust. The interest which prompts that subtle enjoyment is a late acquisition, when the natural preoccupation with external things has ceased to monopolise our minds. And it is small wonder that we should regard our introspection as turning our minds into objects, seeing how largely the language which expresses our mental state has been elaborated in pursuit of practical interests and in contact with physical objects.

Introspection and extrospection. Moreover, we are sometimes victims of a misapprehension as to what it is that we introspect. I am sometimes said to discover by introspection the images that flit before my fancy or the subject of my thoughts. But the landscape I imagine, or Lorenzo's villa on the way down from Fiesole that I remember with the enchanting view of Florence from the loggia, are no more discovered to me by introspection than the rowan tree which I perceive in front of my window as I write. These objects are presented to me by imagination or memory or perception, not by introspection, and are the objects not of introspection but of extrospection, if such a word may be used, all alike. What I introspect is the processes of imagining and thinking or remembering or perceiving. Hence it is that introspection is so difficult to the untrained person to perform with any niceness, unless it is the introspection of some complicated and winding process of mind, as when we describe the growth of our feelings, as distinguished from the objects to which those feelings relate,[1] or some of the less simple mental processes such as desire where it is easy to note how the mind is tantalised by straining after a fruition which is still denied. In so simple a situation as mere sensation of green introspection can tell us next to nothing about the actual process of sensing, only its vaguely enjoyed 'direction.' The green which is the object sensed, the sensum, is observed by extrospection.

Thus my own mind is never an object to myself in the sense in which the tree or table is. Only, an -ing or an enjoyment may exist in my mind either in a blurred or subtly dissected form. When that condition of subtle dissection arises out of set scientific interest, we are said to practise introspection, and the enjoyment is the existence which is introspected. Such introspection displays the complexities of our mind as careful scientific observation of external things displays their complexities and the relations of their parts or features.

If I could make my mind an object as well as the tree, *The angel's view.* I could not regard my mind, which thus takes in its own acts and things in one view, as something which subsists somehow beside the tree. But since I cannot do so, since my mind minds itself in being aware of the tree, what is this but the fact that there is a mind, whose consciousness is self-consciousness, which is together with the tree? Imagine a being higher than me, something more than mind ; let us call him an angel. For him my consciousness would be an object equally with the tree, and he would see my enjoyment compresent with the tree, much in the same way as I may see a tree compresent with the earth. I should be for him an object of angelic contemplation, and he would have no doubt that different

---

[1] Cp. Browning's :

> " Hardly shall I tell my joys and sorrows,
> Hopes and fears, belief and disbelieving : "

these are described introspectively.

> " I am mine and yours—the rest be all men's,
> Karshish, Cleon, Norbert, and the fifty."

These are the objects of extrospection.

as are the gifts of minds and trees they are co-ordinate in his contemplated world, as external things are in mine. Now I cannot do as an angel and contemplate myself, in so far as I am mind (for, of course, I contemplate my body). But in recognising that in the cognitive relation to the tree, the tree and I are distinct and relatively independent existences compresent with each other, I am, under the limitations imposed on me, anticipating the angel's ' vision ' (I have to use mental terms for what is higher than mental and different from it). Hence I have sometimes allowed myself playfully to speak of what here I call seriously the empirical method in philosophy as the angelic method. What the angel sees as the compresence of two objects I experience as the compresence of an enjoyed mind and a contemplated non - mental object. And if you fail, as many persons appear to fail to whom I have spoken, to find in your experience the act of experiencing the enjoyment, but find only the object and nothing else ; for instance, if you find the tree but not the enjoyed perceiving of it ; the reason is that you are seeking for the enjoyed as if it were an object contemplated, and naturally can find no perceiving or imagining or thinking which stands to you in the same relation as the tree, no idea of reflection or inner sense comparable with an idea of sensation. All that you then find that can be called your self is your body. On the other hand, seek for the enjoyment as something which you mind or live through, and which you are, and, beginning with acts highest in the scale like willing or desiring, where the enjoyed act is palpable, descend in the scale through con-structive imagination to remembering, perceiving, and at last to bare sensing of a sensum, where the enjoying act is least distinct,[1] you will assure yourself of the compresence of the non-mental object with your enjoyed mind.

Experience of together-ness. But a word is needed to explain what has been omitted till now, how the fact of compresence or togetherness is itself experienced. It means the bare fact, as the angel sees it, that I and the tree are together. That together-

---

[1] I owe this point to Mr. Laird.

ness is the togetherness of an *-ing* and an *-ed* ; and this is for the empirical method the fact of their belonging together in their respective characters in the situation. But since the one term is an enjoyment and the other a contemplation, and the relation relates the terms, how, it may be asked, is the togetherness experienced ? Is it an *-ing* or an *-ed* ? Now from the angel's point of view I am together with the horse I see and the horse together with me, we are together both. But when we ask how, in the knowing relation, the togetherness is *experienced* we ask the question from the point of view of the being which has the experience, that is, the mind. Thus the mind in enjoying itself enjoys its togetherness with the horse. It does not contemplate the horse's togetherness with itself, the mind. When I say I see a horse, the object is not the horse *as seen* but an object with certain colours and shape. The horse as seen or the seen horse is a description of the horse from the philosopher's point of view in discussing the matter, not from the point of view of the experient himself. What I see is therefore not a horse which I see to be together with me. But in contemplating the horse, I, the experiencer, am experien- cing the fact of my togetherness with the horse. The horse's togetherness with me is experienced by me as my togetherness with the horse ; which I express by saying I see a horse. If we could suppose the horse to rise to our point of view he would in turn enjoy himself as together with me, that is, with what he apprehends of me ; but this would not be the same experience. It would be the horse's experience and not mine. In fact, for me to say that I contemplate the horse as together with my enjoy- ment is merely a linguistic variation, and consequently a repetition, of the statement that I enjoy myself together with the horse. I neither ought to count the relation twice over nor can I in fact do so. I experience the string which unites us only, as it were, from my own end.[1]

Before proceeding further, let us touch lightly on Elucidations.

[1] See, further, *Mind*, N.S. vol. xxi., 1912. 'On relation, and in particular the cognitive relation,' §§ 5, 6, pp. 319-323.

certain points where difficulties are likely to be felt or
doubts to be raised.

1. When in any cognitive experience the mind or
its act is said to be compresent with a distinct and
independent object which is non-mental, it will not be
supposed that the mind is as it were floated off from
connection with the body.   Nothing is said as to the
body because the body does not as such enter into
the experience.   It is commonly believed on sufficient
grounds that when I see a tree there is excitement of
the occipital region of the cerebral cortex.   But it is
certain that I do not experience this cerebral excitement
when I see the tree, and that when I experience the
cerebral excitement as such I do not see the tree, but
think of the excitement.   We are describing experience
as we have it by direct knowledge or acquaintance, not
importing into it what we may know indirectly or, as
it is said, by knowledge 'about' it.   There are indeed
experiences of the contemplated body which accompany
the enjoyment of vision, such as movement of the eyes
or their accommodation.   These are added experiences
and are not part of the experience of seeing the horse,
but are experiences of other objects, located in my body.[1]

2. The analysis of experience is claimed to be true
of any experience.   But it is often urged that the distinction of subject and object is a late experience, and is
preceded by an experience where the contrast has not
yet arisen, an undifferentiated form of "feeling" which
is below the level of relational experience.   We have,
it is admitted, only verifiable approximations to such
experiences ; if they do exist they would be comparable
to a life which was lived within itself, not needing the
stimulus of a surrounding world to which it reacts.
It may be gravely questioned whether they are rightly
described.   In some cases the object felt is a mass of
bodily states.   In other cases, which are more probably
the ones hinted at, the apparent absence of an object
distinct from the enjoyment arises merely from the
vagueness of the object, in which no specific qualities

[1] This subject is discussed in a later chapter, Bk. III. ch. iv. B.

can be detected, no parting of the mass into things with their shapes and colours and smells. Great is the importance in the mental life of the non-mental object which can only be described as 'something or other.'

3. No experience, we have said, ever is isolated or has boundaries which shut it off rigidly from the rest of the world. Rather it is true alike of the enjoyment and of its object that they swim in a surrounding atmosphere or medium. As we turn our eyes, or move our heads, or vary anyhow from one moment to another, the old vague field shifts into a new, and we have the experience of an unending or at least indefinitely shaped and uncircumscribed volume. Every experience has its fringes, or shoots out its corona into some larger whole which encircles it. Some of these surroundings are supplied in memory or imagination, some in present consciousness, and thought with its symbolic process carries us still further beyond. Even the shapes and dates of things are merged into Space and Time as wholes. We have on the side of mind, flashes of light on a dim background of consciousness ; and on the object side, more vivid or interesting particulars rising like peaks out of a continuous range of mountainous country. Thus rather than to say we are definite acts of mind which take cognisance of a definite object, it is truer to say that every object we know is a fragment from an infinite whole, and every act of mind is correspondingly a fragment out of a larger though finite mass.

4. Experience varies from that of 'something or other' through all the grades of mental life, sensation, perception, imagination, memory, thought. In each case the -ing and the -ed are distinguishable and the -ed is non-mental, and in some cases patently physical. All these mental phases are different forms of attention with its accompanying pleasure or pain. The act is cognitive not because there is any act of cognition distinct from the attention or interest, but because that interest is directed upon a cognised object. In sensation we can distinguish the sensing from its object, the sensum, which is external to it. In like manner we have on one side

3. Fluidity ev experience.

4. Enjoy- forms of attention.

the perceiving, imagining, remembering, and on the other the percept, the image, the memory, the thought, the object in every case being attested by experience itself as a non-mental existence. Many difficulties are thus raised which I dare not here discuss for fear of repetition. They will, I trust, be removed or enlightened when the mind appears in its due place in the order of things. The externality and physical nature of sensations is a particularly disputable matter ; for to some they appear to be immediate experiences utterly dependent on mind, though objective in their reference as distinguished from subjective acts like desiring or attention. I will only say that to me every mental act is equally immediate, thinking as much as sensation, and the sensum no less external and non-mental than the thought.

Images not mental.

Imagination, however, requires more than a passing mention. It seems in the last degree paradoxical to ascribe to the image of a landscape regained in the memory, and still more of one which has never been seen, an existence, in this case a physical existence, independent of the mind. However objective in character, images appear to be patently psychical, to be mere ideas and in no sense realities. Impressed by the mental character of images, philosophers have construed the rest of experience in their likeness. If an image is the creature of the mind, may not perception be equally so ? Error comes in to reinforce this procedure, for an error or an illusion is demonstrated by its discordance with reality to be a mere idea. This way of thinking has led in the past to the doctrine that the objects of our minds are but copies or representations of real things which we therefore do not know directly. When Berkeley reduced all sensible reality to ideas, representationism received its deathblow, but its influence cannot be said to have been eradicated.

The circumstances are altered when instead of beginning our inquiry into knowledge with images, we begin it, as we deliberately did, with perception, where there is less difficulty in believing ourselves directly in contact with the sensible thing. We can then construe the more difficult cases in the light of perception, passing through the images of memory which are nearer to perception because the memory is of something which was once perceived ; thence to an image of an object once experienced but presented again in imagination without the consciousness that it is familiar from the past ; and thence to the constructions of fancy. In the memory-image of my friend I have before my mind the revelation of my friend just as much as I have a revelation of him when I see him. The first differs from the second only in the absence of the friend from my organs of sight, in his removal from me in time, and further in that, not being limited and constrained by the presence of the thing to my senses, the subsidiary operations of my mind may introduce into the object features which do not belong to the thing. He is revealed to me through the haze of remoteness in Time and Space, and under the distorting influence of myself adding or subtracting or rearranging. As we pass to constructive imagination the element of personal inter-ference increases. The problems raised by the con-structive action of the mind, and, in particular, how in imagination or error we can be in compresence of an object which is a revelation of something in the world of reality, must again be deferred to their place.[1] Mean-time let us only observe that no action of the mind is possible without its object any more than a plant can breathe without air. In sensory experience compresence with the physical revelation of a physical thing is brought about through the direct operation of the thing upon the senses. In imaging the act of mind is provoked from within, but in the one case as in the other the act of mind is face to face with its appropriate revelation. The very constitution of a perceived object, as already observed, verifies this description. For it is a common-place that only part of it is sensed, the rest of the object is supplied by the action of the mind itself.

5. Lastly, the acts of mind are not colourless. They

1 Bk. III. chs. viii. and ix. B.

are different with every variation of the object. They vary according as the object is a sensum, a percept, an image, or a thought. Moreover they vary according to the qualities of the object. It is not the same act of mind which apprehends green as apprehends red, still less as apprehends sweet, and my response to a tree differs from my response to a man. Briefly, as the object varies, however minutely, so does the corresponding enjoyment vary however minutely. But this variation in the mind is not a variation of quality. The mind to experience has only the quality of being mind, that is of being conscious. This proposition is almost the same thing as saying that cognition is being in presence of, in compresence with, the cognitum. The so-called "content" of the mind is the object which is distinct from it, and is revealed to the mind, but in no other sense in the mind. I call the variation of the mind with its object a variation of 'direction,' but must leave the more exact meaning and justification of the description to a later stage.[1]

Let us now return from pursuing these hints which are intended to smooth the way for acceptance of the fundamental proposition to the fundamental proposition itself; and consider what conclusions of a more general metaphysical nature may be drawn from the character of the fact of cognition; and, further, what problems it suggests. There is nothing in the compresence between the mind and its objects to distinguish that relation from the compresence between any two objects which it contemplates, like the tree and the grass. To the supposed superior being or angel this would be obvious. We only conceal it from ourselves, as has been explained, because we fancy that the experient is himself contemplated. When we take the deliverance of experience without prepossessions, we realise that our togetherness with our object and the togetherness of two objects are so far forth as togetherness is concerned identical. The difference between the two situations is, precisely as the angel would recognise, to be found not in the nature of

[1] Bk. III. ch. vi.

the relation, but of the terms related. In the case of two physical objects both terms are physical. In the case of cognition of a physical object, one of the terms, our mind, is a mental or conscious being. When such a conscious being is in a process or act of mind appropriate to a certain object, we are conscious *of* that object. The little word *of* is the symbol of the compresence. So far then as the cognitive relation is concerned, it appears not only not to be unique, but to be the simplest of all relations, the mere togetherness of two terms, their belonging together to a world.

Not only is there a togetherness between the enjoyed and the contemplated, which is the same as that between two objects contemplated, but there is togetherness in enjoyment, as when two acts of mind are distinguished by us as enjoyed, whether at the same time (*e.g.* I see a friend and hear his voice) or in succession. If we indicate objects contemplated by Roman letters, and enjoyments by Greek ones, we have three instances of togetherness which may be indicated thus, AB, aA, and $a\beta$.

At once a problem is raised. The togetherness of Transition to problems physical things is at least, it would seem, a spatial and temporal relation; the things or events belong to one and Time. Space and to one Time. (It may be observed in passing that togetherness in time or compresence in it includes both simultaneity and succession.) Do mental acts, then, belong together in Space and Time? and is the mind together with its objects in Space and Time? It would be at once admitted that mental acts are related in time, they are either simultaneous or successive, but it would not universally or even commonly be admitted that they are spread out in space. Further, it is clear that the mental act stands in a temporal relation to its object; whether of simultaneity or succession is not obvious from direct experience. I am aware that my act occurs in time, and the event contemplated also, and the two moments belong at least to one inclusive Time. Does the experience declare that the object and the mind are correspondingly together in Space? The object is contemplated in Space.   Even if it is an image, for example of a landscape once seen, not only is it spread out, but also, however vaguely and indefinitely, it is referred to the place to which it belongs in the one Space which we both perceive and imagine.[1]   Moreover I seem to enjoy myself as being somewhere in Space, a place which with further experience I assign to somewhere in the region of the contemplated space of my body.   Whether these experiences are or are not rightly reported, at any rate the problem of whether mind like physical things is not only in Time but in Space, and of the relation of the space and time contemplated to the time and the problematical space which we enjoy, is pressed upon us for solution.

But the tale of experience is not yet completed.   Space and Time are not the only forms of relation or features of things which may make a claim to belong to mind as well as to physical things.   All the so-called categories like causality or substance or quantity belong both to the A order and the *a* order, and where that is possible to the order in which an A and an *a* are together.   Take, for example, causality, which is contemplated as between events in the physical world.   It obtains also as between the mind and some physical objects.   When I receive a sensation from an external object, I feel myself passive to that object ; I enjoy my sensing as an effect of the sensum, which is its object.   This is not a mere postulate made by philosophers for theoretical purposes—that there is an external cause of my perceptions.   It is a direct deliverance of experience, and Locke and Berkeley, who insist (particularly Berkeley) on our passivity to sensations in contrast with our activity in imagination, were rendering a fact of experience and not a dogma.   I enjoy myself as the effect of an object which acts on my senses, and only in this sense do I contemplate the object as the cause of the effect in me.[2]   Moreover, besides causality between

[1] On this last difficult point see later, Bk. I. ch. iii.   That the image is spatial in itself is enough for my purposes ; it indicates a problem.

[2] See the parallel remarks above on the experience of togetherness (p. 21), and further, *Mind*, N.S. xxi., 1912, 'On relations, etc.,' § 7, pp. 323 ff.

things and me, there is causality between my mental acts or processes ; as when the thought of my friend leads me by association to remember a reproof, which in the fashion of friends he administered to me. The causal relation, as we have before observed, is, in fact, more easily noticed and analysed as we experience it in ourselves than as we contemplate it outside us.

What is true of causality is true of other categories. We enjoy ourselves as permanent amid our changes, that is, our mind is in its own enjoyment a substance. It enters into relations within itself as well as with external things. Its processes have at least intensity : they have that species of quantity. Whether it may be qualified by all the categories remains to be seen, and is proposed as a problem. At any rate it would seem that some of them belong both to mind and to things, and that these categories, and, if it is true of all of them, that all the categories, are parts of experience which are features alike of the mental and the physical world. If this is to be regarded as a mere coincidence it is a highly interesting one and would correspond to the superior importance attached in some philosophies to these categories. Is it more than a coincidence, dependent on some deeper reason?

Some, at any rate, of the categories bring us back once more to the earlier problem. Causality is, as physical, a relation which can only be described in terms of Space and Time. What is the connection of this category with Space and Time ? Finally, is there any connection between the other categories and Space and Time ? We are thus faced again with the duty of investigating these two things (shall I call them entities or forms of relation or features of reality ?) as fundamental to any metaphysics.

Thus our analysis of the experience of experience Summary. itself has led us to two results. It has shown us that minds and external things are co-ordinate members of a world, and it has so far justified the empirical method which proceeds on that assumption. In the next place it has suggested, with the help of additional experiences all intimately connected with that analysis, that Space and Time may be in some peculiar fashion basic to all being. At the same time Space and Time, whatever they may be and whatever may be their relation to one another and to the categories, have been treated as something which can be contemplated and cannot therefore be regarded as dependent on mind, though they may be concerned with the constitution of mind as well as of external things. This is only an extension to them of the empirical method.

I have introduced this long review of mind, which is yet far too short to be convincing, for the reasons which I mentioned before, that it is the natural method of approach and the one I have followed in my own thinking. It may, I trust, have removed any prejudice against the empirical method in metaphysics. If I have failed, I can only beg that my readers will be content to treat the fundamental implications of the method as a hypothesis, a hypothesis of method. That is all that is needed for what is to follow. Let the examination be an empirical examination of the world in its *a priori* features, and without demonstration of the position taken up by any particular form of realism, let us put aside any postulate as to the nature of knowledge, and let the relation of mind to its objects develop if it can in the course of the inquiry. The outline which I have given of the analysis of knowledge will at least have served the purpose of an explanation of certain terms which may be used henceforth without commentary.

The plan I shall follow is this : I shall begin with an inquiry into Space and Time, designed more particularly to exhibit their relation to one another, and after this into the categories. This will occupy the first two Books. In the third Book I shall seek to treat, so far as this falls to the business of philosophy, the various types of existents, so as to bring out their relations to one another within Space and Time. We shall have to ask, for instance, whether the relation of mind to body is unique or not, and in the same way whether its relation to its objects is unique or not, a question already answered provisionally by reference to the fact of experience itself.

Finally, I shall discuss what can be known as to the nature of deity, consistently with the whole scheme of things which we know, and with the sentiment of worship which is directed to God. In attempting this enterprise I can but regret that I am hampered at many points by want of relevant knowledge, especially mathematical and physical knowledge, but it may well be that an outline which is defective in detail may be correct in its general movement. Whether this is so or not I must leave to the result to determine.

BOOK I

SPACE-TIME

CHAPTER I

PHYSICAL SPACE-TIME

It is not, I believe, too much to say that all the vital Extension and ura-tion. problems of philosophy depend for their solution on the solution of the problem what Space and Time[1] are and more particularly how they are related to each other. We are to treat it empirically, describing Space and Time and analysing them and considering their connection, if any, as we do with other realities. We do not ask whether they are real in their own right or not, but assume their reality, and ask of what sort this reality is. Kant believed them to be empirically real but contributed to experience by the mind, unlike the varying qualities of things which were contributed to experience from things in themselves. Other philosophers have turned to the alleged contradictions in Space and Time, and while assigning to them their due reality as appearance have denied that they are ultimately real, and have maintained that the whole or ultimate reality is spaceless and timeless. Events which in our experience appear in time, that is, are laid out in succession, lose that character in the absorbing whole. This depreciation of Time in particular is a widely spread sentiment among thinking men. When the dying Pompilia in Browning's poem wishes to assure her priest-lover of their true union hereafter, she

---

[1] I use for convenience capital letters for Space and Time when I am speaking of them in general or as wholes. Small letters are used for any portion of them (thus a space means a portion of Space); or in adjectival phrases like 'in space' or 'of time.' The practice is not without its disadvantages, and I am not sure that I have followed it rigorously.

sends him the message, "So let him wait God's instant men call years." In a famous passage Kant, speaking of our need of immortality in order to approximate to perfect virtue in an infinite progress, says, "The infinite being for whom the condition of time does not exist sees what for us is an endless series, as a whole in which conformity with the moral law is attained ; and the holiness which his command inexorably requires is present at once in a single intellectual perception on his part of the existence of rational beings." Neither the poet nor the philosopher means merely that what is years to us is a moment to God, in the same way as a moment to a man may be hours to a fly with his microscopic measures of duration. A person might well be content to be an idealist in philosophy in order to have the right of saying these noble things.[1] But all these questions arise not before but after the empirical inquiry into the nature of Space and Time, and this inquiry should answer them directly or indirectly in its course or in its outcome. At the present moment the special question of the exact relation of Time to Space has been forced into the front, because Time has recently come into its full rights, in science through the mathematical physicists, in philosophy also through Prof. Bergson, who finds in Time conceived as *durée*, in distinction from Time as measured by the clock, the animating principle of the universe. Unfortunately his conception of the relation of Space to Time is at once the most important and difficult doctrine of his philosophy and the most obscure. But one welcome consequence of

---

[1] Even Mr. Russell writes (*Our Knowledge of the External World*, pp. 166-7), "The contention that time is unreal and that the world of sense is illusory must, I think, be regarded as based on fallacious reasoning. Nevertheless, there is some sense—easier to feel than to state—in which time is an unimportant and superficial characteristic of reality. Past and future must be acknowledged to be as real as the present, and a certain emancipation from slavery to time is essential to philosophical thought. The importance of time is rather practical than theoretical, rather in relation to our desires than in relation to truth. . . . Both in thought and in feeling, to realise the un-importance of time is the gate of wisdom." I should say that the importance of any particular time is rather practical than theoretical, and to realise the importance of Time as such is the gate of wisdom.

his work is that it imposes on philosophy the duty of considering, like the mathematicians in their way, what exactly Space and Time are in their relation to one another.

Space and Time as presented in ordinary experience are what are commonly known as extension and duration, entities (let us say provisionally) or forms of existence, in which bodies occupy places, and events occur at times or moments, these events being either external or mental. We shall deal first with physical Space and Time, leaving mental occurrences to a later stage. Now in order to examine empirically what Space and Time are, it is necessary to consider them by themselves, in abstraction from the bodies and events that occupy them, and this offers great difficulty and may seem to some illegitimate. The difficulty is partly derived from our practical habits, for we are not accustomed to think about Space and Time themselves, but about the things contained in them. But it also has a theoretical basis. For we have not any sense-organ for Space or Time ; we only apprehend them in and through our sensible apprehension of their filling ; by what mode of our apprehension we shall inquire later. I shall call it intuition. It is only by analytic attention that we can think of them for themselves. This leads to two alternative or partially alternative beliefs. Sometimes it is thought that spatiality and temporal character are but properties of sensible things. Extension (to confine ourselves for the moment to this) belongs to colours and touches. In psychology this consideration has brought into authority the doctrine that our sensations, some or all of them, have a certain bigness or extensity just as they have quality or intensity. The other alternative is to declare Space and Time to consist of relations between things or entities, these entities with their qualities coming first, and Space and Time are then respectively the order of coexistence and succession of entities. This is the relational doctrine of Space and Time, and it will come up for discussion in its place, where we shall have to ask how far it is justified and whether relations of space and time (whatever they

Space and Time as experienced.

are) are relations as the doctrine suggests between things or events, or relations between places or times themselves.

At first this relational view seems imperative. The ordinary mind, impressed with things and events, naively thinks of Space and Time as if they were a sort of receptacle or framework in which things and events are found. The helplessness of such a belief, which makes the connection of things with their space almost accidental, drives us into the relational view. But whatever we may learn later about this relational view, which is of course a legitimate and workable one, it seems clearly not to represent our direct experience of Space or Time. For bodies are not only in relations of space to one another, but they themselves occupy spaces and have shapes ; and though we may regard these in turn as relations between the parts of the bodies, this is surely a theory about them and not a description of what the shapes of things look and feel like. They look and feel like extensions. But in fact the relational view is not the only permissible hypothesis. Another hypothesis as to the connection between things or events and the Space and Time they occupy places in is that Space and Time are not merely the order of their coexistence or succession, but are, as it were, the stuff or matrix (or matrices) out of which things or events are made, the medium in which they are precipitated and crystallised ; that the finites are in some sense complexes of space and time. In the language familiar from the seventeenth-century philosophy, things and events are 'modes' of these 'substances,' extension and duration. In the same way instead of supposing that extension is a partial character of a colour or a touch, we may suppose colour to be a character of the extension, that what we see is not extended colour but coloured extension. We may even think it possible, as has already been suggested, that although we on our level of existence can see extension only through colour, extension itself may be an 'experience' on a lower stage of finite existence. A world is capable of contemplation by us (though only through our thinking or analytical attention, and though we can only apprehend Space and

Time through the special senses), which is anterior to qualities and contains nothing else but Space and Time.

These, however, are speculations for the future. But enough is said to show that to consider Space and Time by themselves, abstract and difficult as it is, is not an illegitimate abstraction, but is in fact nothing but the consideration of things and events in their simplest and most elementary character. The reproaches which have been urged against Kant because he said that you may think away material bodies in Space but you cannot think away Space have no justification.[1] Difficult indeed the process is, and in practice I am accustomed in thinking of Space and Time by themselves to keep constantly pictures of material things and events before my mind and then forget their richness of colours and smells and other qualities ; and I recommend this practice to my readers.

Physical extension then is presented to us in experience as something within which bodies are placed and move, which contains distinguishable parts but is continuous, so that the parts are not presented as having a separate existence, and which is infinite. Ultimately when we introduce intellectual construction we may distinguish points within Space which again are not independent but continuous. The parts of Space are experienced as coexistent. In like manner Time or duration is experienced as a duration of the successive ; it is continuous, so that its distinguishable parts are not isolated but connected ; in

The emcharacters of Space and Time.

---

[1] These reproaches suggest a reflection. An eminent philosopher, Kant, declares that things in space can be thought away but Space cannot, and at the same time regards this Space as a 'form' of intuition (*Anschauung*). Another eminent philosopher, Mr. Bradley, declares that without secondary qualities extension is not conceivable (*Appearance and Reality*, p. 16). The conclusion is that the truth of the matter cannot depend on whether this or that person finds himself in possession of a gift denied to others, but upon the facts of experience. If Kant had maintained pure Space to be conceivable by some kind of apprehension and had not asserted it to be a subjective form, and if Mr. Bradley had not denied it altogether to be conceivable in its own right, both of them would have been in fact right. But the decision is a matter of fact and can only be made by examination of the facts conducted with the help of hypothesis.

the end it may be distinguished into moments or instants with the help of intellectual construction, and its parts are successive, and, like Space, it is infinite.

The continuity and infinitude of Space and Time thus spoken of as presented in experience are crude, original characters [1] of them. They do not in themselves imply, though still less do they deny, a theory of the nature of a continuum or an infinite, such as is current in the mathematics of the day. There is something in Space and Time of the nature of uninterruptedness which can be described by no other word than continuity ; and something which is described by the word infinity. Mathematical theories of them are arrived at in the effort to render these crude characters into terms of thought, and they come to crown a precedent reflection which is already contained in ordinary experience of Space and Time.

Spaces and times are apprehended in the first instance just as other things are, if not by sense, at any rate through sense. But sense carries us but a little way in this experience. Only finite spaces and times are presented through sense. But even so our senses give us such evidence as they can of these original characters. For no finite space or time is experienced without a surrounding space or time into which it sensibly flows. And every finite time or space is sensibly continuous or uninterrupted ; it is not an aggregate of parts, but something in which parts can be distinguished as fragments of the whole.

Our further ordinary experience of Space and Time involves the recognition of elements given to us in thought. When we proceed to speak of Space and Time as continuous wholes and distinguishable into points or instants, we are going beyond what we learn through sense and employing ideas, or what are sometimes called intellectual constructions, and are employing also thoughts in the special and proper sense of concepts. Nor is there any reason, supposing the ideas to be well chosen, why we should not do so. For the simplest objects of experience are full of our ideas. A thing of a certain sensible colour

[1] A remark to much this effect which I heard in a discussion induces me to make this explicit statement by way of clearness.

and shape is seen as a man. Half the object is ideal, due to our interpretation of what we see. What we perceive is the object which we sense as supplemented by what we image or think. Space and Time are only in the like case with other experienced things, and to apprehend them we need to use imagination and conception. I can see and touch only limited spaces. But I discover that one space is continuous with another, or is included within a larger space, and I can think of a very large space, such as a country two hundred miles square, partly by imagination but largely by conceptions founded on experience of the plan of construction of one space out of smaller ones, and on exact measures of length. We take a sensible space and elaborate and extend it by ideas and concepts. It is still plainer that infinite Space is apprehensible only with the help of thought. Similarly there are no perceptible points or instants, but only durations and extents. But we discover in experience that an extent or a duration admits division continually. Space and Time are so constituted. Accordingly we can construct the idea of a point or instant in a way the reverse of that by which we construct an infinite Space or Time. We start with a finite extent or duration, we imagine it divided, and then we interpret this imagination by the concept that there is no end to the division. A point is thus something which, founded on apprehended reality, is constructed by an act of analytical imagination, which involves also besides the image or idea of a point, the concept of point as the element out of an infinitude of which an extent is made. Such an intellectual construction, or construct, is legitimate, provided at least we make no assumption that the point or the instant can be isolated from other points or instants. By using the constructive idea of point or instant we do not falsify the experienced object, Space or Time, but dissect it into its elements, following the plan of its construction. We must not imagine that the elements are unreal because they are ideal constructions, as the word construction is apt to suggest, any more than we must imagine that a man's back is unreal because I do not see it but only imagine it or have it in idea. For sense has no monopoly of reality. We reach reality by all our powers. All we have to be sure of is that we use them rightly so that the whole, by whatever powers of ours it is apprehended, shall be itself and self-consistent. When we come to the mathematical treatment of Space and Time we shall return to these intellectual constructions.

Infinity
d on
tinuit as
compre-
hended.

The infinitude of Space or Time is another of their experienced features and like their continuity is a percept extended by thought. It is indeed the other side of their continuity. It expresses not their uninterruptedness but their single wholeness. And, as with continuity, our thinking discovers but does not make, it only finds, an element in Space which is not discoverable by unaided sense. The sensible or perceptual datum is that each finite space is part of a wider one. The infinite Space is the perceptual datum as qualified by the introduction of this conceptual element. The something or other which we feel to be the larger space of which a finite space is a fragment becomes extended into totality. Thus the infinity of Space does not merely mean that we never can reach the end of it however far we go, though it implies that as a consequence. That would be to describe Space in terms of our infirmity. But we are not concerned with our ways of thinking Space but with Space itself. The infinite Space is thus the positive object of which the finitude of any given portion, apprehended as finite, is the limitation. Infinite Space is positive ; finite space is negative. The infinite is not what is not finite, but the finite is what is not infinite. In this sense Space (or Time) is presented as an infinite thing which is prior to every finite piece of it. " How can finite grasp infinity ?" asks Dryden. He had already been answered by Descartes that however difficult to comprehend, the Infinite is known or apprehended directly and before the finite things which are easier to *comprehend*. It is thus that infinite Space is given to us in experience.

To *comprehend* it, reflective (mathematical or philosophical) thought is needed which does not merely embody a formulation of the surface aspect of space- or time - experience, (for that is all the thought that is needed to be aware of infinite Space, so patently is its infinitude displayed), but analyses and probes. What philosophers have adumbrated in this regard, the mathematicians have made luminously clear. Space is infinite because it is self-contained. Choose any selection of its parts according to some law of selection and you find that that selection is itself infinite and contained within the original. It is thus that the sphere or the circle have been used as symbols of a totality because they return with revolution into themselves. An infinite class is defined by mathematicians as one to which a class can be found corresponding, one to one, to the original class and yet a part only of the original class. The series of integral numbers is infinite, not because it has no end,— a mere mental or subjective criterion,—but for that reason. Double, for instance, all the numbers of the series 1, 2, 3, etc. The series 2, 4, 6, etc., corresponds to the whole series one to one, but falls wholly within it as a part of it. In this case on account of the infinity of the derived series we cannot say that the whole is greater than its part. Whereas if we take a finite series, 1, 2, 3, 4, the doubles of these numbers fall some of them outside the original series, and there is no operation we can perform on them which will yield a different result. Space and Time are infinite in this comprehensible and again perfectly empirical sense.

In like manner, reflective thought attempts to comprehend the given apprehended feature of continuity of Space or Time (or any other continuum). But for convenience I defer the few remarks I can make upon this difficult matter to a later page.[1] It is enough to say that, in a continuum, between any two members another can be found.

Space and Time then are presented to us as infinite and continuous wholes of parts. I shall call these parts points and instants, availing myself of the conceptual description of them, and meaning by their connectedness or continuity at any rate that between any two points or

[1] Ch. v. p. 147.

instants another can be found. To me, subject to what may be said hereafter, this is a way of saying that the points and instants are not isolated. But if any reader jibs, let him substitute lengths and durations ; he will find that nothing is said in what follows except what follows equally from the notion of parts.

The interdependence of Space and Time. (me and Space.

Other features will declare themselves as we proceed, some obvious, some less so. But they will be found to require for their understanding the understanding of how Space and Time are related to each other. These are often thought, perhaps commonly, to be independent and separate (whether treated as entities as here or as systems of relations). But a little reflective consideration is sufficient to show that they are interdependent, so that there neither is Space without Time nor Time without Space ; any more than life exists without a body or a body which can function as a living body exists without life ; that Space is in its very nature temporal and Time spatial. The most important requirement for this analysis is to realise vividly the nature of Time as empirically given as a succession within duration. We are, as it were, to think ourselves into Time. I call this taking Time seriously. Our guides of the seventeenth century desert us here. Besides the infinite, two things entranced their intellects. One was Space or extension ; the other was Mind. But entranced by mind or thought, they neglected Time. Perhaps it is Mr. Bergson in our day who has been the first philosopher to take Time seriously.

Empirically Time is a continuous duration, but it is also empirically successive. Physical Time is a succession from earlier to later. As Mr. Russell points out,[1] the succession from past through present to future belongs properly to mental or psychical time. But so long as we take care to introduce no illegitimate assumption we may conveniently speak of past, present, and future in physical Time itself, the present being a moment of physical Time fixed by relation to an observing mind and

[1] *The Monist*, vol. xxv., 1915, 'On the Experience of Time,' pp. 225 ff.

forming the boundary or section or cut between earlier and later, which then may be called past and future. In a manner, earlier and later are, as it were, the past and future of physical Time itself. I shall therefore use liberty of phrase in this matter. Now if Time existed in complete independence and of its own right there could be no continuity in it. For the essence of Time in its purely temporal character is that the past or the earlier is over before the later or present. The past instant is no longer present, but is dead and gone. Time's successiveness is that which is characteristic of it as empirically experienced, in distinction, say, from Space, which also is continuous. This is the plain conclusion from taking Time seriously as a succession. If it were nothing more than bare Time it would consist of perishing instants. Instead of a continuous Time, there would be nothing more than an instant, a now, which was perpetually being renewed. But Time would then be for itself and for an observer a mere now, and would contain neither earlier nor later. And thus in virtue of its successiveness it would not only not be continuous but would cease even to be for itself successive. If we could suppose an observer and events occurring in time, that observer could distinguish the two 'nows' by the different qualities of the events occurring in them. But not even he could be aware that the two 'nows' were continuous, not even with the help of memory. For memory cannot tell us that events were connected which have never been together.

Descartes did, in fact, declare the world to be perpetually re-created. For him the idea of a Creator presented no problem or difficulty, and with his imperfect grasp of the real nature of Time the step he took was inevitable and imperative. For us the case is not the same, even if re-creation at each moment by a Creator left no difficulty unsolved. But in any case the universe at the stage of simplicity represented by mere Time and Space has no place for so complex an idea as creation, still less for that of a supreme Creator. Time and Space are on our hypothesis the simplest characters of the world, and the idea of a Creator lies miles in front.

Thus the mere temporality of Time, its successive-ness, leaves no place for its continuity or togetherness and seems to be contradictory to its continuity. Yet the two are found together in Time as we experience it. If, therefore, the past instant is not to be lost as it otherwise would be, or rather since this is not the case in fact, there needs must be some continuum other than Time which can secure and sustain the togetherness of past and present, of earlier and later. ('Togetherness' here is used obviously to mean merely connection and not as in ordinary usage contemporaneity.) This other form of being is Space ; that is, Space supplies us with the second continuum needed to save Time from being a mere ' now.'

The same conclusion follows if, for instants, we sub-stitute durations. The earlier duration, if Time stood by itself, would not be continuous with the later. We should but have a duration, a particle of time, per-petually re-created. There would then, moreover, be the additional problem of how a particle of duration could be temporal if it did not itself exhibit differences of before and after.

It was not open to us to say that since the successive-ness of Time and its continuity are contradictory Time is therefore not real but only appearance. Time is an object given to us empirically. We had thus to ask whether this Time is independent of Space, as it appeared to be. With the necessity of Space to the existence of Time the contradiction is removed. It may, in fact, be suggested that the reason why Time and Space are believed to be contradictory in themselves is that the Time and Space in question are not really Time or Space, as they are experienced. Time is considered apart from Space and Space from Time.

The only other way of evading the force of this analysis of facts is on the relational view of Time where an instant is defined by events in relation. But this method is contrary to our hypothesis, and it would be out of place to consider the alternative here.

One word to anticipate misunderstanding. I said that to supply continuity to the successive there must be a non-successive continuum, simulating by the word 'must' the deductive form. But I am making no attempt to prove the existence of Space. There is no room for 'must' in philosophy or in science, but only for facts and the implications of them. I might have said simply the continuity is, as a matter of fact, supplied by the connection of Time with the other continuum Space. The apparent 'demonstration' was a piece of analysis of an entity given in experience.

But if Time cannot be what it is without indissoluble (2) Space relation to Space, neither can Space be except through and Time. indissoluble connection with Time. For Space taken by itself in its distinctive character of a whole of co-existence has no distinction of parts. As Time in so far as it was temporal became a mere 'now,' so Space so far as merely spatial becomes a blank. It would be without distinguishable elements. But a continuum without elements is not a continuum at all. If Space were without elements it would be open to the difficulties urged with so much force against Spinoza's conception of the infinite Substance or of its attributes : that it swallowed or absorbed everything which might be said to be contained in it, but left no means for the existence within it of the multiplicity of things or indeed of anything. Thus the empirical continuity or totalness of Space turns out to be incompatible with the other empirical feature of Space, that it contains distinctness of parts. That distinctness is not supplied by the characteristic altogetherness of Space. There must therefore be some form of existence, some entity not itself spatial which distinguishes and separates the parts of Space. This other form of existence is Time. Or in order once more to avoid the appearance of an attempt to demonstrate the reasons for the universe, let us say that Time is discovered to supply the element in Space without which Space would be a blank.

Thus Space and Time depend each upon the other, but for different reasons. But in each case the ultimate reason of the presence of the other is found in the continuity which in fact belongs to each of them as we find them in fact. Without Space there would be no connection in Time. Without Time there would be no points to connect. It is the two different aspects of continuity which compel us in turn to see that each of the two, Space and Time, is vital to the existence of the other.

It follows that there is no instant of time without a position in space and no point of space without an instant of time. I shall say that a point *occurs* at an instant and that an instant *occupies* a point. There are no such things as points or instants by themselves. There are only point-instants or *pure events*.[1] In like manner there is no mere Space or mere Time but only Space-Time or Time-Space. Space and Time by themselves are abstractions from Space-Time, and if they are taken to exist in their own right without the tacit assumption of the other they are illegitimate abstractions of the sort which Berkeley censured. How they come to be distinguished apart from one another and on what terms this is legitimate and useful will appear in due course. But at least they are not merely two concurrent though correlated continua. The real existence is Space-Time, the continuum of point-instants or pure events.

Repetition in Space and Time.

The characters which Space and Time present to experience and the relation of the one to the other as founded on those characters are not exhausted by the simple statement that each is necessary to the existence of the other. So far as the exposition has gone, their correspondence might be a one to one correspondence, to each instant a point. As a matter of fact it is a one-many correspondence. One instant may and does occupy several points, that is, Time is repeated in Space. In the more familiar but less elementary and more complex language of our experience of things and events with their qualities, several such physical events may occur in different places at the same time. Again Space is repeated in Time; one point may and does occur

---

[1] I speak of pure events in distinction from events with qualities or 'qualitied' events, *e.g.* a flash of red colour.

at more than one instant ; or to revert to the familiar language of unspeculative experience, several events at different times may occupy the same place. Time, as it were, returns to its old place at a later instant. These mere empirical facts are sufficient to show that the correspondence of point to instant is not one to one. Now it may be seen that our previous statement of the relation of Space and Time was defective, and besides not making provision for the repetition of Space in Time and Time in Space, would be insufficient even to account fully for the continuity of either Space or Time, either an extended continuum or a successive one.

If the correspondence were unique, neither would Space be able to perform its office of saving the instant from perishing, nor Time its office of saving Space from blankness. For each would in that case be " infected," if I may borrow from Mr. Bradley a picturesque habit of speech, with the character of the other. Consider Time first. If the point corresponded uniquely to the instant it would share the character of the instant, and Space would cease to be the Space we know. The point would lack that element of permanence, that is, independence of its particular instant, in virtue of which it can as it were detain the instant and save it from perishing utterly and being a mere 'now' without connection with other instants. But the repetition of a point at many instants, its recurrence, secures to the point this capacity ; or if the more demonstrative form of words be preferred, in order that Time should linger Space must recur, a point must be repeated in more than one instant. All that our previous analysis effected was to show that a continuous succession depended on something different in itself from a succession. But just because of its intimacy of relation to Time, this something different must be something more than merely different from Time, and that more which it has is what I shall call, for reasons to be made clearer hereafter, the intrinsic repetition of a point in several instants.

Similarly, if there were unique correspondence, Time would share the character of Space, be infected with bare blank extendedness, would in fact be mere extension and cease to be the Time we know, which is duration in succession. In order that it should be in its own nature successive and so be able to discriminate points in Space, the instant of Time must be repeated in or occupy more points than one ; that is to say, the occupation by an instant of several points gives 'structure' to the instant, and thereby enables it to distinguish one point of space from another.[1]

This abstract or elementary relation of Space and Time lies, it will be seen, at the bottom of our experience of empirical substances. They possess temporal permanence and spatial structure : the parts of a substance are always changing. There would be no substance were it not that at any instant of its life several parts were of the same age, and each part of its space could be occupied by different moments of time. If the substance changed all at once and its parts were not repeated in time, or if none of its parts occurred together at the same instant it would not be a substance. What I have done above is to exhibit these same relations in respect of any part of Space and Time themselves. Later on we shall realise the importance of this analysis of permanent structure in things, when we come to speak of categories, a topic which I must not here anticipate.

The three dimensions of Space, and the characters of one-dimensional Time.

The relation of Space and Time is, however, still more intimate. So far as we have gone Space might be one-dimensional like Time, but physical Space as presented in experience has three dimensions. Time also, besides being a one-dimensional continuum of duration in succession,[2] has two other features as experienced. It is irreversible in direction, that is, an instant which is before another cannot be after it. In technical phrase the relation of instants is

---

[1] Observe that only the point or the instant is repeated. The point-instant is not repeated.

[2] By succession I mean bare succession. In ordinary usage a succession would be understood to include the two other features of irreversible direction and betweenness.

asymmetrical. Secondly, each instant is *between* two instants, before the one and after the other ; or, to put the same thing otherwise, the relation of 'before' is transitive, that is, if an instant A is before an instant B, and B before C, A is before C. Now the three dimensions of Space are, considered spatially,[1] independent : position may vary according to each independently of the others. To say that Space is a three-dimensional form of externality is the same thing as to say there are three independent one-dimensional forms of externality. It is not so obvious that the three features of Time, its successiveness, the irreversibility of the succession of two instants, and the transitiveness of 'before,' or 'betweenness,' are independent. The second is clearly enough different from the first, there is nothing in the relation of successiveness as such which makes it irreversible. But even if Time is irreversible it is not necessarily uniform in its direction. The movement of Time might be pendular, and a movement might be from A to B and from B to C and both irreversible, but that from B to C might be in the opposite direction in spatial representation. It would not in that case necessarily be true that if A is before B and B before C, A is also before C.

| C | A | C | B | C. |

Any of the three relative positions of C is possible, and it could not be said whether A is before or after C—the relation of A to C is indeterminate. In fact, movement in time might be subject to constant reversals of direction by jumps, and any one interval would be irreversible, but the whole Time not uniform in direction, which is necessary to 'betweenness.'

Now the three features enumerated in Space and Time being independent, we might content ourselves with saying that as between spatiality and successive duration there subsists such a connection of interdependence that each new feature in Time is rendered possible by a new dimension of Space and conversely renders it possible. But I do not like to leave the matter in this vague

---

[1] See note 1 on p. 59 for the reason of this limitation.

condition ; and therefore I shall try to make the connection of Time's properties and the dimensions of Space more explicit ; hazardous as the undertaking is. It is essential to bear in mind the one-dimensionality of Time and the independence of the three dimensions of Space of one another. I shall use capital letters to designate instants and small ones to designate points.

Irreversi-
bility of
Time and
a second
dimension
of Space.

, Let us begin with the fact of irreversible, that is, determinate, order in time ; we can see then that a one-dimensional Space would not suffice to secure it. aA and bB are two point-instants. The points a and b which occur at those instants suffice to distinguish the instants as well as making them possible, but not to determine whether A is prior to B or posterior. So far as the points are concerned A might be before or after B in time. ⤫ For the instant A is repeated in space at say the point a_1, and if there were only one dimension of Space and we take the line ab as we may to represent the time-dimension as well, there would be nothing to distinguish aA from a_1A, which has the same time. But a_1 might be on the other side of b from a and thus A might be either before or after B.[1] Hence since the order is irreversible it follows that the instant A cannot be repeated in the one-dimensional line ab. For it is clear

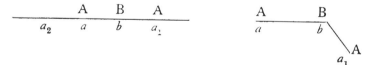

that A cannot be repeated at two points a and a_2, both on the same side of b, because in that case their dates

---

[1] I assume the one-dimensional Space to be spatially ordered, as it empirically is (for our inquiry is an empirical analysis). Since order of Space is said later (p. 56) to be due to Time this may seem to be a circular procedure ; but it is not really so. The argument is that, empirical Time being intrinsically repeated in Space, its irreversibility is not secured by a one-dimensional Space, but requires a second dimension. In the end we see that its irreversibility in one-dimensional Space as expressed in the difference of right and left implies a second dimension, and that a one-dimensional Space is in fact an abstraction.

would be different.[1] Now with a second dimension of Space A can be repeated outside the line *ab*, and since this second dimension is independent of the first, the possible contradiction is removed. The point *a* is before *b* so far as one dimension is concerned, and the point a_1 before *b* so far as the other is concerned. The second dimension is accordingly not only necessary but sufficient. Thus if succession is irreversible there needs more than one dimension of Space.

Conversely if Space has two dimensions succession is irreversible. Let XB now represent the one-dimensional time-line, X and B occupying the points *x* and *b* ; and let *a* be a point outside *xb* occurring at the instant A, which is before B.[2] Now every point is repeated in time and *a* therefore occurs at some other instant A_1 which may

$$a \ (A)$$

X	A_1	A	B	A_1
			b	

x

be represented on the time-line on either side of B from X. But unless the order in time is irreversible there is nothing to distinguish A from A_1 since they both occupy the same point, though the two point-instants are different. A might be before B or after it, so far as Space is concerned.

[1] This does but represent the empirical fact that in a motion in one dimension no date recurs on the line. A friend who has favoured me with valuable criticism urges that this assertion is made without sufficient ground. In a purely one-dimensional Space, *a* and a_2 might still be on the same side of *b* and yet contemporaneous, that is, have the same instant. We might imagine a subsequent movement along *ab* which arrived at a_2 at the same moment as the previous movement at *a* ; for instance puffs of smoke might be blown along at intervals. But directly we realise the extreme simplicity of the data we are dealing with, we see that such a suggestion implies the ordinary three-dimensional world we are familiar with. We should be thinking in terms of physical things and their movements in Space, not of the pure movements which constitute Space-Time itself. Whereas we are in this inquiry watching in thought the generation of Space in Time, and we cannot go back and think of the world as beginning over again.

[2] The instant of *a* is represented on the time-line A. I write A beside *a* in the figure, but in brackets, merely to indicate that *a* has an instant.

There must be something therefore in Time to distinguish
the two-point instants aA and aA$_1$.   This is secured by
the irreversibility of the time-order.   A$_1$ is after B, or if
before B at a different date from A.

Note in passing and by way of introduction to what
follows that nothing has been said as to whether A is or is
not before A$_1$.   All we need is that A$_1$ if after B shall not
also be before B, and irreversibility secures this.   It is
therefore not only necessary for distinguishing aA from
aA$_1$, but it is sufficient for the purpose.

Betweenness of
Time and
a third
dimension
of Space.
The third correspondence, that of the betweenness of
Time to a still further independent dimension of Space, is
more difficult to establish.   Suppose, in the first place, that
succession possesses betweenness or is a transitive relation.
Then it may be seen that two dimensions of Space are
insufficient.   Let there be a movement in such Space
from a to b and from b to c, so that the instant A of a is
before B and B before C.   Since Time is one-dimensional
we may represent times, as was done before, on the line
ab ; and on this C also may be represented.   Now the

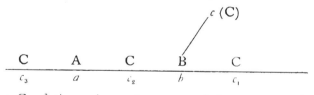

instant C of the point c is repeated in space, and not in
the line bc, and since ab represents the time-line, we may
represent the various repetitions of C in space by points
on the line ab.   But C is then represented ambiguously
by any one of the three points c_1, c_2, or c_3.   For whichever
of the points repeats the time C, the postulate of irreversible succession is satisfied.   If C is at c_3, A is before B,
but B may still be before C, for Time may change its
direction within the line ab, but still C will be after B.
So, for example, there is irreversible succession in the
swings of a pendulum, but as represented by the excursion
the time changes its direction.   There is irreversible order
in each of the two times AB, BC ; but there is no betweenness unless C falls at c_1.   There is thus no guarantee

of betweenness of Time if the repetition of C be confined to two-dimensional Space. But this is possible if C be repeated outside the plane *abc*. Moreover, since the third dimension is a new dimension and independent of the other two, the necessary condition is also sufficient. For if the relation of A, B, and C is transitive, we must represent the priority of B to the instant C in the new independent dimension by the same spatial convention as we represent priority on the line *ab*, that is, C occupies c_1 and not c_2, or c_3.

Conversely, if Space is three-dimensional Time is transitive, there is not merely irreversibility of direction in Time but uniformity of direction. Let the line XB represent the time-line, these being the instants of *x* and *b*. B is before C, which is the instant of the point *c*, and there is a point A

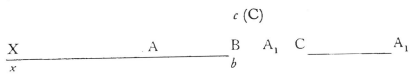

$$c \; (C)$$

X ————————————— A ———————— B A$_1$ C ————————— A$_1$

x   b

outside the plane of the paper whose time A is before B. But *a* is repeated in time at the instant A$_1$, which may be represented on the time-line on either side of C from B. Whether *a* occurs at A or A$_1$ there is irreversibility of succession. But there is nothing so far as Space is concerned to distinguish A and A$_1$ since they occupy the same point *a*, although the point-instants *a*A and *a*A$_1$ are different point-instants. Hence if we only know that *a* occurs at an instant A before B, we cannot tell where that instant is to be represented on the one-dimensional time-line, unless there is some property of Time which is different from irreversibility. On the other hand, betweenness secures the definite place of *a* upon the time-line, and is thus not only necessary but sufficient if there is to be a third and independent dimension of Space. As in the earlier case of the proof of determinate order as necessary with a second dimension, the reasoning depends on securing the unambiguous distinction of point-instants. For no point-instant can be repeated, while both the point and the instant may.

It follows as a matter of course that since every instant is connected with other instants continuously, in definite order and in the transitive relation, every point is related to other points in three dimensions, and is therefore voluminous. The physical point is in fact the limit of a volume.

Order. It is difficult in discussing the elementary relations of Space and Time to avoid questions which belong to a later stage of our inquiry. One such question will have at once arisen in the minds of some. Irreversibility and betweenness have been on the faith of experience attributed to Time, and tridimensionality to Space. But why, it may be asked, is not Space credited with irreversibility of order and betweenness? Certainly if a is to the right of b, b is not to the right of a; and if a is to the right of b and b to the right of c, b is between a and c. Has not the character of Time been represented by a line in Space so as to imply these characters of points of Space? The truth is that these are characters of order, and are so because they belong intrinsically to Time, and they belong to order because all order presupposes Time. Points in space are ordered in virtue of their time-character. This does not mean that they assume an order through our act in arranging them or selecting them by a process which takes time. Our procedure in dealing with positions in space or time has nothing to do with these positions themselves; at least it is the hypothesis of the present inquiry that the mind is merely contemplating what it finds in Space and Time. Our proposition means that positions in space are really ordered themselves, but that they are so ordered in virtue of the time-character which is essential to them. Merely as points, as positions in space, they do not possess order, any more than instants merely as temporal possess position in time—supposing that it is possible to think of points apart from their time or instants apart from their space, which we have seen it is not. Order arises out of the temporal character of positions in space; and it is this fundamental or elementary order which is presupposed in any order of more complex or qualitative things which are in any way ordered, like pebbles in a row, or terms in a progression, or officials in a hierarchy.[1]

Let me, at the conclusion of this inquiry (which, be   A caveat. it observed, is entirely non-mathematical) into the precise relation between Space and Time, once more remark that it contains no attempt at a construction of Space and Time, as if we were giving reasons for them and for their experienced features, and in a manner affecting to preside over their creation. Such an attempt would be as foolish as it is unscientific. I have merely attempted to show how the various features of the one depend for their character on those of the other. The reason why Space has three dimensions is that Time is successive, irreversible, and uniform in direction. If we could imagine a Creator who had determined to make Time an asymmetrical transitive succession, he would, to carry out his purpose, have made a Space of three dimensions ; and *vice versa* if he had determined to make a three-dimensional Space he would, to carry out his purpose, have made Time a transitive asymmetrical succession. This does not mean that one who knows the characters of Time could conclude from them to the three dimensions of Space, but only that he finds on examination that there is an intimate relation between the one and the other, a relation which requires reflective analysis to discover. The word 'must' or 'needs' which I have occasionally used means no more than that we are forced to look for something, which we may or may not find. We cannot say that Time implies Space in the sense in which the working of two laws in conjunction implies their resultant. The point is of sufficient general importance to be worth a few remarks even here. Suppose a man thought, I will not say that he could see a reason why there must be Space, but that he could see a reason why if there was to be Space there must be Time or *vice versa*, he might be asked how in the absence of an experience of Time he would be able to invent the idea of Time. All that he can do is to see that in Space as empirically presented there are features which are those of Time as empirically presented, and that the mutual relation

[1] See further later, Book II. ch. v.

,of Time and Space is so close and ramified that they cannot be considered as separate entities but only as the same entity described in terms of its different elements. Other 'must' metaphysics does not recognise—except the must of logical implication, and wherever I have spoken of implication I have been careful to limit it to what the experience with which I have been dealing itself demands, and only so far as it demands it. The undertaking is hazardous and even presumptuous enough (and I cannot feel complete confidence that some error may not have crept in) not to be burdened with the suspicion of pretensions which are foreign to it.

Space-
Time.
, , in
mathe-
matics ;

We have thus by purely analytical or metaphysical and non-mathematical methods applied to a subject-matter presented in experience, arrived at a notion of Space-Time which at least in spirit is not different from the notion of a world in Space and Time which was formulated by mathematical methods by the late H. Minkowski, in 1908. The underlying conception had been used or implied in the memoirs of Messrs. Lorentz and Einstein, which along with Minkowski's memoir laid the basis of the so-called theory of relativity, which is now, I believe, common property amongst certain mathematicians and physicists. In Minkowski's conception the Universe is a system of world- or cosmic points ; it is assumed that at each point-instant (the name [1] is due to Mr. Lorentz, *Ortszeit*) there exists some perceptible "substance," and the course of such a substantial point is called a cosmic line (world-line, *Weltlinie*). Space and Time are described us being shadows of the Universe. Only the Universe has self-existence. Every point has four co-ordinates, the time co-ordinate being the fourth. Hence it follows, as Minkowski writes, that geometry with its three dimensions is only a chapter in four-dimensional physics. There are infinite Spaces in the physical world, just as there are infinite planes in our Space. In fact, Space

[1] The term point-instant is used by Mr. A. A. Robb in *A Theory of Time and Space* (Cambridge, 1912).

becomes merely the assemblage of all events which belong to the same moment of Time.

Now I understand the essential spirit of the doctrine to be that Space and Time are not independent of each other but united in the one four-dimensional world, and with this the result of our empirical or metaphysical inquiry is in agreement. But there are some respects in which there is (as I must with becoming misgivings admit) divergence. I take for granted that to think of Time as a fourth dimension in a world in which the other three dimensions are spatial is a legitimate and the only possible way of representing mathematically the nature of the world or Space-Time. But if the empirical analysis is correct, this representation cannot be regarded as other than a means of mathematical manipulation. For it seems to treat Time as an additional dimension, not of course a spatial one, much in the same way as the third spatial dimension is additional to the other two, that is, as a further order in which three-dimensional Spaces are arranged. But the relation between Space and Time which we have found empirically appears to be of a much more intimate kind than is thus suggested. For not only are Space and Time indispensable to one another (as in the conception of Minkowski), but Time with its distinctive features corresponds to the three dimensions of Space, and in a manner of speech Time does with its one-dimensional order cover and embrace the three dimensions of Space, and is not additional to them. To use a violent phrase, it is, spatially, not temporally, voluminous. Metaphysically, (though perhaps mathematically), it is not therefore a fourth dimension in the universe, but repeats the other three. Space, even to be Space, must be temporal.[1] At a later point I shall propose a non-mathematical formula which seems to me to express this relation with metaphysical propriety, without attempting to question the mathematical

[1] It follows also that the three dimensions of Space, just because they correspond to the characters of Time, are not in reality independent of each other (see before p. 51, note).

[2] Book III. ch. ii. A.

appropriateness of Minkowski's formulation. Beyond this, I call attention only to two other matters. According to the method customary in mathematics, it is taken for granted that there is a substance, electricity or matter or what not (the word substance is used expressly in order to avoid the question), which occupies the point-instant. On our hypothesis, whatever substance there is must be a fragment of the one stuff of Space-Time, and therefore is not to be assumed within the metaphysical account of Space-Time. Secondly, as will be mentioned presently, the definition of Space as the assemblage of events at one instant, which may be derived from Minkowski's doctrine and is formulated so by M. Langevin,[1] is connected with the same assumption of material events occurring at a point-instant, and while legitimate in one way, and true, does not tell us the essential character of Space but a consequence of it.

Space-
"   .
(2) in
meta-
p ysics.
Meantime, I may proceed with the metaphysical exposition. We have then to think of Space and Time in much the following way. (a) By themselves each consists of elements or parts which are indistinguishable so long as the elements of the other are excluded. (b) In reality each point of space is determined and distinguished by its instant in time, and each instant of time by its position in space. The elements of the one reality which is Space-Time, and not either Space or Time alone, owe their distinctness in either kind to the complementary element. We have not yet arrived at an examination of the notions of identity and diversity. But using these terms in their common sense, either of the two we may regard as playing the part of identity to the other's part of diversity. It is worth while observing this, because previously Time was shown to supply discrimination in the otherwise blank Space. But Space may equally well be regarded as introducing diversity into time. For without Space Time would be a bare 'now'

---

[1] *Le temps, l'espace et la causalité dans la physique moderne.* Bulletin de la Societé Française de Philosophie, 12ᵉ annee, No. 1, janvier 1912. Paris.

always repeated, and there would be no such thing as diversity. But the reality of Space and Time is in Platonic phrase[1] the "substance" which contains the identity and the diversity in one.

Space must thus be regarded as generated in Time, or, if the expression be preferred, by Time. For Time is the source of movement. Space may then be imaged as the trail of Time, so long as it is remembered that there could be no Time without a Space in which its trail is left. It would be inept to say that Time is in its turn the trail of Space, for Space of itself has no movement. The corresponding proposition is that Time as it moves from past through present to future (from earlier to later) is the occupation of a stretch of Space.

Space-Time thus consists of what may be called lines of advance connected into a whole or system in a manner to be described. In a line of advance $c\ b\ a$ we have the displacement of the present from c through b to a, so that a becomes present while b becomes past and c still further past. The present means as before the point of reference. In terms of earlier and later, b having been later and c earlier, a becomes later and cb earlier. Now this is the meaning of motion. Points do not of course move in the system of points, but they change their time-coefficient. What we ordinarily call motion of a body is the occupation by that body of points which successively become present, so that at each stage the points traversed have different time-values when the line of motion is taken as a whole. Thus Space-Time is a system of motions, and we might call Space-Time by the name of Motion were it not that motion is in common speech merely the general name for particular motions, whereas Space easily and Time less easily is readily seen to be a whole of which spaces and times are fragments. Hence Descartes could identify Space with matter, and there is nothing astonishing in the hypothesis that Space as qualified with Time is the matrix of all being. But Motion we find it difficult so to represent to ourselves. It seems paradoxical consistently with the ordinary use of

---

[1] In the *Timaeus* (ουσία).

language to speak of a single vast entity Motion, though to do so is to do the same thing as to speak of Space-Time.

But the notion that Space is generated in Time in the form of motion is apt to be misinterpreted. We may think of fresh Space as being swept out in Time. We figure advance in Time, the growth of the world, as an advance in column, and it is then easy to go on and treat the present moment as determining a section along this advance, so that Space becomes the arrested events of the present or any one moment. We then have the idea of an infinite spatial present sweeping forward in Time. Space is defined as the assemblage of events at one moment. We shall find that this proposition has under proper conditions a good and important meaning. But both it and the previous proposition that Time sweeps out fresh Space in its advance are open to fatal objections.

First of all, to suppose that Time generates new Space is to neglect the infinity of Time (and indeed of Space). It supposes a part of Space to be generated at the beginning and pushed forward. But a beginning of existence is itself an event in Space-Time which is the system of point-instants or pure events, and it is clear therefore that Space-Time as a whole begins either everywhere or nowhere. Infinity is understood here as explained before in its true sense of self-containedness.

Secondly, the notion that Space is what is occupied by any moment fails to give a true insight into the intrinsic nature of Space. A present which occupies the whole of Space would suffer from the same defect as a mere instant disconnected with other instants. We saw that an instant which was not through Space connected with its past would not be an instant of Time at all, because its past would have perished and it would perish too. The present so described would be all that there was of Time, a ' now ' perpetually re-created. If it were spread over the whole of Space, it and its Space would need to be re-created at each moment.

We have then to abandon the notion of an advancing

column and of Space as a mere instantaneous section of that advance. We have to think of lines of advance as displacements of the present in relation to past and future over positions in Space. In this way we conceive of growth in Time, or the history of the Universe as a whole, or any part of it, as a continuous redistribution of instants of Time among points of Space. There is no new Space to be generated as Time goes on, but within the whole of Space or the part of it the instants of Time are differently arranged, so that points become different point-instants and instants become also different point-instants. I believe that this very abstract (I mean very simple, yet highly concrete) conception lies, in fact, very near to our common notions of a growing world.

But an abstract conception is difficult to retain without a pictorial and more complex representation, and there are several at hand to replace the misleading image of an advancing column. The simplest way is to imagine a limited space, and motions taking place within it. We may choose a disturbed ant-heap or the less pleasing instance of a rotten cheese seen under the microscope. But a severer and more useful picture is that of a gas in a closed vessel, conceived according to the kinetic theory of gases. The molecules of the gas dash against the sides of the vessel and each other in all manner of lines of advance, whether straight lines or not is for us indifferent. The molecules stand for instants of Time with their dates, some being earlier and some later, in various degrees of remoteness, than the point-instant which is the centre of reference ; some simultaneous with it, that is, possessing the same date. The gas is not considered as it is at any moment but as it exists over a lapse of time. We are not supposing the internal motions to be arrested at a given instant which is taken as the point of reference, which would be to suppose arrested what is intrinsically a movement. For us it is perfectly easy to contemplate the motions of the gas over such a lapse of time, for we have memory to help us and expectation, and we can keep in our minds at once a limited piece of the history of the gas. Subject to this explanation we can revert to our

usual form of speech and say the molecules are some of
them present instants, some past, and some future instants,
and the incongruousness of future instants disappears,
for they are objects of our minds, that is, objects in
expectation, equally with present and past instants.   Like
all pictures which symbolise a conception the image halts ;
and in two respects.   First, the instants of identical date
are separate molecules, whereas simultaneous instants, as
we have seen, are the same instant, and have no temporal
but only spatial difference.   Here both the molecules
and their places are distinct.   Secondly, there need not
always be a past molecule to take the place of the
'present' one as the present one moves on to a new
point in space, leaving its old place to be past or earlier.
There are places in the gas empty of molecules.   But in
Space-Time there is no place without time.   Still the
picture conveys fairly well the notion of redistribution of
instants among points.   In some respects the streaming
of protoplasm in a cell would be a more manageable
image.   Best of all perhaps, and certainly very useful, is
the picture of the condition of a growing organism where
we find a perpetual alteration or redistribution among the
cells of distance from maturity ; some being mature (the
present), some moribund, in different stages of senescence,
and still others adolescent.

We have now to see how Space is to be thought of
more accurately as saturated with Time, that is to say, as
the theatre of perpetual movement ; and secondly, in
what sense it is true to say that any instant occupies
the whole of Space, or that any point occurs in the whole
of Time.

CHAPTER II

PERSPECTIVES AND SECTIONS OF PHYSICAL SPACE–TIME

THE physical universe is thus through and through No empty historical, the scene of motion. Since there is no Space or immoveable Space. without Time, there is no such thing as empty Space or empty Time and there is no resting or immoveable Space. Space and Time may be empty of qualitative events or things, and if we are serious with Time there is no difficulty in the thought of a Space-Time which contained no matter or other qualities but was, in the language of Genesis, without form and void before there was light or sound. But though empty of qualities Space and Time are always full. Space is full of Time and Time is full of Space, and because of this each of them is a complete or perfect continuum. If this might seem a quibble of words, which it is not, let us say that Space-Time is a *plenum*. Its density is absolute or complete. There is no vacuum in Space-Time, for that vacuum would be itself a part of Space-Time. A vacuum is only an interval between bodies, material or other, which is empty of body ; but it is full with space-time. Hence the old difficulty that if there were no vacuum motion would be impossible is without foundation, and was disposed of by Leibniz in answering Locke.[1] If it were completely full of material bodies with their material qualities there would be no room for locomotion of those bodies with their qualities. But it is only full with itself. Material bodies can move in this absolute plenum of Space-Time, because their motion means merely that the time-coefficients of their spatial outlines change.

[1] *Nouveaux Essais*, Preface (Erdmann, p. 199*b*, Latta, p. 385).

In the next place, there is no immoveable Space. In one sense, indeed, Space is neither immoveable (or at rest) nor in motion. Space as a whole is neither immoveable nor in motion. For that would suppose there was some Space in which it could rest or move and would destroy its infinitude. Even when we speak of Space as a whole we must observe that it is not a completed whole at any moment, for this would omit its temporality. Under a certain condition, to be explained presently, we may indeed contemplate Space as an infinite whole when we consider only the points it contains. Directly we allow for its Time, we realise that while there may be a complete whole of conceived timeless points there cannot be one of real point-instants or events. For incompleteness at any moment is of the essence of Time. Neither strictly can the universe be said to be in motion as a whole. It *is* motion, that is in so far as it is expressed in its simplest terms.

But it is not Space as a whole which is understood to be immoveable. The immoveable or absolute Space of Newton is the system of places which are immoveable. Now since every point is also, or rather as such, an instant, a resting place is only a place with its time left out. Rest, as we shall see more clearly presently, is only a relative term.

Perspec-
tives and
sections.
With this conception of the whole Space-Time as an infinite continuum of pure events or point-instants let us ask what the universe is at any moment of its history. The meaning of this obscure phrase will become clearer as we proceed. The emphasis rests upon the word history. Space-Time or the universe in its simplest terms is a growing universe and is through and through historical. If we resolve it into its phases, those phases must express its real life, and must be such as the universe can be reconstructed from in actual reality, they must be phases which of themselves grow each into the next, or pass over into each other. We are to take an instant which occupies a point and take a section of Space-Time through that point-instant in respect of its space or time.

The point-instant in question we may call the point or centre of reference. What will this section of Space-Time be, or what would it look like to an observer supposed to be looking at it from the outside, if we make such an impossible assumption of an observer outside the whole universe? The natural and immediate answer would be, the time-section consists of the whole of Space as occupied in every point by events occurring at that moment. For we are accustomed to think of Space as so occupied. It is true that at this moment some event or other is occurring at every point of Space. I may not be aware of them directly, but I can know of them by report, and can anyhow think of all those events that occur at this moment. Accordingly it would seem that any moment a section of the universe would be nothing other than the whole of Space ; and Space may then be described as the assemblage of events which occur at the same moment of time. Now I shall try to show that this Space so described is under certain conditions something real and legitimately conceived. It is a legitimate selection from the whole of Space-Time. But it does not represent what Space-Time is at any moment of its history. The fuller reasons will appear later. At present it is enough to observe that if Space is the assemblage of all events occurring now, it is open to the same objections as were urged against the notion of a single point or a single instant. It does not matter whether the instant occupies a point or the whole of Space ; the universe cannot be composed in reality of such sections. An integration of such sections does not represent the history of the world. The world would need to be re-created at every moment. To insist on this is but repetition. For the moment which is now would be a now which perished utterly and was replaced by another now. Time would cease to be duration and would be nothing but a now, for the different nows would have no continuity. We should vanish utterly at each moment and be replaced by something like ourselves but new ; to the greater glory perhaps of a Creator who would be completely unintelligible, but to the confounding of science in his creatures.

We have to distinguish from this legitimate but artificial selection a selection of point-instants which shall be the state of Space-Time at any historical moment of its continuous history. I shall describe such a section as Space-Time considered with reference to the point-instant which is taken as the centre of reference, and I shall call it a 'perspective' of Space-Time taken from that point of reference; and for convenience I shall speak of the previous selection distinctively as a ' section.' Both are in fact sections of Space-Time, but in different senses , and it is useful to have different terms. The justification of the term perspective will appear presently. The perspectives of Space-Time are analogous to the ordinary perspectives of a solid body. They differ from them in that these are taken from some point outside the body, whereas the point or instant from which a perspective of Space-Time is taken is included in the perspective itself. The choice of the word is suggested, of course, by Mr. Russell's use of it in recent inquiries in his work on 'External Reality,' as that in its turn is affiliated with Leibniz' conception of the monads as mirroring the universe from their several points of view. Meantime we may contrast the two conceptions by illustrations. At any moment of a man's history his body is a perspective at that instant of his whole life. But it consists of cells at all degrees of maturity. We have the space of his body occupied by parts, some mature at this moment, and others which are immature or senescent. In other words, his space is of different dates of maturity. We might, on the other hand, think of his space as occupied with cells of the same maturity, and we should have the same space, and it would all be of the same date, but it would not be the man's body as it is at any moment whatever but a selection from various stages of his history. It would, however, give his shape. Once more the illustration limps because the man's space changes in volume with his growth. But we may suppose him not to alter; and in Space-Time since Space is infinite the difficulty does not arise. Or we may illustrate by a section of a tree. As mere dead wood the space of the section is given to us at one moment. But in the history of the plant, the concentric rings of the wood are of different dates. To the eye of the botanist the section is variable in its time ; to the eye of the carpenter, or better still of the person who sits at it when it is a table, it presents no such variation.

When therefore we consider Space-Time with reference to an instant of time, that is to a point-instant in respect of its time, we shall have the whole of Space, not occurring at one instant but filled with times of various dates. There is a continuum of events filling Space but divided by the point of reference into earlier and later, with the exception of those points in which the instant of the centre is intrinsically repeated, and which have the same instant. The other points will be earlier and later at various dates, and since any date is repeated in space there will be at each date points contemporaneous with each other,[1] but earlier or later than the centre and its contemporaries. There are, if we choose to use a technical term, equitemporals or isochrones in space (just as there are in a perspective from a point equispatials or isochors in time). Call O the instant of reference. One of its points is o ; there are points intrinsically contemporary with o. A point a is earlier than o, and if we call the time of o the present, a is past. The point a is of the same date as b and is earlier than c. For example, a and b may be contemporary points of the same structure, e.g. my hand ; ac may represent a transaction of causality, for example a bullet killing a man, that is, with reference to o, a and c are occupied by the events in question. Now the meaning of such reference in date to o is that the events a, b, and c lie on lines of advance which connect them with o. Directly or indirectly o is connected by spatio-temporal events with every point in Space, as for instance the cells in a body are connected directly or indirectly with one another. The lines of advance need not necessarily be straight (as when, for instance, we see events in space by light, which proceeds, or is thought to

---

[1] E.g. all the points on the same spherical surface if the lines of advance are those of light.

proceed,[1] in straight lines) but may be of the most complicated character. The comparison with light is the reason why the term perspective is appropriate to such a picture as we have drawn. For not only is it true that to an outside observer the various points of space would be at different dates, but he would get that perspective by being situated at the point of reference.

Accordingly I may illustrate the difference of dates in Space in the perspective from any instant by reference to a human percipient, supposed to be at the point of reference. Only whereas in his case the lines of advance by which he apprehends events outside him are the very developed and differentiated movements by which his senses are affected, with a pure event or point-instant the lines of advance are but the movements in Space-Time by which the centre is related however circuitously to the other points of Space. Moreover, in using the illustration, we assume according to our hypothesis that what the man perceives and the act of perceiving it are separate events whose reality is not dependent on or does not owe its existence to the reality of the other. As an example of a line of advance connecting the past or earlier point with the centre, I might take any sensation, for it is certain that the act of sensing a flash of light follows by a small but measurable interval the flash itself as a physical event. A better instance is the familiar case of apprehending Sirius and his place in the sky by means of the light from him which reaches my eyes some nine years after the event. What I see is an event which happened nine years ago at the place where I see it (though I see the distance very roughly); and Heaven knows what may have happened to Sirius between the date of what I see and now when I see him.

In the same way I may apprehend in my imagination a later event which, in reference to now, is future. Nine years hence I may apprehend what is taking place at Sirius at this moment, if Sirius now exists. (We have yet to

---

[1] I add the reservation because I understand that according to Mr. Einstein's most recent work light may not travel in perfectly straight lines.

see how we can with propriety speak of Sirius as existing at this present moment at all, since I only see him nine years late.) I mean by thinking of Sirius and his position in the future that there is a system of transactions now begun which will end by enabling me to see Sirius then. This system of transactions is begun on my side by the expectation in my mind of seeing Sirius ; it was begun on the side of Sirius by the causes which lead to his continuance. Generally, the point c is future to o in that transactions in Space-Time are set up which will enable me at some future time to date c as contemporary with my present moment. There is a line of advance from o to c as well as a line of advance from some other event before c to c. Again, when a and b are contemporary events in the past they are connected by different lines of advance with o ; and when a is before c the two points are successive in reference to o as when a percipient follows the causal succession in a bullet's hitting a man.

Continuing the human metaphor, which we shall find[1] at long last[1] to have its justification, we may personify Space, and having regard to the differing dates of its points with reference to the centre, which is the present of that perspective, we may say that Space at any moment is full of memory and expectation. The objection may be made, how can reality contain at this moment the past, for the past is past and exists no longer ? But the difficulty is only apparent. It arises from identifying reality with the present or actual reality ; it assumes in fact that Time is not real. The past event, it is true, does not exist now, and if existence is taken to be present existence, the past clearly does not exist. But if we avoid this error and take Time seriously, the past possesses such reality as belongs to the past, that is, to what is earlier than the point of reference ; it does not exist now but it did exist then, and its reality is to have existed then. As to the later or future, there is at bottom no greater difficulty in speaking of the future as being real and existing really than there is in respect of the real existence of the past. A future or

---

[1] See later, Bk. III. ch. ii. A, where it will be suggested that the instant of a point is its 'mind.'

later point does not occur now, and therefore it is now not-yet, just as the past is now no longer.   It has what reality belongs to it in the real Time.   Thus in describing Space-Time in reference to a centre of reference which is now— its perspective from that point of view—we are not sup-posing that the universe is stopped at that moment arti-ficially, in which case there would, as some think, be a now spread out over infinite Space.   They are mistaken ; for there would then be no Time and no Space.   We are determining which among the instants of the whole of Time belong to the points of Space in their relation to the centre.   We find that so far is it from being true that at any moment in its *history* Space is completely occurring now, that the only points which occur now or are filled with the present are the points in which the instant of reference is intrinsically repeated.

Empirical verifica-tion.

This proposition that Space considered at any moment is of various dates is very elementary and in that sense abstract.   But before proceeding I may note that as an empirical fact Space, when we apprehend it through the senses and, therefore, as filled with 'qualitied'[1] events, and not merely with pure events, is not pre-sented to us as simultaneous.   I assume, for the reasons just mentioned, that what we sense is anterior to our act of sensing it, because of the time it takes the physical event to stimulate our organs.   Bearing this in mind we can conclude what the time-relations are, not so much to ourselves, for that is not relevant to our purpose, but among the different objects perceived.   If I am using eyes to apprehend Space through (I am not saying that we apprehend Space by sight but we do apprehend it through sight), it is clear that since different points of space are at very different distances from the eye, and the light reaches it from them in different times, however slight the difference of distance from my eyes may be, more

---

[1] The word has Dr. Johnson's authority.   "Lord Southwell was the highest bred man without insolence that I ever was in company with, the most *qualitied* I ever saw" (Boswell, March 23, 1783, G. B. Hill's ed., vol. iv. p. 174).

distant points must in general have occurred earlier than nearer ones, in order that my acts of seeing the various sets may occur at the same moment. This applies not only to vast differences of distance, as between my lamp on the table and Sirius, but to points only slightly remote from one another. There will also be certain points which are equidistant from the eyes and are simultaneous with one another. So much for sight. Even with the hand it would be difficult to prove that all points touched by the hand can send their messages through to our mind in equal times, as they must if the sensing of them is to occur at the same time. Empirically then, though we may take in an immense space in an act which, however complex, occurs all together, the Space which we apprehend is presented with different dates, though to discover this may need reflection.

Two kinds of retort may be imagined to this statement. It is based on the deliverance of the senses ; and the senses deceive. To which the answer is, that with all allowance for the feebleness and treachery of the senses, they have established themselves, if there is any truth in the doctrine of natural selection, by adaptation to the very objects which it is their office to observe. We *are* " miserably bantered by our senses," and, moreover, we shall learn that, since we only apprehend Space and Time by the help of the senses, we pay for the privilege of seeing colours, and for the delicate touches and movements of the wood-worker or the etcher, by making mistakes about position in space or time. But we cannot believe that though the senses may confuse our apprehension in this respect, they are there to pervert it.

Let me add the application of this remark, or its extension, to the bare point-instant which is the point of reference. There, too, it might be asked how we can be sure that two contemporary points a and b, in which the same instant repeats itself intrinsically, are contemporary for O, or if a is really before c, that it will precede c for O. The date in reference to o is determined by the line of advance from the point to o. How can we know that the dates are, as it were, 'apprehended' accurately by o O ?

The doubt is really suggested by humanising o O and treating it as if it were a sensitive subject, with all the drawbacks possessed by such. But consider o and a, b, and c in their purely spatio-temporal character. If a and b are intrinsically isochronous and a A and b A are in the perspective from O, that means that Space-Time is such, and its point-instants so connected with each other by lines of advance, that two intrinsically isochronous points belong to the same perspective of Space as o. If they were not isochronous relatively to o, they would not appear in the perspective from O. For o is itself part of the perspective. It is only because we suppose it to be looking on at Space from the outside, and endow it with something like our sensibility, that we think of it as open to misapprehension. Being so simple, it is infallible. On the other hand, if any two points x and y are not intrinsically isochronous, but only happen to be so for this perspective, they may not be so in a different perspective.

The second retort is that perhaps it is true that, perceptually, empirical space-positions occur at different times ; but, conceptually, they are all simultaneous. Something will be said hereafter of the relation of concepts to percepts. But at least it is not the business of concepts to distort perceptual objects but to indicate the pattern on which they are built. If perceived Space is full of Time there is no conceived or conceptual Space which is unfilled with Time. On the contrary, the concept of Space must all the more urgently provide for the change of Time within Space. It is true that our familiar notion of Space as a framework in which events occur all over it at the same moment is, as we have said, a legitimate and real notion, and we are yet to explain how it arises. But though it implies thought, it does not rest on the difference of conceptual and perceptual Space but on another distinction, namely on the distinction between partial and total Space-Time, between spatial perspectives of Space-Time and Space-Time as a spatial whole.

Perspectives from a point. Hitherto I have been dealing with perspectives of Space-Time from the point of view of a single instant as located at a point. But in the same way there are perspectives from the point of view of a point of space as located in its instant of time. Once more the section of Space-Time across a point might seem to be the whole of Time, and Time might be described as the assemblage of events which occupy a single point. Metaphysically this would be open to the same objections as the notion of Space as an assemblage of events occurring at the same time. The point would be discontinuous with other points, would be a mere 'here,' and would require as before re-creation of the world in each 'here.' But when we take not the section of the world through a point but its perspective, we shall have the whole of Time occupying not the same point but points of Space at all manner of distances from the central point of reference. That is just as a perspective from an instant is spread out over the whole of Time and presents all variety of dates, a perspective from a point is spread out over the whole of Space and presents all varieties of locality. It would be tedious to enter into the details which correspond to the details of the preceding picture. I will only note that in our empirical experience this state of things is as much a fact as in the other case. Still, assuming the hypothesis that what I remember and what I expect are distinct existences from me, we realise that in thinking of the history of the past or divining the future, the events are located not in one place and still less in no place at all, but in the places where they occurred or will occur, however inaccurately we may apprehend their positions. The full development of these matters belongs more properly or more conveniently to the next chapter, and I must ask something from the sympathetic imagination or patience of the reader. There is a machinery of imagination and memory for sorting out events into the places to which they belong.

A perspective from an instant of time and one from a point of space are different perspectives, and cannot be combined into a single perspective. This may at first present a difficulty. The instant from which a perspective is taken occupies a point or points. O occupies o and its contemporaries. But *o* is itself intrinsically repeated in time. Why are these repetitions of *o* in time left out of the perspective ? The answer is, that if *o* is repeated at O' and *o*O' is taken into the perspective, the perspective would be taken not from the instant O but from O' as well. We include in the point of view O all the contemporary points occupied by O, but we cannot include the other times which occupy *o*. In fact, a perspective from an instant gives us a picture of Space ; a perspective from a point gives us a picture of Time. If we attempted to combine the two pictures, and to get a 'perspective' of Space-Time from the point of view both of the place and time of the point-instant *o*O, we should have, as a little consideration will show, not a perspective at all but the whole of Space-Time. Space-Time considered in reference to a point-instant from the point of view both of the point and the instant is nothing but Space-Time.[1]

Relation of the perspectives to one another.

Total Space-Time is the synthesis of all partial space-times or perspectives of Space-Time. I use the awkward word 'total' in order to avoid two others, either of which might be misleading. The one is the adjective 'universal,' which is ambiguous and might suggest just what it is desired to avoid, namely, that the whole continuum of point-instants is a concept derived from special bits of Space-Time or even from perspectives or partial space-times. Whereas it is, to use language borrowed from Kant, which may pass muster at present, a single infinite 'individual.'[2] The other adjective 'absolute' I avoid because of its historical associations with Newton's doctrine of Absolute Space and Time.

What we have to see is first, what information we can draw from our experience, in pursuit of our empirical method, as to the differences between different perspectives ; and secondly, that these perspectives are of themselves connected with one another, so that the synthesis

[1] See later, Book IV. ch. i., for the connection of this with the so-called ontological argument.

[2] Later it will be seen that Space-Time is not an individual.

of them is not an operation which we, human subjects who think, perform upon them, but one which they, as it were, perform on themselves. For a perspective of Space-Time is merely the whole of Space-Time as it is related to a point-instant by virtue of the lines of connection between it and other point-instants.

The information we get from experience is first, that points of space which are simultaneous in one perspective may be successive in another, and points which are successive in one may be simultaneous in another. A simple instance of the first is that on one occasion two points in my hand may be isochronous for me or my brain, but on another occasion, when the time has changed and the point-instant of reference therefore with it, the one may precede the other. For example, in a new perspective an electric current may have been sent from one point to the other, and the points are successive. Observe that it is not the physical or qualitied events at the two points of my hand which have changed their relation in Time ; but only that in the two perspectives the points of Space have become differently dated. Again, suppose that *a* is earlier than the centre *o*. In a different perspective *a* may have the same date as *o*. Thus let us go back to Sirius, and merely for simplicity's sake (and because without some simplification, however impossible in fact, the mind is apt to reel before the complexity of things) let us assume that Sirius and I remain fixed with relation to each other. The event which I now see in him by the light from him is nine years old. But, on a different line of advance in the universe from the path of transmission of light, an event may be, and probably is, occurring in Sirius which is nine years later than the event there which I now see. If it comes into my present perspective at all it is as a future event. For simplicity let us suppose I am not expecting it and that it does not enter into the perspective. Still, it occurs in fact at the same instant as *o* ; that is, from some point of reference different from *o*O the points *o* and *a* will be of the same date. Again I observe, that it is not the real physical events, my sight of Sirius now and the

(1) Differences of perspectives.

past physical event in Sirius, which will have, as it were, become contemporary, but only that the points at which they occur have become differently dated, that is, in the new perspective are occupied by different physical events. In the new perspective the future event in Sirius enters as contemporary with my present sight of him. It is not the same event as aA, but it occurs we are supposing at the same point. In other words, the points of Space are filled with different instants owing to that redistribution of instants among points which makes the history of Space-Time. Thus there are isochrones of o in the whole of Space, which are not related to it as its isochrones are in its own perspective, and which do not appear as isochrones in that perspective.

In general a perspective of Space-Time from one point-instant differs from the perspective from another point-instant, whether the perspectives be taken in respect of the instants or points. Points which were simultaneous in the one may be successive in the other ; the interval of time or space may be altered, and even two points may reverse their dates in the different perspectives. For though a perspective takes in the whole of Space or the whole of Time, it does not take in the whole of Space-Time, the totality of point-instants ; it would otherwise not be a perspective. If we endow point-instants with percipience, all these changes in the distribution of points among instants will be perceived accurately ; for the percipient sensibility of so simple percipients must be also supposed perfectly simple.[1] We are here within the region of Space-Time pure and simple, before qualited events, like the fall of a stone or the birth of a flower, or the existence of complex percipients like plants or ourselves. Hence I have been obliged to repeat so often that qualited events do not occur in different places or at different times because their dates and places may be changed in two perspectives. The place at which they occur or the time which they occupy, if the event in question remains within the perspective,

---

[1] For the questions raised by this idea (cp. above, p. 74) of the perfect accuracy of perception of point-instants, see later, Bk. III. ch. vii.

alters its date or its place ; their place or date in the first
perspective is now occupied by some other event. We
must add that such changes may not be noticeable to more
complex percipients, because the extent of them may not
fall within the limits of the discrimination of the percipient
or class of percipients even with the help of instruments
of precision, or because the difference is for them of no
practical importance. Simultaneous events may seem
to them still simultaneous, or the intervals, spatial or
temporal, not to have altered, because the change is not
perceived or is not interesting. One illustration we have
already had, in the belief that what we see of Space is all
contemporaneous.

Next let us note that the various perspectives of the (2) Their
universe viewed from points or instants, or the contents connection.
of the universe as referred to a centre of reference, are of
themselves connected, and together constitute the whole
universe. Each perspective leads on to some other.
The redistributions of dates among points are linked in
one continuous process. For a point of reference is a
point-instant. Its place is temporal, and merely an ideally
separated position in a movement ; is, in fact, a movement
at its limit. Whether we consider the time-element or
the space-element in it, both alike are transitional. Point
merges into point and instant into instant, and each does
so because of the other. Our centre oO is the next
instant at the time O' and becomes oO', or to keep our
notation uniform oO', and the world referred to this new
point-instant is a different selection from the world of
point-instants.[1] The mere fact that each perspective is
from the beginning a selection from a whole, and not a
construction by the centre to which it is referred, is
enough to show that the perspectives are in their own
nature united, and need no combining hand. It is in
this sense that the whole of Space-Time is the synthesis

[1] Not of course from the world of points. Every perspective includes
the whole of Space and the whole of Time, but not the whole of
Space-Time. That is, every point in Space is there with some date,
and every instant in Time with some place ; but not the whole mass
of point-instants.

of partial space-times or perspectives. At a later stage[1] we shall see how important this consideration is for understanding the relation of perspectives, in the ordinary sense, of finite things like houses.

Corresponding remarks may be made about perspectives from points. Moreover, the two sets of perspectives are not only internally connected but connected with one another. The instant from which a perspective is taken being located at a point, the perspective from it is connected with the perspective from the point.

Total Space and Time.

Total Space-Time is thus the synthesis of all perspectives, which is, in fact, only another way of saying that the perspectives are real perspectives of it or are its historical phases. Owing to the infinite interconnection of point-instants on different and independent lines of advance, independent, that is, of those which pass through any given point of reference, there is an infinity of such perspectives. Not limiting ourselves therefore to any one centre of reference but admitting infinite such centres, we can see first of all that when we are considering all the perspectives from every instant, any point of Space is occupied, not as in the single time-perspective by some one moment of Time but by the whole of Time. The whole of Time in the totality of such perspectives streams through each point of Space. Thus while the state of Sirius nine years hence may not enter into my present perspective (except in expectation) it occurs on some independent line of advance (not included in my perspective) at the present time in the total ; and extending our view to all perspectives, we see that the position of Sirius is occupied by some time or other through infinite Time. The position in Space is occupied by only one time in a given time-perspective, but by all Time in the totality of perspectives.

In the same way consider the totality of point-perspectives, that is, perspectives from the point of view of a point. In a single such perspective an instant is localised in only one position of Space. But in the

[1] Bk. III. ch. vii.

totality of them each instant is localised in all positions in Space. We saw that it was a condition of the very nature of Space-Time that each instant was repeated in space and each point in time. But we now see that while for any perspective (which is of course three-dimensional and possesses the corresponding characters of time) there is this intrinsic repetition, every time having its appropriate isochors and every point its appropriate isochrones ; in total Space-Time each point is in fact repeated through the whole of Time and each instant over the whole of Space. Now when these particular selections are made of point-instants, the one from the total of one set of perspectives and the other from the other set, we have a total Space which occurs at one instant and a total Time which occupies one point.

The total Space and Time so arrived at are what we called, in distinction from perspectives, sections of Space-Time. They do not represent what the world of Space-Time is historically at any moment or at any point. For at any moment of its real history Space is not all of one date, and Time is not all at one point. But Space and Time so described can be got by an arbitrary selection from the infinite rearrangements of instants amongst points. And the result of the selection is to give us Space apart from its times and Time apart from its places. That Space and that Time are what is meant by the definitions of them as assemblages, the one of all events of the same date, the other of all events at the same place. Moreover real Space with its varying dates coincides with this total Space when the variation of dates is omitted ; and correspondingly for Time. Hence from considering the true perspectives of Space-Time we can arrive at the notion of Space occurring at one time or Time occupying one place. But from these sections we cannot arrive at the notion of true perspectives or at true Space-Time. I need not now repeat the reasons why.

It is because Time is intrinsically repeated in Space and Space in Time that it is possible at all to speak of Time or Space by themselves, when in fact neither exists apart

Absolute Space and

from the other. They get shaken apart from each other in thought, just as the shape of billiard balls of varying colour gets shaken apart from the varying colour. But when we go on to consider the whole of Space-Time and discover that the whole of Time when you choose from all the perspectives, or when you make an arbitrary selection of space-points, streams through every point, and the whole of Space can be filled out with places of the same date, we then formulate the two conceptions, one of a Time which flows uniformly on and the other that of a Space immoveable : what are commonly known as Absolute Time and Absolute Space, and, so far as I can judge, the ordinary or 'common-sense' notions of Time and Space. Arbitrary as the selections are, they are possible, and it is easy to see under what conditions the conceptions are valid, or the Space and Time in question can be regarded as real. They are valid so long as Absolute Space is understood to be total Space and not supposed to exclude Time, or Absolute Time to exclude Space, with their respective variations of date and place. They are the fully formulated Space and Time when these are shaken apart from each other. What is false in them is to suppose them real if Space is understood to occur at one instant or Time at one point. But if no such assumption is made, (and I believe no such assumption is made in mathematics, but the two are considered merely apart from one another without any ulterior view as to their relations,) then the whole of Space is the same frame-work as belongs alike to the real and the arbitrary selection from Space-Time at any instant ; and the whole Time is the framework of the real and the arbitrary selection from Space-Time at any place. So understood, not only are they useful and valid conceptions, but they are real, in the same sense as the material body of an organism can be said to be real and the life of it also real, though the life does not exist without a body of a certain sort, and the body, to be the kind of body that it is, depends on life. In other words, the reality of Space-Time may be resolved into the elements total Space and total Time, provided only it be remembered that in their *combination* Space is always variously occupied by Time and Time spread variously over Space.

Hence we may note the impropriety of distinguishing total Space as conceptual from empirical Space (the only *Space* we know) as perceptual. Space and Time are shaken apart from each other. But total Space is no more the concept of Space than the shape of the billiard ball is its concept while the whole ball is a percept. Total Space is the same as real Space with the Time left out, by an abstraction which is legitimate or not according to the use made of it. If the concept of Space were got by omitting Time which is vital to it, the result would be not a concept but a false product of thought. The separation of the Space from its Time involves abstraction and, so far, thought, but concepts are not arrived at by abstraction.

I have so far spoken of total Space and total Time. In dealing with the conceptions of them as absolute I am partly beset with the historical difficulty of interpreting Newton's ideas, a task to which I am not equal, but mainly I am concerned with the question how far we can validly speak of an absolute Time and Space. I leave it to others to say whether it is not the idea of what I call total Space and total Time, Time and Space taken as wholes, which is in the background of Newton's mind. His familiar illustration of absolute motion at any rate, which I give in the note,[1] suggests this interpretation. What is defective in Absolute Space is the notion of

Rest relative.

---

[1] *Principia*, Bk. I., Scholium to Definitions.

"If the earth is really at rest, the body which relatively rests in the ship will really and absolutely move with the same velocity which the ship has on the Earth. But if the earth also moves, the true and absolute motion of the body will arise partly from the true motion of the Earth in immoveable space ; partly from the relative motion of the ship on the Earth : and if the body moves also relatively in the ship ; its true motion will arise, partly from the true motion of the Earth in immoveable space, and partly from the relative motions as well of the ship on the Earth as of the body in the ship ; and from these relative motions will arise the relative motion of the body on the Earth."

In other words, the true or absolute motion is the motion when you take it in the whole of Space and not in relation to any one body in Space.

resting places. Space as a whole we have seen is neither immoveable nor in motion. But neither can a place be at rest if Space is only one element of Space-Time. Rest, in fact, appears to be purely relative and to have no real existence. Every place has its time-coefficient and is the seat of motion. In general, we speak of rest only where-ever the motion is irrelevant for our purposes. This may arise from various reasons. Two motions may be the same, and the moving bodies, though each in motion, are at rest relatively to each other. Or I may rest in my chair while the mosquitoes move around me, but I am moving with the earth. I neglect that motion because I am interested in the mosquitoes, and because the mos-quitoes also in following me move with the earth. But while I do not change my position relative to the earth they do. It seems, in fact, clear that if anything could be absolutely at rest everything must be at rest. For if any point in space retained its time, this would dislocate the whole system of lines of advance within Space-Time, a point being only a point on such a line.

Thus if absolute rest means the negation of motion, there is no such thing in reality. Rest is one kind of motion, or, better, it is a motion with some of its motional features omitted. But if absolute rest means merely position in space with its time left out, it is a legitimate abstraction if so understood. It may be gravely doubted whether anything else is ever intended by those who speak of absolute rest, though once more I do not enter into the interpretation of Newton, as being beyond my competence.

It is important to distinguish the different antitheses into which the idea of Absolute Space or Time enters. Absolute may be opposed to relational. Space may be treated as a stuff or as a system of relations. Or absolute may be opposed to relative. The two questions are not easily separable. It may be doubted if Newton, for whom Space and Time are non-relational, distinguished them ; but they are distinct. Now with the relativity of position in time or space or of motion as commonly understood nothing in our conception of Space-Time conflicts. When motion or position is declared to be relative, we are thinking of the material bodies or the qualitative events which occupy times and places and are moving. Relative for Newton refers to the sensible measures of space or time. In regard to them all the commonplaces of the subject are evident. A thing is to the right of A and to the left of B ; or more important, A which is to the right of B is also from the point of view of another observer to the left of B. An event is before another event and after a third. A train may be at rest with respect to another moving train but in motion with respect to the telegraph poles. Or the train may seem at rest and the telegraph poles to move. In fact a motion of A with respect to B which is at rest is equally a motion of B with respect to A which is at rest. This relativity has sometimes been urged by philosophers to demonstrate that Time or Space is self-contradictory and therefore unreal. A present event is next moment past and some other event is present, as if to call both events by the same name in different connections made any difference to the real position of an event.

But the case is different when instead of qualitied bodies or events we think of the pure events or point-instants which in their continuity make up Space-Time. It is true that these events are related to each other. But to call position or motion absolute is merely to say that these positions and motions are what they are in their own right. It is simply untrue to say that two point-instants or pure events may be indifferently either before or after each other. The same points may be occupied by times which are before or after each other, but the two point-instants in total Space-Time are not the same in the two cases. We may help ourselves in this situation according to our custom by reference to human affairs. All good actions are relative to their circumstances and good under those circumstances ; and it is sometimes thought that they cannot therefore be absolutely good or good in their own right. Absolute goodness is then regarded as some ideal which serves as a standard to which we can only approximate. On the contrary, it is because good actions

Absolute position or motion.

are relative to or determined by their circumstances that they are absolutely good. Other good there is none. We fancy a perfect good because there are certain rules of action which apply to sets of circumstances comparatively so simple and perpetually recurrent, like telling truth and respecting life, that we confuse the universality of these rules with some special sort of absoluteness and construct an ideal of a perfect good. In analogous fashion point-instants and, what is the same thing, motions are related ; to be an unrelated point-instant (absolute rest) is a contradiction and does not exist ; it is in fact a contradiction because it is incompatible with the nature of Space-Time. A point-instant is essentially an element of a movement and is between other point-instants. Motion is related to other motion. But each point-instant and each motion is what it is and is in this sense absolute. The bare framework of such absolute order is Absolute Space or Time or Absolute Motion. Again, I leave it to others to judge if this is or is not the meaning of Newton.

From this point of view I may approach the old controversy whether it makes any difference to say the earth goes round the sun or the sun round the earth. To an influential school of thought, headed by the late E. Mach in our day, the difference is one of convenience and economy in description. Neither is truer than the other. Now it is quite true that a motion round the sun may be represented equally well by a motion round the earth. But in doing this we are representing either motion as merely a series of points in space, and omitting the intrinsic time. We are giving, in fact, a purely geometrical account instead of a physical one. Physically the two descriptions are not indifferent. It is, rather, because there is only one physical description that we can find two indifferent spatial descriptions. Let us say then that total Space-Time involves as two elements total Space and total Time, these two being the framework of places and instants within which point-instants (and with them the material or psychical events which occupy them) exist. Each of them is an abstraction from the real world of Space-Time ; not an abstraction in the sense of a mere creation of the human mind, but each of them real under the limitations before described. Absolute Time and absolute Space mean for us only these two elements or factors in the whole, factors which are not juxtaposed but interrelated in the complex history of point-instants.

Having ventured to suggest that absolute Space and Time, interpreted as of total Space and Time, have a very good meaning as understood within the one Space-Time or world from which they never do exist in abstraction, I am impelled in spite of natural hesitation to go further and make some brief remarks upon the philosophical bearing of the current principle of relativity which claims to displace the Newtonian conceptions of Space and Time. Our purely metaphysical analysis of Space-Time on the basis of ordinary experience is in essence and spirit identical with Minkowski's conception of an absolute world of four dimensions, of which the three-dimensional world of geometry omits the element of time. The principle of relativity as enunciated by Mr. A. Einstein is taken up, as I understand the matter, into the body of Minkowski's doctrine. And it would be strange, therefore, if our metaphysical doctrine should be in conflict with it, considered as a mathematical doctrine. The principle of relativity means that the laws of physics are the same for all observers in uniform motion with respect to each other ; so that in Mr. Paul Langevin's phrase purely mechanical observations interior to two such systems would not reveal the motion of the systems relatively to each other.[1] The principle was suggested by certain experimental evidence which need not be mentioned here, and it carries with it certain consequences of which, for the layman like the writer, the simplest and, at the same time, the most paradoxical are these. Time, it should be mentioned, is determined by means of clocks whose synchronism is tested in a certain method by means of a flash of light flashed from one clock to the second and then flashed back : the clocks are synchronous when

The Principle of Relativity.

[1] *L' Temps, l'espace, et la causalite,* p. 6.   Referred to in note on p. 91.

the reading of the second clock is half the two readings on the first. Now it follows from the relativity principle that two clocks which are synchronous with one another in one system supposed to be at rest will for an observer who moves along with them not be synchronous, and hence events simultaneous to one set of observers are not so for the other set in uniform movement of translation with respect to the first. Secondly, a stick of a certain length lying in the direction of the translation will not be of the same length to the two sets of observers but will shrink for the resting observer in a certain ratio. The conclusion is that Space and Time are entirely relative and vary for each observer.

This is precisely what we should expect on the metaphysical statement (apart from the exact numerical determinations) if different sets of observers have different views or perspectives of the one Space-Time. Each such perspective is perfectly real and in no sense illusory, just as the perspectives we have of solid objects are the object as seen under certain aspects and are perfectly real.[1] The motion of the one system S' with regard to the other system S changes the perspective for the two sets of observers. Consequently though the material events of sending and receiving flashes of light at two stations are not altered in their relations in Space-Time, they will have different dates in the two cases ; for the places at which the events occur will change their dates relative to the observers. In the same way, to take the case of the stick, times appropriate to the ends of the moving stick will occupy different places for the two sets of observers, and the stick will alter in length. There is no such thing as a purely spatial or temporal interval. A distance in space is a system of events, whether it is distance pure and simple or is occupied by a stick. The length of the stick in total Space-Time does not alter, but the dates of its points do, according to the perspective. Only when we forget this does it seem paradoxical to us that the length should vary to different observers. So, too, the retardation of the clock may seem paradoxical, for though we are familiar with the spatial character of Time,

[1] See later, Bk. III. ch. vii.

since we estimate it for purposes of accuracy by spatial marks, as in clocks, yet we forget that these spatial measures are themselves temporal.

The same thing may be expressed otherwise thus. We are dealing in the theory not with point-instants or pure events as such, but with the measurements of Space and Time by means of sensible or material events; in fact, by light-signals. What the theory does is to establish the relations between Space and Time as thus sensibly measured in such a way as to express the persistence in an identical form of physical laws for observers in uniform motion of translation with respect to each other. But this is not in any way inconsistent with there being pure events or point-instants which have their 'absolute' position in Space-Time. To illustrate the point, let me take the conclusion drawn by Mr. Langevin that under certain conditions events may have their order of succession reversed for the two sets of observers; if, that is to say, the distance between the events is greater than can be travelled by light in the time between them. It is inferred that there can be no causality between events at such a distance. But if the time of events were measured by sound-events at comparatively inconsiderable distances, events which are known to be in causal relation would have their succession reversed for observers in appropriate positions.[1]

Now the principle of relativity is a physical or mathe- Its meta-
matical principle, and is not primarily concerned with p ysic l
metaphysics (or even theory of knowledge, which for me is bearing.
only a part of metaphysics). But we are concerned here with the metaphysics of it. It would seem at first sight to mean that while the laws of physics are the same for

---

[1] I do not of course mean slightingly that the principle of relativity is a mere affair of measurements, but rather that measurement when you press it to its ultimate foundations always implies the introduction of time considerations into spatial quantities and space considerations into temporal quantities. This is a matter of the highest importance, and it is of a piece with the principle that a space without its time or a time without its space is a fiction. This second point is what I miss in Mr. Broad's treatment of the subject of relativity in his Appendix (*Perception Physics and Reality*, Cambridge, 1914, pp. 354 ff.), from which I have learnt much on the relation of the principle of relativity to measurement.

every observer, each one has his own Space and Time and lives in that world. But if that conclusion is drawn, and I do not feel sure that it is, the relativist seems compelled philosophically to go beyond his own Space-Time and arrive at a total Space-Time in our sense. It is sometimes said that the very reasonings which establish the relativist results (those paradoxes which are so beautifully natural) presuppose and postulate an absolute world ; but I cannot find that this can be maintained. But they certainly seem to me to lead on to it. For the different sets of observers compare notes, or if they do not, the mathematician who supplies the formulas of transformation whereby equations expressed in the co-ordinates of one world can be expressed in the co-ordinates of another world, thereby contemplates a world in which the worlds of the two sets of observers are unified. Moreover, even within one world the various persons who read the clocks are supposed to communicate with each other, and they are not the same persons and may have a slightly different perspective. The only way in which the conclusion from this comparison of the observers at least in the two systems (to say nothing of observers within each system) can be turned is by the reply that the formulae are numerical and independent of Space and Time. For reasons which I cannot at present explain, I should regard this answer as unavailing, because number is itself dependent on Space and Time.

Thus the position metaphysically of the relativist is apparently one of solipsism, or rather the same question is raised as in solipsistic theories of knowledge. Solipsists, as has often been pointed out, could not talk to each other. Moreover, as Mr. Bradley has shown, a solipsist at one moment could not talk to himself as he was at a previous moment ; he would have no continuous self. Now all such metaphysical difficulties are avoided if we start with the empirical fact that we do communicate with one another about a common world which each sees from his own view, and moreover that each remembers himself. If relativism means philosophically (and I repeat that I do not know that it does mean this) that

Space-Time for each observer is his own, it inevitably leads on to a total Space-Time which combines these worlds.

I venture, therefore, to suggest that the importance of the doctrine does not lie in any supposed annihilation of absolute Space-Time as understood in the sense explained here, but in two other respects. Of the first a philosopher can judge. It is the truth that the world is not a geometrical but a physical one, and that Space and Time are indissoluble. This seems to me a result of the last importance and fundamental to metaphysics. The second is the exact determination on the basis of experimental evidence of how formulae are to be transformed in the case where one system moves in uniform translation with respect to another system. Such transformations are required in the Newtonian mechanics, but the contention of relativists is that they are only a first approximation. Later knowledge shows the transformations to be less simple.[1] If this contention is well established, and this is a matter for physicists and certainly not for me, the principle means a vast advance for physics itself over and above the fundamental reconstruction of the relation of Space and Time. But whatever modifications it introduces into the Newtonian mechanics it leaves Time and Space and Motion in their ancient reality, or rather it leaves us still with Space-Time in itself as a total from which perspectives are selections ; and therefore in that sense absolute and independent of the observers. And I do not feel sure that any relativist would object to this in a metaphysical sense. Time and Space in their ancient pure reality remain as the *framework* of history, and the new doctrine is a new doctrine of their sensible measures.[2]

[1] Possibly this new system may not be final. See this suggestion as made by Mr. Langevin, p. 27, "Peut-etre des experiences nouvelles nous obligeront-elles a retoucher le groupe de Lorentz, comme nous venons de retoucher le groupe de Galilee," and Mr. Silberstein (*Theory of Relativity*, London, 1914, p. 108).

[2] There is a very serviceable statement with very little mathematics of the relativity doctrine by Mr. Langevin in the *Bulletin de la Societe Française de Philosophie*, 12me Annee, No. 1, Jan. 1912, whose language I have several times used. (See also his paper in

'Report of 4th international philosophical congress at Bologna,' 1911, vol. i. p. 193, and in *Revue de Metaphysique*.) I quote some words of his used, not in the paper but at the close of the discussion which followed it, p. 43. "We must conclude to the existence of a new reality, the Universe, of which the Space and Time particular to a group of observers are but perspectives, more immediately given, but relative and variable with the movement of the system of observation." One of the speakers in the discussion of Mr. Langevin's paper suggests, only in order to disavow it, the idea I have used of different perspectives of a solid object. I imagine the disavowal to be based on the belief that such perspectives are therefore illusions, instead of being as they are realities and physical realities. See later, Bk. III. ch. vii. and Mr. Russell's treatment of perspectives in recent works.

The memoirs of Messrs. Lorentz, Einstein, and Minkowski are now conveniently collected in a single volume, *Das Relativitätsprincip*, Leipzig and Berlin, 1913. On p. 58 above I have omitted to mention the name of the late P. Fitzgerald along with these writers.

CHAPTER III

MENTAL SPACE AND TIME

By mental or psychological time I mean the time in which the mind experiences itself as living, the time which it enjoys ; by mental space I mean, assuming it to exist, the space in which the mind experiences itself as living or which it enjoys. They are contrasted provisionally with the space and time of the objects of mind which the mind contemplates. I hope to show on the strength of experience that mental space and time possess the same characters and are related in the same intimacy of relation as physical Space and Time ; that the time of mental events is spatial and their space temporal precisely as with physical Space and Time, and further that mental time, the time in which the mind lives its life or minds its mind, is a piece of the Time in which physical events occur ; and similarly of mental space. In many respects it would have made the task of analysing physical Space and Time in the preceding chapters easier if, following the method of the angels and assuming mind to be an existence alongside of physical existence, I had examined first the simplest elements in mind rather than in physical objects, and with the results of the analysis of the familiar thing mind, had passed to the analysis of the less familiar external world. But I felt myself precluded from this procedure because it would have meant before approaching physical Space and Time that we should need to accept two very disputable propositions, first that the mind is spatial, that is, is enjoyed in space, and second, that this enjoyed space is at any instant occupied not merely by the mind's present but also by its enjoyed past and future.

93

Accordingly I have endeavoured to examine physical Space
and Time without encumbrance by these difficulties.

That the mind as the experienced continuum of
mental acts (the nature of what underlies this continuum
is a subject for later inquiry) is a time-series, and in
that sense is in time, or has Time in its very constitution,
would be admitted on all hands. By continuity is meant
mental or felt continuity, so that, by memory or other
means, in a normal mind no event occurs which is
disconnected with the rest. There may be intervals of
time, as in sleep without dreams, or in narcosis, when the
mind apparently ceases to act : "the mind thinks not
always." But consciousness, as William James puts it,
bridges these gaps, so long as it is normal, and it feels
itself one. The elements of this continuum are conscious
events or processes. There is no rest in mind but a
relative one. We only think there is, because with our
practical interests we are concerned with the persistent
objects—the trees and men, which we apprehend in what
James calls "substantive" conditions of mind. If we
overlook the transitions between these objects, their
repugnances and likenesses, how much more easy is it to
overlook the transitions in our minds, the feelings of
'and,' and 'but,' and 'because,' and 'if' or 'like'—the
"transitive" states. We catch them for notice when we
happen to be arrested in our thinking, when we leave off,
for instance, in a sentence with a 'because,' when the
forward and defeated movement of the mind is directly
made the centre of our attention.[1] The sense we have in
such cases that the flow of our meaning is stopped is
accompanied by caught breath or tense forward bending
of the head or other bodily gestures, but it is not to be
confused with the consciousness of these gestures. They
are but the outward bodily discharge of the mental arrest.
It is these transitive conditions which betray the real
nature of the mind. The substantive states are but

[1] There are many happy examples in Humpty Dumpty's poem in
Through the Looking-Glass : "I'd go and wake them, if ", "We
cannot do it, Sir, because——"

persistence in movements which have the same character and correspond to objects of the same quality. In itself the mind is a theatre of movement or transition, motion without end. Like all other things it has the glory of going on.

But not only is mind experienced in time, but the direct deliverance of our consciousness of external events is that the time in which we enjoy our mind is part of the same Time in which those external events occur. It is only when philosophy steps in with its hasty inter-pretations, that we can say that Time belongs, as Kant believed, to external events because they have a mental or internal side in our experiencing of them. On the contrary, to be aware of the date or duration of physical events is the most glaring instance, derived from direct experience, of how an enjoyed existent and a contemplated existent can be compresent with one another. In this case the compresence is a time-relation which unites both terms within the one Time (I am assuming, let me remind my reader, the hypothesis of direct apprehension of the external object). In memory or expectation we are aware of the past or future event, and I date the past or future event by reference to the act of remembering or expecting which is the present event. An event five years past occurred five years before my present act of mind. We have seen, in fact, that physical Time is only earlier or later, and that the instants in it are only past, present, or future in relation to the mind which apprehends. Now without doubt, when I remember that a friend called at my house an hour ago, I mean that that event occurred an hour before my present condition of myself in the act of remembering that event, and that the mental and the physical event are apprehended within the one Time.

Only in regard of present physical events does doubt arise. We are accustomed to call those physical events present which are contemplated by us in sensory form in the present moment of consciousness. Now it is certain that the physical events which I contemplate precede by a small but measurable interval my sensory apprehension of them, and this is true not only of events

outside me but of the events in my body which I
describe as occurring at the present moment. They are all
anterior to my apprehension of them. But this is not the
deliverance of unsophisticated experience, but a fact which
we learn about our process of perceiving external events,
and is not given directly in our acquaintance with them.
Ask an untrained man whether the events which he sees
occur at the same time as his perception of them, and he
is merely puzzled by the question. For him the present
events are those which he perceives, and he has not
asked himself, and does not understand, the question
whether they really are simultaneous with the perceiving
of them or not. Further experience of a reflective sort,
experimental experience of the times of reaction to
external objects, shows him that they are not. But
equally he may find by reflection or scientific methods
that the event he remembers as occurring an hour ago
occurred in reality an hour and five minutes ago or
longer. Thus the philosophical question of the precise
time-relation between our perception and its objects does
not arise for us in practice. It remains true that all our
mental events stand in some time-relation, whether
rightly apprehended or not, to the contemplated physical
events. The enjoyed mind is compresent in a time-
relation with those objects. This is the whole meaning
of a time-relation in which the terms are not both contemplated, as they are when we are dating two physical
events with reference to one another in physical Time,
but when the one is contemplated and the other enjoyed.
That the mental duration or instant stands thus in relation
to the contemplated instant in time shows, then, so far as
experience directly gives us information, that the times of
both terms are parts of one Time.

From this mere vague experience that I who enjoy
am in Time along with the event contemplated which is
in Time, we may easily pass to a more definite statement.
We may date the physical event with reference to the
physical events going on in my body at the 'present'
moment. Then I am contemplating a stretch of time
between the event and me (I may even, as we shall see

later when we come to discuss our memory of the past, *enjoy* the interval between me and my apprehension of the physical event). At a later stage in my experience, when I have learnt that my mental act occurs really at the same time as a certain physiological process which corresponds to it, I may contemplate the time-interval between that process and the cognised physical event, and then we have a still exacter notion of the time-relation, but clearly one which is only possible for more advanced experience and not given in the mere cognition, in the mere memory, for example, of my friend's visit an hour ago.

Turning to Space, we find that mind enjoys itself spatially, or is extensive, in the same sense as it is successive and endures in enjoyed time. But while it is admitted that mind as experienced is in time, the proposition that it is extended meets with direct and even contemptuous opposition. Partly the repugnance is moral; it seems to some to savour of materialism. Now if materialism in philosophy were forced upon us by inquiry we should have to make our account with it and acquiesce. Nothing can in fact be further from the spirit of the present investigation, as the whole issue of it will demonstrate. But even now it is plain that if mind is spatial like matter, Space is as much in affinity with mind as it is with matter and the fear of materialism is groundless. The other objection arises from the mistaken belief that a spatial mind must be apprehended like a spatial physical object. This, however, would be to imagine that the mind is asserted to enjoy itself in contemplated Space; whereas the assertion is that mind enjoys itself in enjoyed space, and we shall presently see that the space which we enjoy as occupied by our minds may also be contemplated as occupied by a physical thing. Bearing this proviso in mind, turn to experience itself. My mind is for me, that is for itself, spread out or voluminous in its enjoyment. Within this vague extension or volume the separate and salient mental acts or processes stand out as having position, and 'direction.' My mind is streaked with these more pungent processes, as when a shoot of painful consciousness is felt or a sudden thought produces a new distribution in this extended mass. These streaks and shoots of consciousness have the vaguest position, but they have it, and such position and direction are most clearly marked in the higher acts of mind, imagination, or desire, or thinking, and especially when there is a change in what we call the direction of our thinking. There is verifiable truth in the words of Tennyson "As when a great thought strikes along the brain and flushes all the cheek"; though he has described the enjoyed direction in terms of its position in contemplated Space.

Thus just as we enjoy a time filled with mental events, so we enjoy an extension or space filled with mental events. Further, as with time, so here the deliverance of experience is that in apprehending physical extension, say a physical object in space, we are aware in our act of enjoyment of an enjoyed space as related to the extension of the physical object within the one Space. Our mental space and our contemplated space belong experientially to one Space, which is in part contemplated, in part enjoyed. For all our physical objects are apprehended 'over there' in spatial relation to our own mental space. This is evident enough, when once the terms are understood in the case of sensible apprehension of objects in space. The contemplated and the enjoyed spaces are in spatial relation, though distance is only vaguely apprehended as somewhere there away from me. But what is true of perception is true also in imagination. The contemplated space is now only imagined, but it is still somewhere there away from me. Once more I cite Tennyson. The words on Gordon "Somewhere, dead, far in the waste Soudan" illustrate the relation of enjoyed to imagined space, both of them being equally real space, though their distance if vague in perception is still vaguer in imagination. I will add two less simple examples which I have used elsewhere.[1] Let any one who at all possesses sensory imagination think of the lines

---

[1] *Mind*, vol. xxi., 1912, 'On relations.'

> The same that ofttimes hath
> Charmed magic casements, opening on the foam
> Of perilous seas, in fairy lands forlorn ;

and ask himself whether he is not conscious of the object described as somewhere in Space along with himself, that is, does not enjoy himself in an enjoyed space, along with an object somewhere in contemplated Space. Here the Space is the Space of fancy, of fairyland. Or let him try the same experiment on

> The antechapel where the statue stood
> Of Newton with his prism and silent face,
> The marble index of a mind for ever
> Voyaging through strange seas of thought alone,

when he will enjoy himself in space, not only along with the statue of Newton somewhere there in Trinity College, Cambridge, but also with the strange seas over which Newton's mind is supposed to be travelling, the world of contemplated things before Newton's mind.

In saying that when I imagine an object I locate it somewhere in the same Space wherein I enjoy myself, I do not mean that I locate it somewhere in front of my eyes.[1] On the contrary, I locate it in the place in Space to which it actually belongs. If it is the image of the Soudan I locate it in the south of Egypt. For the imaged Space is but perceived Space as it appears in an imaged form. All images of external objects are themselves spatial in character, and their parts have position relatively to each other. But also they have position in the whole of Space so far as we imagine the rest of Space. Now images are for the most part isolated objects,

The place of an image.

---

[1] I believe that I have said so in one of my papers. From this disloyalty to my own principles I was saved by the admirable treatment of this subject in Mr. E. B. Holt's *Concept of Consciousness* (London, 1914), chap. xii. pp. 230 ff. I borrow from him the statement that the image taken by itself has no position at all. But I doubt if an image ever is cut off completely. And so I persist in holding that the image of a town belongs to the actual place of the actual town, only of course under the indistinctness and falsification which attach to any imagination. The matter becomes clear only at a later stage when we come to speak of illusions and imagination. See in particular the mirror experiment described in Bk. III, ch. vii.

cut off more or less completely from their surroundings, and so far as this is the case the image as a whole cannot be said to have position at all. But directly we ask where the image is we begin to supply in image the rest of Space. Thus if I can remember the map and bear in mind the way I am facing, I image the Soudan more or less accurately where I know it to be, or in other words where it actually is. The place of an image is its position in imaged Space, and according to the fulness of that imagination will its place be determined accurately or become so shadowy as almost to vanish. How the place in imaged Space is correlated with the place in perceived Space which is imaged in imaged Space, is discovered by experience, as for example, to take a very simple case, I recognise that the image of a person in front of me when I first look at him and then shut my eyes belongs to the same place as the percept of the same person. When the image is not the image of anything actual its place in actual Space is of course not actual either. This only means that the object imaged is not actual in the form which it assumes. It purports to have a place in Space, which is not actually filled by any such object. The Space which is imaged is still the same Space as is perceived, but it is occupied with imagined objects. Further discussion of the problems thus suggested belongs to a later part of our inquiry.[1]

Place of mental space
But this vague experience of interval in space between myself and the place of physical objects in space becomes more definite when I ask where is my mind and its enjoyed space in the whole of Space. I cannot ask where I am in enjoyed space, for the space and time I enjoy are the whole of enjoyed space and time. I can date a mental event in my past ; and I can dimly localise a mental event in my space : I can distinguish the outstanding point, or if it is a connected event, the streak in my space which it occupies. But when I ask when I occur in Time as a whole I answer by reference to some physical event in my body with which I am simultaneous. When I ask

[1] Bk. III. ch. vii.

where I am in the whole of Space I answer by reference to my body. My mind is somewhere within my body, or within my head, or when I have acquired knowledge about my central nervous system it is for me recognised as being *in the same place* as that system or more specifically as the brain or some part of it. In this way I localise my mind in Space by recognising it as occupying the same place as some physical object. Now this is our constant and early acquired experience. I feel myself somewhere in my body or more particularly in my head. I am now contemplating the whole of Space and localising my enjoyed space in the same place as a contemplated object my body ; just as I localise myself in time in the same part of physical Time as is occupied by my bodily ' present ' events.

All this will seem to some to be founded on an elementary blunder of confusion between the locality of consciousness and the sensations derived from the scalp or the movements of the eyes. All our mental life is accompanied by these experiences, and when we talk of enjoyed space we are thinking of and misinterpreting what we learn about our head. And this kind of localisation is an arbitrary matter. Did not Aristotle regard the mind as seated in the heart, and the brain as merely a cooling apparatus to the heart? He attended to the cardiac region, we to the head and brain. The case of Aristotle is really not damaging to our contention as it seems, but rather supports it. For though Aristotle is so far removed from us in time, it may reasonably be supposed that like us he felt his headaches and fatigue of attention in his head. If then he still located his mind in the heart, he must have done so, not because he was guided by direct experience of the parts most affected in mental process but from imperfect anatomy. His mistake is therefore irrelevant.

But, Aristotle apart, there is a clear distinction in experience between the contemplated sensa (or objects of sensation) belonging to the body and the movements of consciousness itself. In my own case a change of thought is nearly always accompanied by sensations of movement

in the eyes ; but I distinguish these from the acts of
thought. The consciousness of colour is different from
that of eye-movement, and is particularly easy to distinguish from it because vision is not localised in the body
like touch, but projected. I see a colour in the external
coloured object but I do not refer it (I mean in my plain
experience, apart from theories) to the eye. In localised
sensations like touch, the bodily object, say the hand,
does intrude into the felt pressure, and so it is easier here
to imagine that when we speak of the enjoyed place of a
touch sensation, we are thinking of the place where the
touch occurs. But even here it is possible to get a faintly
accentuated experience of the movement of consciousness
in sensing a touch as distinct from the actual sensum or
pressure *of* which we are conscious. This is best done
when there are two distinct sensa in the mind at once, as
when, leaning against an armchair, one is seeing a bright
light. There are then two differently localised movements of consciousness. Thus in the first place we may
distinguish the course of the thoughts from the accompanying bodily sensations. And in the next place in sensation
there is besides the sensum (the object sensed) the mental
act of sensing it, and it is this, not the other, which is
enjoyed. Thus it cannot be because we have sensations
from the region of the head that we assert our experiencing
of external objects to be located in enjoyed space within
the head. For the same problem arises with regard to
these sensations from the head, it is their objects which
are in the contemplated head ; the enjoyments of apprehending them are in an enjoyed space, whose place
is identified with the place of the head. It is indeed
difficult, if not impossible, to understand how we could
ever correlate a particular mental process as we do with a
particular neural process possessing its contemplated or
physical character, had not mind already its own spatial
enjoyment. The correlation, if that is the right term to
use, is the identification of an enjoyed space with an
observed or contemplated one.

The identification of the place of mind with that of

the body which begins by locating the mind roughly within the body and ends by the more accurate correlation of mental with physiological processes within the central nervous system is not mere matter of theory but is derived from empirical experience ; and experience which in its earlier stages is of a quite elementary character.   It is an essential part of the history whereby we become aware of ourselves as a union of body and mind, a body organic to a mind, a mind whose functioning is conditioned by a body.   I shall call this union of mind and body the person.   In every stage of the growth of our self or person two elements are palpably present, one the body and the other the subject or consciousness.   Sometimes it is the body which is predominant, as when I say I have a headache or a cold and do not feel quite myself ; sometimes it is the subject or mental factor, as when I say I am most myself when I let myself go dreaming by day, or I never feel like myself when I am doing something so distasteful as reading examination papers or books of travel, or that I wish myself "like to one more rich in hope."   In the first case myself is an embodied self, in the second it is the inner self, the self which thinks, desires, imagines, wishes, wills.   The most developed stage of the person is the personality, the persistent stable organised set of habits of action, thought, and feeling by which I am to be judged, by which I stand or fall.   I say, for instance, I was not myself when I lied or cheated. The person is in the first case mainly a body, in the second it is mainly something psychical, in the third it is something spiritual.   The two elements are, however, traceable everywhere in the history ; the one the body, what Locke called the man, the other the subject, the element of consciousness itself.[1]

The bodily self or person is the one with which we are chiefly concerned.   We experience it in the form of organic and motor or kinaesthetic sensations as well as the special sensations of touch, sight, or other sensations derived from the body itself.   The body is a percept, in

[1] For fuller treatment see 'Self as Subject and as Person' (*Proceedings Aristotelian Society*, 1910–11, vol. xi.).

which various sensa or sensed elements and corresponding ideational elements are revealed. It is like other external things a synthesis of these various sensa, some felt, some suggested. But the bodily self or person is never the body alone but the body with the apprehension of it. It is the experienced body along with the experiencing of it, these two forming a whole. This bodily self is the nucleus of the later stages of the self; but it is only the person with its two elements which could thus serve as their foundation, and not the body alone. How intimately the bodily experience is involved in the inner self or in the personality is easy to recognise. For motor sensations in a very high degree, and organic sensations as well, are present in all the higher life of thought, emotion, and will, and sustain that life and give it richness and resonance. Thinking is not, indeed, identical with the tense movements and strains of attention, but it is sustained by them, and the emotions without organic sensations and the other sensations of the expression of the emotion would be like an old vintage of port wine which has lost its colour and 'body.' Even where these elements are less apparent they betray themselves to closer inspection. When I feel myself ill at ease, or not myself, in the company of a person whom I dislike, what may be uppermost in my mind is the hindrance which his presence offers to the free working of my inner thoughts and wishes. But I may soon discover that these impediments to my spiritual activity mean also restriction of my motor freedom, or other reactions of bodily uneasiness. I recognise here that I am both spirit and body, and the one will not work freely without the other. Other facts of the normal and the abnormal life of mind supply additional and familiar evidence. Changes and disturbances in the organic and motor sensations or, apart from them, in the organs of sense and connected parts of the body, though we may not be aware of them through means of organic or motor sensations, may and do alter the tone and build of the whole personality. Such changes occur normally at the climacteric epochs of life, like the time of teething or adolescence. In abnormal cases, failures in organic or tactual or visual sensibility, or any functional breakdown, may be an important factor in violent alterations of temper and thought, or even lead to division of personality.

The difference of the bodily stage of the personal life and the higher stages is in fact mainly one of emphasis. We are absorbed in the practical urgency of our bodily needs and changes and the subject-side of the self does not stand out in our experience. Even in ideation or volition, it is still the things we think about, or imagine, or desire, which interest us most. If we were confined in our inner life to the sensations we have from external objects we should still have an inner life, but should hardly notice it. But imagination, and, above all, willing and desiring, which go on in the absence of sensory objects corresponding to our ideas, begin to bring the mental action as such into relief. Even then it may be doubted whether the inner life of the subject would be attended to for its own sake were it not that in the intercourse with other persons, to which we chiefly owe the unfolding of the personality proper, we are thrown back upon ourselves by the effect of contrast, or imitation, or co-operation or rivalry, and we become definitely aware of ourselves as subjects of experience. It is then we can begin to see that even in sensation it is we who have the sensations, and it is then that the conditions arise for the birth of the science of psychology.

The higher self is thus in all its stages a continuation and expansion, and refinement of the bodily self. The body, it may be observed, is capable of indefinite extension. We feel the ground at the end of the stick we carry, not at the finger which holds the stick : the stick has become part of our body. So may anything in contact with our bodies ; like our dress, injury or offence to which we resent as we do offences to our body. All this has been described by Lotze in a well-known passage.[1] But my 'body' may include things not in contact with me, or indeed any of the external objects I am interested in—my room, my

---

[1] *Microcosmus*, 'On dress and ornament,' Bd. ii. pp. 203 ff. Engl. transl. vol. i. pp. 586 ff.

books, my friends, and all the things I care about, philosophy or psychology, which are systems of knowledge,
the works of Plato, the history of my country. All these
things may become extensions of my body and the experiences I get from them may be for a time of a class with
my organic and other bodily sensations. The self, if I may
quote a happy phrase of Mr. Henry James in one of his
novels, " overflows into " these objects. Damage to my
property, or disaster to philosophy or my country, is like
a blow in the face. I may in certain moods feel myself
one with the universe : the universe has become part of
my body. Many or most of these extensions of the
body are only possible to a life which has gone far beyond
the interests of the body itself. But still these higher
objects of interest may become as intimately organic to
me as my proper body. This is the interpretation of that
exchange of the self and the not-self which has sometimes
been thought to demonstrate the ultimate unreality of
the self. The not-self becomes part of the self and I may
even turn myself outside me so that it becomes part of
the not-self. Yet the not-self in such cases never becomes
part of the subject nor the subject part of the contemplated
world. I may take external things into my body or loose
my body into the external world. But it is but a shifting of the borders within which I have the experience of
intimacy or organic connection. My body may expand
to include the world or it may shrink and be lost in a remote and independent system of things outside me.

Subject and
od r
f rred to
same place.
    The bodily person is thus the type and beginning of
all forms of the self, and we may return to the question
of the experience by which in the self the subject and the
body come to be apprehended as unified into a whole
or person, which is more than a mere aggregate. Their
unity is known in its simpler stages through very elementary experiences. In the first place we have the direct
identification of the place of mind and body. The enjoyed
space of the one is identified with the contemplated space
of the other in precisely the same way as we identify a
colour as occupying roughly the same space as a hardness
or a tone, or as we identify again roughly the place of an

organic sensum of, say, cramp in an area of the skin with a touch sensum in that area of the skin.   In both these cases we have two external objects localised within the same contour.   In the case we are considering we localise the mind and the body within the contour of the body and declare it to be in the body or even more narrowly in the head.   There is no difference in the two cases except that one of the things whose space is identified is spread out in enjoyed and not in contemplated space. This identification is accomplished experientially.   More-over, we do not necessarily refer the consciousness always to the place of the body, we may refer the body to the consciousness as being in part of it in the same place. Here too we have a parallel in external experience.   Pain in the toe is an organic sensum and the toe itself is seen. But W. James has said with as much truth as wit that when a baby feels a pain in its toe it is really feeling the toe in the pain.   Now the pain, though a sensum and not a mere feeling of painfulness, is notwithstanding more personal, nearer to mind than the seen toe.   It is but a step from this to identifying the seen space of part of the body with the enjoyed space of the mind.   Mental events and bodily events are thus realised to belong to one place, and we may add by similar considerations, roughly speak-ing, to one time.   Mind and body are *experientially* one thing, not two altogether separate things, because they occupy the same extension and places as a part of the body.

Besides this direct spatial identification, the union of mind and body is experienced by us in the bodily movements into which the mental response to external things is continued.   The mental process of perception of the apple is continued into the movement of seizing the apple, which movement in its turn is perceived. Moreover, there is a difference in these responses with the difference in the mental processes—with their more or less vaguely experienced differences of locality within enjoyed space.   In securing its ends the mind's actions issue into appropriately distinct bodily actions.   The body is experienced as an instrument of the mind.

Mental process on-tinued in bodily movement.

This is true not only in the life of the senses and appetites, but also in the life of intellect. We experience that these activities issue in bodily movements which sustain them and affect the external world, were it only in the form of speech. Thus the person is experienced as no mere aggregate of mind and body, because these have place (and time) in common and their movements are in experienced connection. And all the facts before referred to which indicate how changes in the one determine changes in the other come in, when the person reflects, to swell the tide of evidence flowing in that direction.

The map of mental ace.

So much, except for such phrases as imply a slightly more extended knowledge or reflection, may be taken as describing the ordinary history of how mind and body come to be recognised as connected ; and it is compatible with different hypotheses as to the ultimate nature of that connection. That experience teaches us that the mind is somewhere within the body and is felt in particular within the head ; and it answers roughly the question, Where is the enjoyed space of mind in the whole Space which is contemplated ? But from what we learn about our own bodies and from the bodies and, above all, the brains of others, we are able to establish a much more detailed and intimate connection between mental processes and physiological ones. Let us assume for shortness that consciousness is conditioned by physical events in the cerebral cortex.[1] This must not be taken to mean that there is some place in that cortex at which the mental event is located, as if the rest of the brain or the central nervous system were indifferent. No conception could be so naïve. Rather what is meant is that certain processes occurring in specific parts of the cortex are so vital for a particular sort of mental event that unless the affection reached this part

---

[1] Written before the appearance of Dr. Head's recent paper in *Brain*, xli., 1918, on 'Sensation and the Cerebral Cortex.' (Cp. later, Bk. III. ch. vi. Suppl. Note.) The precise localisation of mental process is, however, indifferent for our purpose here.

of the cortex the mental event would not occur. We learn then that specific consciousness such as vision is correlated with specific movements in the occipital region of the brain. Plainly this kind of knowledge is not direct experience of my own vision or of its relation to the brain. For it is a commonplace that in seeing a tree I know nothing of the occipital movement, and when I think of the occipital movement I am not seeing the tree. But it is knowledge *about* my own vision, and extends my experience of vision, for when I see I can think of these processes in my own brain, in ideal contemplation, and when I think of them I can think of vision in ideal enjoyment. Having learnt from other brains what underlies vision I can use that knowledge to understand my own.

Now if we accept the commonly held results of correlation between specific mental acts and specific neural processes, we arrive at a much closer conception of how the psychosis is related to the neurosis. Instead of roughly feeling our mind within our heads we can think of a psychosis as occupying the place of its correlative neurosis. Once more no particular theory is here implied of the ultimate connection of psychosis and neurosis. The doctrine that they are correlated or even parallel, regarded as a bare compendious statement of facts, is sufficient for our purpose. There may be interaction between mind and brain ; there may be, as indeed I believe to be the case, identity of psychosis with its own neurosis.[1] But this is not necessary here to affirm. Those who think that secondary qualities like colour and sound interpenetrate, that is, are found in precisely the same place, may well believe that a psychosis may occur in the place of a neurosis and yet be something distinct from the neurosis. We have made no such supposition as to the coincidence of a colour and a smell, for we have only supposed them to coincide in the rough.[2] The question may be left open and we may be content with the hypothesis founded on cerebral

---

[1] See later, Bk. III. ch. i. A.
[2] See later, Bk. II. ch. vi. A, p. 275.

localisation that mental events, with their specific enjoyed place, are in the very contemplated place of their neurosis. This is a mere extension of the experienced rough identity of place between mind and body.

This picture of our neural space is painted by inference. But it enables us to derive two results. First it substitutes, as said, for the vague blur of enjoyed space a map of that enjoyed region, and we can attach a definite meaning to the proposition that our mental states are enjoyed as having place and direction. So far as any one mental process is defined against the general mental background, its direction is that of its specific anatomical or physiological path. The direction is defined within the brain itself and it does not change if I alter the position of my body by turning round. For my brain, or at least my central nervous system, is the whole region which I can experience in enjoyment. I am my own microcosm so far as enjoyment goes. When I turn round, my brain processes may change their direction according to the compass used in contemplated Space, but not in relation to my brain as taken by itself. The orientation of its constituent movements does not change when the orientation of the contemplated brain changes in the rest of contemplated Space. It is therefore irrelevant if any one objects that a mental direction would vary with every movement of my body.[1]

Some of these anatomical or physiological paths are occupied by present states of mind ; some of them by

[1] I may note here that the direction of a mental process is thus understood by me literally, in its spatio-temporal sense. Sometimes it is said, and I have myself on various occasions said, that in any act of cognition, e.g. in seeing a tree or colour, the mental act is directed upon the object contemplated. I suppose it is this which may have led to the criticism that the direction of a mental process alters with the position of the head. But direction is understood in these other statements metaphorically, as when we speak of directing our attention to an object. It means strictly in such phrases little more than being concerned with, and expresses the correlation of the mental act with its object, the parallelism of mental act (or its neural process) with the external object with which it is in my language compresent. (See later, Bk. III. ch. i. A.)

the mental states which are the enjoyments of remembered
or expected objects, that is, which are in ordinary language
memories or expectations of ourselves.   Not all of our
brain is necessarily at any one moment occupied by
mental events, except so far as the whole brain may be
needed to function in order that there may be specific
functioning of any one path within it.   This apparent
lapse or abeyance of mental action in certain parts of
our neural system raises a problem.   But we need not
discuss it now.   The fact is that not every part of our
brain is mentally effective at once : we may see without
hearing.

Secondly, with our picture before us, we can begin
to understand better the connection of enjoyed space
and time.   For mental events are processes in time
and occupy our enjoyed space, and different mental
events are connected together either as contemporaneous
with or following one another within this space.
Hence in this microcosm of enjoyed space and time,
time, that is, enjoyed time, is laid out in space,
primarily in enjoyed space but also in the contemplated
space which is identical with it.   It is therefore no
mere metaphor or illusion by which we represent the
passage of mental life in time by spatial pictures.   For
now we recognise that in fact mental time enjoyed in
mental process occupies space, or like physical Time it
is experientially spatial.

So far we can see ; but what we learn is little more
than a recognition that mental processes which occur in
time, and which are related in time-relations, occupy
space.   But to go further requires us to determine the
relation of the time of the mental process, that is, the
enjoyed date, to the time of the physiological process
which corresponds to it.   This is a matter which presents
great difficulty.   Strangely enough, though we accept at
once the proposition that the mind is in Time and with
difficulty the proposition that it is in Space, yet it is easy
to see that if the mind is in Space the place of a mental
process is identical with that of its brain process, but the

*Mental
space-
time : the
problem.*

question, Are their times identical or not ? seems to us half unnecessary to ask and exceedingly difficult to answer. The reason is, that the time of a present mental event is clearly and palpably itself the date from which we reckon Time, and we need to ask no more about it. But we can only give definiteness to the place of a mental event by correlating and identifying it with the place of some contemplated event.

Let us state the problems before us more distinctly. I am at this moment seeing a colour and hearing a sound. The corresponding parts of the brain in the occipital and the temporal regions are excited at one and the same time : certain phases of the movements are contemporaneous. But suppose that while I am at this moment seeing a colour I am remembering part of a friend's conversation in which the predominant images are auditory. The corresponding enjoyments which occupy my brain are the present enjoyment of the colour, that is, the seeing of it, and the renewal in memory (I purposely leave the phrase vague) of the hearing of the conversation. Is that renewal by way of memory wholly a present enjoyment ? If so, then, since the like would apply to expectations, and my mind is filled with present thoughts, images, rememberings, and expectations, my brain would be occupied at this moment by a mass of present enjoyments. The time of an enjoyment would be identical with the time in contemplated Time of its corresponding neurosis. Since the time of every part of the brain corresponding to mental action would be the same, we should have in mental space an exception to what we have learned of contemplated Space, that it is primarily not all simultaneous. We are forced, therefore, to ask ourselves whether the time of a mental enjoyment is always that of its underlying neural process, or in other words whether a remembered enjoyment is not itself a past enjoyment, not a present one. We shall find, strange as the statement may seem, that this is the truth. But the inquiry cannot be an easy nor a short one.

CHAPTER IV

MENTAL SPACE-TIME

LET us for the sake of clearness begin, not with the Memory of objects. memory of ourselves, but the memory of objects, that is to say, of things or events which we have experienced before, and in remembering are aware that we have so experienced them. This is the fully developed kind of memory, to which other acts of so-called memory are only approximations. James writes : [1] " The object of memory is only an object imagined in the past (usually very completely imagined there) to which the emotion of belief adheres," and in substance there is little to add to this statement. I prefer to say the object of memory (what I shall call ' the memory ' as distinguished from the mental apprehension of it, which is ' remembering ') is an object imagined or thought of in my past. I say ' my past,' for I may believe in the assassination of Julius Caesar as a past event without being able to remember it. The object, then, is before my mind, bearing on its face the mark of pastness, of being earlier than those objects which I call present. In the mind there corresponds to it the act of imagining or conceiving it, and there is in addition the act of remembering it, the consciousness that I have had it before.

The pastness of the object is a datum of experience, directly apprehended. The object is compresent with me *as past.* The act of remembering is the process whereby this object becomes attached to or appropriated by myself, that is, by my present consciousness of myself which has been already described, in which may be distinguished

[1] *Psychology*, vol. i. p. 652.

a subjective and a bodily element unified in the person. The past object is earlier than my present act of mind in remembering, or my equivalent bodily state, whichever may happen to be more predominant in my mind. When the past object is thus appropriated by myself I am aware of it as belonging to me, as mine, as occurring in *my* past. This is the consciousness that the object is remembered. In precisely the same sense as I am aware of a perceived object when I have before me a sensory experience, I have a memory when I have before me an experience of the past and appropriate it to my personality. The object is then not only past but belongs to a past in which I contemplate myself (that is my body) as having been existent also and related to the object.

No refer-
e   .o he
erceived

    In this as in many other psychological inquiries, error may arise from reading into the experience more than is there. The actual past event as we once perceived it is remembered as the memory of it which has been described. I may not say that in memory I am aware of the memory as referred in thought, or in some other way, to the actual object I once perceived. It is true that I can in reflection, in a sophisticated mood, so speak. But this is not the deliverance of the experience itself called having a memory. For example, I may see a man and remember that I heard his conversation yesterday. Here I have the actual man before me ; but my memory of his conversation is not first taken by itself and then referred to him as I heard him yesterday. The memory-object is itself the object, and the only one I have, of the consciousness that I heard him yesterday. So far as I remember that, there is no reference to any former perception of the man, even though he is now also present in perception. The percept of him and the memory of him are two different appearances which in their connection reveal the one thing, the man, whom we now know to be to-day by perceiving, and to have been yesterday by remembrance. Moreover the memory is as much a physical object as the percept. He is physical in so far as, in Mr. Russell's happy phrase, he behaves according to the laws of physics. The remembered man does not speak now, but he is remembered as speaking, or, to vary the example, the memory-object is the physical man cutting physical trees yesterday.

Thus we have not in memory itself any reference to the perceived. The memory itself is the only knowledge we have that there ever was something perceived. But there is a real truth misrepresented by the erroneous statement. Like a single perception, a single memory is incomplete. The particular percept is full of movement towards other aspects of the thing perceived, and the memory in like manner throws out feelers to other memories. These memories through their internal coherence and continuity build up for us our memory of the whole thing of which they are partial representations, and, as in the case just given, may blend in turn with fresh perceptions, or, again, with expectations of the future. It is then that in our unsophisticated experience (as distinct from the sophisticated deliverances of the reflective psychologist or philosopher) we can think of our friend as the same thing compresent with us in more than one memory. Even then we only introduce into our experience of him the element of his having once been perceived, through familiarity with the blending of perceptions with memory-ideas of the same thing.[1] For this reason it is that, as has often been observed by psychologists, we learn so much more directly about the nature of Time from expectation of the future than from remembrance of the past. Expectation is precisely like remembering except that the object has the mark of future, that is of later than our present, instead of past or earlier. Now we are practical creatures and look forward to the satisfaction of our needs, and the past interests us only theoretically or, if practically, as a practical guidance for the future. But in expectation the anticipated object

---

[1] For the synthesis of many objects or appearances of a thing into a thing see the discussion later, Bk. III. ch. vii. vol. ii., where it will be seen that the unity of a thing which underlies its various appearances, the objects of perception or memory, is the volume of space-time which it occupies. That volume is filled by each of its appearances, and that is why a single percept or a single memory can be the appearance or 'presentation' of the thing.

is, or very often is, replaced continuously and coherently by the percept, and the expected object may now become a memory. I remember now how the object appeared to me an hour past when I expected it. But whereas the expectation is in the ordinary course succeeded by fulfilment in perception, memory need not be so succeeded and most often is not.

Now it is not the whole thing which we need have before us in memory, but only its appearance altered by the lapse of Time, seen through the haze of Time, as things distant in Space are coloured by their remoteness. The lapse of Time may distort, and when to Time is added the subjective prejudices of the experient the memory of the thing may be highly distorted. But it remains what it declares itself to be when supplemented by similar appearances, nothing but the revelation of the thing through that mist of intervening Time, and the thing itself is only given in the actual memory through the mere reaching out of any experience to other experiences of the like sort.

A memory not a present object.

Thus we avoid the first error of interpreting memory to mean more than it contains. No wonder memory is regarded as so mysterious if it is supposed also to inform us of the perceived past, as if that perceived past could be thought of except through some idea other than the memory. A second error is to suppose that the memory is in some sense present and that it is referred to the past through certain indications of a subjective or personal kind. In one form or another this doctrine is very common. Our ideas come to us in succession it is said, but the succession of ideas is not the idea of their succession. To be distinguished as past or future from the present they must all be present together. "All we immediately know of succession is but an interpretation . . . of what is really simultaneous or coexistent." [1] Even for James the feeling of the past is a present feeling. How far this is true of the *feelings* of past, present, and future we shall inquire presently. Of the objects, it is, I

[1] J. Ward, *Psychological Principles* (Cambridge, 1918), p. 214; Art. *Encycl. Brit.* ed. ix. p. 64b.

venture to think, in flat contradiction to experience which declares the memory to have the mark of the past on its forehead, and the expected that of the future. Not all the subtle and important discovery of temporal signs,[1] whereby places in time are discriminated as local signs discriminate positions in space, avails to explain how objective past or future could be known as past or future were they not already so presented. For whether these temporal signs are drawn from the movement of attention or are bodily experiences with a rhythmical character like the breathing or the heart-beats, they tell us of our person or rather of our body, but they tell us nothing directly of the objects remembered or expected.[2] When we have correlated these personal acts of mind with the time-order of physical events we can use them to compute more accurately the dates of external events. They are indirect measures of succession, but not direct apprehensions of it. On the contrary, they are themselves successive and require some other indication of their own time-order. But if they carry their time-record with them, then past and future need not be simultaneous with the present in our apprehension of events.

The truth is that remembering and expecting do occur at the present moment ; but we are not entitled, therefore, to declare their objects simultaneous with the present. To be apprehended as a memory in the act of remembering simultaneously with an act of present perception is not to be apprehended as simultaneous with the 'present' object. The simple deliverance of experience is that it is apprehended as past. The notion that it must be simultaneous with the present in order to be referred to the past is thus the intrusion of a theory into the actual experience.

Remembering has been described as an act whereby a memory is appropriated by the self and recognised as my

[1] J. Ward, Art. *Encycl. Brit.* p. 64b, *Psychol. Princ.* pp. 197 ff.

[2] The same thing is true of the local signs. They tell us directly of our own bodies, but not of the external extension or position, except through correlation and indirectly (see later, Bk. III. ch. vi.).

past object.   The features of the act of appropriation are more easily seen in the act of expectation.   There the mind reaches out towards the imagined future event, and as the expectation becomes more distinct and intensive the image rises out of isolation and is incorporated with the personality.   At first there is an image with a future mark but relatively disconnected from the personal life. Gradually it acquires what James calls intimacy, becomes warm with the personal attachment, is attended by emotion. Think of the expectation of some promotion or the fear of some disaster.   Expectation is thus a desire or aversion whose aim is not practical but theoretical ; it is satisfied by fuller cognition ; and in turn all desire is, on its cognitive side, expectation.   If we turn to remembering with this clue we discover the same features.   There, also, is an isolated image, the memory with the mark of the past.   As we remember, it invades us, comes out of its isolation.   If the image is of Caesar's death, which we cannot remember, it may be vivid but it fails to invade our personality and link up with our life.   It is not a memory but only an imagination and a conceptual extension of past time into a past century with which we had no personal touch.   Let it be the thought of a verse once heard but barely rising and in fragments into our mind.   We search for the missing or defective words until they at last spring into view and our aim is achieved and we remember that we heard them once.   Thus remembering is a kind of desire, but, unlike expectation, directed backwards.[1]   It is a retrospective desire ; and just as in expectation we find it difficult at times to distinguish the calm contemplation of a future event from the passionate movement to meet it, so in remembering, especially if it does not proceed with ease, we can feel sometimes the passionate effort to drag up the remembered event into clear vision of it.   When Odysseus meets his mother in the shades, he asks her the manner of her death, whether it was by disease or the arrows of Artemis. She answers him that it was none of these things, " but longing for you and your counsels, Odysseus, and for

[1] See Art. 'Conational Psychology,' *Brit. J. of Psych.* vol. iv., 1911.

your loving-kindness, which robbed me of my sweet life." [1]
Substitute in this passage remembering for longing ; the
tenderness of the passage would in part disappear, but its
psychology remains unaltered.   Just as expecting is part
of the practical effort towards bringing the desired future
object before us, so remembering is the speculative desire
of reinstating the past or rather of reinstating ourselves
in compresence with it, or, as we say, in presence of it.
And it brings the past out of the depths in that form in
which an event or thing which was really past can be
apprehended at a later date.   For Time is real and the
past is real as past.   It is not real as being present ; it is
now no longer.   But it was real, and reveals itself to
speculative or theoretical desire in the form of a memory
which is made the personal property of the experient.

So far, we have been concerned with memory proper, Quasi-
where the object is an image or thought with a date, memories.
however imperfectly the date is apprehended.   It is not
necessary for our purpose to describe how we come to be
aware of the accurate date, which involves conceptual
processes, even in dating a past event five minutes ago.
This is a question of the measuring of Time.   But partly
because of the intrinsic importance of the subject and
partly for future use we may make certain observations
about the time-characters of ideas in experiences which
are not proper memory, but are often loosely called so.
In every contemplation we enjoy ourselves, as we have
seen, in a time-relation with our object.   But the object
may have no date.   It has its internal time-character, as
when I call up in my mind a picture of a man running,
or even a thing like a landscape where there is no movement but where the spatial extension involves Time in its
intrinsic character.   In such a case the image, being a
time-saturated object, is contemplated as somewhere in
Time, but the position of it as a whole in Time is not
dated.   This distinguishes a mere revival without
memory, or a mere fancy, from a memory proper.   It
belongs to Time but has no particular date.   In the next

[1] *Odyssey*, xi. 202-3.

place, there are reproduced mental objects or characters of things which are not even images at all. Such are the ideal supplements which qualify a sensory object and with it constitute a percept. This supplement has again its internal time-character, but it is not an object distinct from the sensory object. A simple example is the perception of a certain group of colours and shapes as a man. The human characters are only elements in the total which are supplied in ideal form. Consequently they share the date of the present sensum, and in this qualified sense the past is contained in the present.[1] Lastly, I may have ideas which are apprehended as past, which are parts of a successive experience and are retained in the mind but are not memories proper. For instance, the first words of a sentence which are still in my mind at the end or in the middle of the sentence. It would be a mere misdescription to say that the idea was first present and then referred to the past. It is a past object. But it is not a memory ; for, though retained from the past, it is not, like a memory, recovered from the past.

The 'specious present' a succession. Thus an image may either be dated and remembered, or, like Caesar's death or other non-personal event, be dated but not remembered, or it may have no specific date, or having a date it may be merely retained. But further, an object may be in the past and yet not an image at all but a sensum. We are thus led to the so-called 'specious present.' Sensory objects, though as a matter of fact they precede the moment of apprehending them by a very small interval, which is not experienced as such but only discovered by reflection and experiment, are in general called present in so far as they are the objects of the present sensing, and this is a mere matter of words, for such objects are the point of reference for earlier or later objects. When I apprehend a sound and a light at the same moment, they are for practical purposes taken as simultaneous though they are not so in fact. But we have mental processes which take place successively where yet the objects are present in sensory form. Such an

[1] See later at end of the chapter.

experience is an example of what is called the 'specious present,' because it is not a 'mathematical' moment but experienced as a duration. The familiar example is that of the path of the meteor where the whole movement is sensory and the path of light is seen at once. We never sense an instant of time, which is, taken by itself, a concept or implies conception. Our sensible[1] experience of Time is primarily that of a duration ; and experiment has determined what are the smallest intervals between two stimuli of sound or other kinds which are experienced as durations, and what interval of time filled by intermittent experiences of certain kinds, for example the strokes of a bell, can be held together at once in the mind. The specious present does not mean necessarily a duration which is filled with sensa. It is commonly taken to include also the fringe of past or future objects which have ceased to be sensory, or are not yet so, and approach the state of images, as in the case of a succession of sounds retained together in the mind, for example, in hearing strokes of a metronome, or the words of a connected sentence. Let us confine ourselves to the span of sensory consciousness. In that duration some of the elements though sensory are not only past in the order of the actual occurrence of their stimuli, but are past to an unprejudiced experience of them. Thus though the meteor's path is given to us in a line of light, we are aware of the meteor's movement through that line. Rapid as the movement was we are aware of the meteor's having been at one end before it was at the other. Two reasons may blind us to this truth that the meteor's path is seen as a succession. The first is the fear that the movement would, on this account of the matter, be resolved into a mere series of successive separate positions and its unity be destroyed. The movement is unitary and it is apprehended as such. Undoubtedly, but equally it is apprehended as occurring in a space and occupying a time. How groundless is this fear that a movement so

---

[1] I use this word for convenience. It does not imply that Time (or Space) is sensed but only that it is apprehended through sense. (For the proper apprehension of Time and Space, see later, Bk. III. ch. vi.)

described is a mere succession of separate point-instants, as if these could be discontinuous, is clear enough from the general notion of Space and Time, and will be more fully seen in the next chapter. The other reason for neglecting the successiveness experienced within the duration of the meteor's path is the fact that, owing to persistence of the sensory stimulation in the retina, the line of movement is before the mind as a stretch of space. This arises from the character of our vision. The separate stimuli leave their after-effects along the retina. This does not carry with it, as is hastily assumed, the consequence that the sensory object is seen all of it in the present. On the contrary, not only is this in ex-perience not so, but the spatial path of the meteor seen 'all at once,' that is, taken altogether in vision, is the best illustration of the essentially temporal character of Space. The visual arrangements actually enable the path to be dated instead of occurring all at one moment. The sensa earlier than the point of light directly present do not in this case fade away into real images. In the case of a specious present occupied by strokes of a metronome I will not undertake to say whether the preceding strokes are retained as after-sensations or are images. I have not the requisite experimental intimacy with the facts. But if they are ideas they are at least past, and if they are not sensations it is because there may be no apparatus in hearing for retaining past sensations in different places, as is the case with the eye.

The c n bread h but not depth.   Thus the 'specious present' is not present at all, but includes within it distinctions of past and present. We may add of future as well. For the broad present may contain at least dawning ideas of what is to come, and even dawning sensory objects, for in vision anyhow we have, corresponding with after-sensations, 'before-sensa-tions' in the process during which a colour sensation is gradually rising to its full intensity or saturation. ('Anklingen der Empfindung,' H. Ebbinghaus calls it [1]). Within this broad duration there is succession experienced

[1] See H. Ebbinghaus, *Grundzüge der Psychologie*, Bd. i. p. 230 (ed. i., Leipzig, 1902).

as such.   It has been compared by James to a saddleback as
opposed to the present instant which is a knife edge.   But
there is no reason in the facts to declare that the present is
saddlebacked, except so far as sensory objects are simultaneous and not successive as when we see red and blue at
once.   In other words we should distinguish the 'broad'
from the 'deep' present.   The present always has breadth
as including many simultaneous objects.   But it has not
depth, that is, breadth in time.   Its depth is a succession
within duration.   No doubt 'the specious present' is a
useful conception if it serves as a reminder that we never
sense the present instant or the present object by itself, but
that we always apprehend a bit of duration, and as a rough,
practical description of the present, as rough as the habitual
description of present objects as present when they are
really slightly past.   But otherwise we are compelled to
conclude that what it describes is not a fundamental fact
of our time experience, and that rather it misinterprets
that experience.   It describes merely the interesting and
important fact that our minds are able to hold together
a certain number of objects without having recourse to
memory proper, and in particular that a certain number
of sensa occupying time in their occurrence can thus be
held together in our minds.   The length of the time
interval so filled varies with the sensory events which
occur in it.   If the specious present is understood in a
different way it is specious in the other sense of deceiving
us.   Perhaps it may be compared with that other interesting and important fact of the existence of a threshold of
sensation below which amounts of stimulation are not
felt.   This was interpreted by Fechner to mean that the
threshold was in some special sense the zero of sensation.   Whereas any sensation whatever may be taken as
zero if we make it the beginning of our scale.[1]

The 'specious present' is a comparatively considerable time interval of some seconds.   The minimal duration
which we apprehend as duration is vastly smaller.[2]   But

---

[1] On this topic see the discussion in Ebbinghaus, Bd. i. pp. 507 ff.
[2] For the data see ch. i. of *Psychologie der Zeitauffassung*, by
V. Benussi (Heidelberg, 1913).

if we learn by experience that the first contains succession within its duration we may conclude that the elementary duration is successive too, that in fact there is no duration which is not a duration of succession, though the successive moments in a very small duration may not be and are not distinguishable. Or if this is too much to say, then we must urge at least that succession is not something new and additional to duration, but past, present, and future represent distinctions drawn within duration. There is as much difficulty in conceiving elementary durations succeeding one another within a longer duration as in conceiving any duration to be intrinsically a lapse in time and therefore intrinsically successive. We have yet to see how mathematical or conceptual instants can be real. But that our elementary experience of Time should be extensive and yet admit of succession within it is no more difficult to understand than that a blur of red blood should under the microscope reveal itself as a number of red bodies swimming in a yellow plasma, or that sensations we cannot distinguish from one another may under other conditions be known to be distinct. The conclusion is that our sensibility to succession is not so great as our sensibility to duration. Where both can be apprehended the duration and the succession are seen to be of the same stuff. This is true of contemplated or objective Time. In what sense it can be held that Time as we experience it in ourselves is other than a duration which is intrinsically successive passes my understanding.

We have been dealing hitherto with the time of objects and have found that the past is in no sense present but is revealed as past. We have now to turn to the much more difficult matter of enjoyed time. It may be said : past physical events are presented as past, but when the past is declared to be somehow present, the reference is to the apprehension of it, as when, for instance, the feeling of the past is called by James a present feeling or the immediate apprehension of a short succession of events a specious present. I do not feel sure that this is what is meant in all cases. But we may use the easier analysis of the experience of past and future objects as a clue to understanding our enjoyments of Time. We shall find that past enjoyments are not experienced in the present but as past, and future ones as future. Let us analyse the experience of remembering a past state or act of mind as distinguished from the past object. I never indeed do remember myself without the object, for without an object a mental state is nothing. Even when I project my personality back into the past or forward into the future, I have before my mind either the external objects about which I was engaged or at the lowest the bodily and contemplated constituents of myself. But I may attend to the self rather than to the object, or in other words it may be the self which predominates in my experience. This most often happens when the past event was highly coloured with emotion, and the emotion is renewed in memory. I remember how elated I felt at a piece of good fortune or how depressed with a misfortune. Even without emotion I can faintly remember how highly invigorated I felt by my first bicycle tour when I was young. But though we do not often attend to our past mental states, we never remember a past object without some consciousness however faint of the past state. I remember hearing my friend's conversation, and do it by an act of imagination which is the renewal (to use a neutral term) of that past. Let us suppose ourselves then to be remembering our past state. There are two elements in the mental condition. First, there is the act of remembering, and secondly, there is the imagination (or thought) of my past self. The mere process of remembering offers no difficulty. The imagined state of my mind is lifted from its relative isolation or indifference into intimate connection with myself, and is appropriated by that self. It is from the beginning continuous with the rest of the mind, for otherwise it would not be the image of a past state of *mind*, but it is in the act of remembering attached more closely to the present consciousness of my personality. And as it grows into intimacy the remembered state of mind deepens and expands (always of course with the help of the past object), and its emotional colour is more vividly revived until it approaches the character of hallucination and we seem half to be actually repeating the old experience.

This act of remembering is enjoyed as present; it is contemporaneous, for instance, with the sight of the friend whose past conversation his renewed visit puts me in mind of, or I remember him at the same moment as I hear a voice like his. We say I remember *now* that I heard him say such and such a thing *then*, or I remember vividly *now* how much moved I *was* at reading his letter. I enjoy here the imagination of the past event. Is this enjoyed imagination of my past state of mind enjoyed as past or as present? Now with regard to the object there was comparatively little difficulty in the answer. The object remembered has the mark of the past. But the object is an existent distinct from the mind and contemplated by it. On the other hand, the remembered state of myself is not an object of contemplation, but is only enjoyed. It is itself a mental act which is in the act of remembering welded into the present personality. Once more we must turn without prepossession to the experience itself, and the answer which it gives is that the imagination of myself which I have in remembering myself is not enjoyed as present but as past. Its enjoyment has pastness written upon its face. What we remember is past as much in our own case as in the case of the external event which is remembered. The remembering is present, but both its object and what we may call its mental material (the past act of mind which experienced it) are past. The appeal is to the bare facts. There may be a good meaning to be assigned to the statement that the renewed mental past is present. But it is not so enjoyed by the experient himself. It can only so be described, if at all, from the point of view of the looker-on, who separates the renewal of the past state from the mind of the experient, and cuts it off from its intimacy both with that experient's self and above all with the object. But as so described it is not the remembered state at all. Looking at it from the outside the psychologist may note that something is happening to the patient

which is present *for the psychologist*, but it is not therefore present for the patient, and if the psychologist so
misreads it, he is not putting himself inside the patient's
mind and is failing of his duty as a psychologist. Or,
again, there is a physiological process in the patient's
brain which is simultaneous with the patient's present.
But it does not follow so evidently that the mental
process which 'accompanies it' is felt or enjoyed as
simultaneous. There may be something present in one
sense which is not present in the vital sense of being
the patient's present and therefore enjoyed by him as
present.

In like manner the expected future event, *e.g.* that I
shall be seeing a friend, is enjoyed not as present but as
future. It has the mark of the future on it. The act of
expecting it on the other hand is present.

This result appears strange only because of the persistent intrusion into the observation of fact of a theory that all mental process is experienced *in* the present or *as* present. Once the facts are accepted as experience supplies them, their interpretation offers no more difficulty than the interpretation of a past object in memory. My enjoyment is a past enjoyment, and it is thus that a being which does not make its own states objects to itself is aware of its past. Precisely so, the past object of memory is the appearance to me of the past thing in the present act of remembering. The past enjoyment, which I have called the material of the act of remembering my past state, is the way in which the actual past of the mind is revealed in the present. But it is not revealed *as* present. Nor is it revealed *in* the mind's present, though it forms one part of the total of which another part is the mind's present. Because it forms one part of that total it is imagined to persist into the present. And so it does, but it persists as past. If Time is real, if the past is not a mere invention of the mind, and this is our original hypothesis, the mind at any present moment contains its past as past. Otherwise, to fall back on an argument used *ad nauseam* in respect of physical Time, there would be no mind at all but a continual re-creation

Difference of 'present' and 'at the present.

of quite independent and molecular mental states, which is contrary to elementary experience.

Thus a remembered mental state is a past enjoyment, as it is enjoyed after the lapse of time, the machinery for such awareness of the past being the process by which for one reason or another the brain is thrown into a corresponding, or a partially identical state with the actual past state of the brain during the past experience. The past is revived in imagination of my mental state just as it is revived in imagination of a past object. I know my own past only through the enjoyment of it as past.[1]

Illustration
memory of
emotion.

The truth that the renewal in memory of a past state of myself is not merely a fresh excitement of myself in the present may perhaps best be seen in the memory of emotions. It is sometimes thought that there is no such memory, but only memory for the exciting object of the emotion and a new present emotion aroused by this memory. An interesting census was taken by Th. Ribot, the results of which will be found in his *Psychology of the Emotions*, ch. xi. He concludes to the existence in some cases of an emotional type which does remember emotions. But the question is rather how emotions are remembered? Are they really memories or are they real or actual new emotions which are excited by an image? that is to say, not different from a present emotion. All revived feeling is new feeling, it is said, attached to an ideal object. This seems to be the meaning of the poet Sully Prudhomme, quoted by Ribot, who says, speaking of some past incidents of an emotional character, that he is now a stranger to the feelings he remembers in connection with them; " but as soon as by an effort of recollection I make these memories more precise they cease *ipso facto* to be memories only, and I am quite surprised to feel the

---

[1] On the whole question of experience of the past, see a very useful discussion by A. Gallinger, *Zur Grundlegung einer Lehre von der Erinnerung*, Halle, 1914. "To be aware of something at the present is not the same thing as to be aware of it also *as present*" (p. 92). "In remembering we have a knowledge of past experiences (*Erlebnisse*), but not a knowledge of the present consciousness of past experiences, nor even of present memory pictures of past experiences" (same page). But I do not claim the writer's support for my general doctrine.

movements of youthful passion and angry jealousy revived in me. And again I am almost inclined to ask myself if every recollection of feeling does not take on the character of an hallucination " (p. 155).

So far as I can trust my own experience I believe we can observe a distinction between a remembered and a present emotion. I remember the feeling of shame felt at a social blunder ; and the more vividly I represent the circumstances the more intense the emotional excitement becomes, and the more completely it includes the bodily expression proper to the emotion and invades me. Still all this personal experience is detained in attachment to the past object, and despite the urgency of the feelings I am lost in the past, and the whole experience, object-side and subject-side alike, has the mark of the past. But suddenly I may find myself arrested ; I forget the past object and I become aware of the emotion as a present state, in which the object is for the most part the bodily reactions, the flushed face and qualms about the heart. I change from a past enjoyment to a present one. What the difference is I find it hard to say ; the pastness of the image seems to draw the feeling after it into the past as well. It may be that the whole difference lies in the compresence with the past object. But the difference is for me palpably there. Thus a new or actual emotion, with its sensorial character, ceases to be a present emotion when it is com-present with a past object ; whether it is neurally or mentally slightly different from the emotion roused by a present object or not, it becomes a past enjoyment in this connection. Its *actuality* no more makes it a present emotion than the sensory character of the beginning of the meteor's path in the sky makes it present, when the real present is the end of the path.

Before pursuing further the ideas suggested by these facts let us note briefly that where there is not memory proper but only retention in the mind, the earlier stages of the mental enjoyment are past and not present, and that the specious present, the present with a depth, is not really a present in enjoyment, and that consequently, to sum the whole matter up, we cannot hold that the experience of the past is a present feeling, whether we speak of the past object or the past state of mind.

What is present in an enjoy-ment of the past.

We may now ask ourselves what is really present in the strict sense when there is a past enjoyment ; what it is which lends colour to the belief that the remembered state of mind is actually present. The answer is that the underlying neural process is present, and that process is partially at least the same whether the act of mind be a perception of a present or a memory of a past object. I do not raise the vexed question whether images occupy the same places in the brain as their corresponding per-cepts, or different places. If the same, then the same tract of brain may be occupied at one time in the observer's present and at another in his past. If not, yet since a percept already contains elements of an ideal character complicated with the sensory elements, the seat of per-cept and image is at least partially the same. Moreover, it is quite possible that though image centres may not be the same as sensation centres, yet since they cannot be supposed disconnected, the excitement of ideas may over-flow into sensory centres. Thus a revival in imagination partially at any rate occupies the same place as if it were a sensory experience. A present and a past enjoyment may be in the same contemplated or enjoyed space but belong to different enjoyed times, or, to put it otherwise, a tract of brain may be occupied either by a present or a past enjoyment.

The case of remembered emotion illustrates this matter well. Why is it, the question is asked, that we do not confuse an image of a past event with a present event, and yet a remembered emotion is or tends to be hal-lucinatory ? The answer might be suggested that an image becomes hallucinatory only when sensation is involved. Now, normally, sensations require the presence of the actual stimulus from without. Thus, for instance, the imagination of a coloured disk is not usually sensory, for although it may lead to various movements of the eyes or other organs, those movements do not excite colour sensations. But the case is different with the emotional excitement produced by such an object. That excitement issues or tends to issue in the appropriate bodily movements of the emotion, and these movements are felt in the form of actual sensations, organic or kinaesthetic. The bodily resonance which forms so large a part of an emotion is brought into existence by the imagined emotion itself. On the other hand, the movements induced by an idea of a picture do not reinstate in a sensory form the details of the picture, because that is outside the bodily organism ; they only give us bodily sensations, not sensations of colour or smell. To have an hallucination of colour, the internal conditions must be the exceptional ones under which an image overflows into the sensory centres.[1]

It is a familiar fact that to an observer in motion two events may occur at different times at the same place

[1] Though my interest here is not primarily psychological I may stop to raise in a note the question, which is naturally suggested by the above, of the revival of organic and kinaesthetic sensations. I find it very hard myself to get images of them, but others do, and there is no reason why these sensa which are external though personal should have no images. There are real reasons, however, which distinguish these sensations from specific sensations. For their sensibles or sensa are bodily conditions, and the neural process which underlies the sensation, the sensing of them, is also bodily. Whereas, as explained in the text, in the case of colour the sensing has a bodily neurosis which underlies it, but the sensum is outside the body. But a kinaesthetic image leads to a movement which continues the excitement. The movements of reaction produced by the image sustain the image, and do so in a sensory form. The reaction is, in Mr. Baldwin's phrase, a circular one. Hence, like emotions, these representations tend to be hallucinatory, as in my case they generally are. Thinking of moving means really beginning to move. Now it may very well be with these and the organic sensations that though their representations tend to be hallucinations, their associates may give them a pull into the past or future, and in that case they would still deserve to be called images. The same thing applies to organic sensations. Some psychologists declare (and I followed them myself in a paper in *Arist. Proceedings*, 1909-10) that they do not admit of representation at all. At any rate their behaviour in this respect puts them for purposes of knowledge in a class by themselves. Seeing that our minds are correlated with our bodies, and these are the sensations from our bodies, it is not surprising that they should occupy a peculiar position in the rank of sensations. (The sensa are in fact living conditions which we apprehend directly in our bodies. See later, Bk. III. ch. vi.)

which to an observer at rest occur at different places. Mr. Langevin's instance is that of dropping stones through the floor of a railway carriage in motion. To the traveller in the carriage two such events will occur at different times but at the same place. To the outside observer at rest the stones will fall at different places. In both cases the space is contemplated. Take now enjoyed and contemplated space. The space I enjoy is that of a part of my body. But my body, say my head, may change its place in the wider contemplated Space to which it belongs, but its parts retain their internal relations as enjoyed, and, as we have seen, mental directions remain unaltered. Thus what is the same place for enjoyment may be in two different places for contemplation.

A similar account applies to the connection of enjoyed and contemplated time. My remembered time is past in enjoyed time. But it occurs in a space which is the same or partially the same for the outside observer, whether the mental process is a present or a past enjoyment. Let us recur to the old case of a conversation remembered at the moment I hear a voice or see a photograph. The physiological process underlying the remembered past is occurring to the observer at the same time as my sight of the photograph. And the enjoyment of the past occupies, at least in part, the same place as if the event were present. To the experient the event is past. To the outsider it might, for all he knows, be either past or present, at least so far as the identical parts of space are concerned. The contemplated present neural event may be either a present or a past enjoyment. Suppose, now, an angel contemplating me. For him my mental process is exposed to his contemplation as well as the neural process, while to me or you it is not. The angel would see the neural process physically synchronous with my present. But the mental event would be seen by him to have the mark of the past, because he could see into my mind as I enjoy it. He would distinguish the past enjoyment from the present enjoyment at the same place, and would see that two events by way of enjoyment might share the same neural process. He would, I suppose, make the distinction of past or present directly in the mental events, and would also, I suppose, see differences in the neural process before him which we might with sufficient knowledge see. When I take the point of view of the angel I can understand how my enjoyed time may return to its old place and partially at least occupy a present contemplated process, whether it is a past or a present enjoyment. If I am right in my account above of the change from an emotion referred to the past to the emotion referred to the present, this is what I actually do experience in such a case.

Thus when a remembered state of mind is declared to be a present feeling, we are, as I said, making a psychological mistake which can be accounted for either because, being an enjoyment, it enters into the total mass of our enjoyment at our present moment ; or because the neural process corresponding to it does occur at the present in the neural space as contemplated from outside.

Whether in the study of past and future objects or in that of past and future states of ourselves, we have thus seen that our consciousness of past and future is direct, and is not the alleged artificial process of first having an experience of the present and then referring it by some method to the past or future. There is no such method given in our experience, and we have therefore no right to assume it just because we start with the fancy that all our experiences must be present. If difficulty is still felt in the unfamiliar notion that we enjoy our past as past and our future as future, the answer must be that in the first place facts, however strange the description of them may be, must be accepted loyally and our theories accommodated to them ; secondly, that as to the special explanations suggested above, of how a present neural process may be felt as a past enjoyment, an explanation like this is theoretical and designed to remove a theoretical difficulty. For immediate acquaintance with our past and future tells us nothing about neural processes, and if we confine ourselves to our enjoyment of ourselves, we find that the memory or the expectation of a past or future state is the way in which we enjoy past or future, and that there is no

Mental space-time

more to be said ; just as our memory of the past object is that past object as contemplated now in the act of remembering, and there is no more to be said.

But now that by an appeal to experience we have rid ourselves of the confusions as to our past and future enjoyments which were engendered by a mistaken reading of experience, we can proceed to examine the space and time of the mind in their mutual relations, and we shall see that they do not exist separately but are only elements in the one mental space-time which exhibits to inspection of ourselves the same features, with such qualifications as may be necessary to note, as the Space-Time of the external world, with a part of which it is identical.

Mental
space and
volve each
ot er.
We have in the first place at any moment a mass of enjoyments (that is, experiences of ourselves, or experiencings), part of which is present, part memories or remembered enjoyments, part expected enjoyments with the mark of the future. These enjoyments occupy diverse places in the mental space. Present enjoyments are in different places from past and future ones. The enjoyed space is not full of mental states all occurring at one and the same time, but it is occupied, so far as it is occupied, with mental events of different dates. But, as we have seen, what is now a present enjoyment may at another moment be replaced by a remembered one ; and what is now a memory may on another occasion be replaced by a present occupying partially at least the same place ; the dates or times being on different occasions differently distributed among the places. Thus enjoyed space is full of time. In the same way enjoyed time is distributed over enjoyed space, and spreads over it so as not to be always in the same space. Thus empirically every point in the space has its date and every date has its point, and there is no mental space without its time nor time without its space. There is one mental space-time. Our mind is spatio-temporal. The easiest way to make ourselves a picture of the situation is to suppose the identification of mental space with the corresponding contemplated neural space completed in details, and to substitute for the enjoyed space, for pictorial purposes, the neural space with which

it is identical, that is, to think of specific mental events as
occurring in their neural tracts.   When we do so, we see
mental past, present, and future juxtaposed in this space ;
or the places of mind succeeding each other in their
appropriate times.

Such a picture of mental space-time at any moment
is the perspective we enjoy of it at any moment or from
the point of view of that moment.   But the picture
is not complete.   The present enjoyment and the
remembered   one   are   enjoyed   as   juxtaposed.   But
they are not in bare unrelated juxtaposition.   For a
remembered past state is in remembering linked up with
the present.   There is a felt continuity between them.
The same thing is more obviously true where there is
not memory proper but a past condition is experienced
as retained in the mind only, being at the fringe of a
total experience, as when we retain in our minds at this
moment the lingering remnants of our past condition, in
going through some complex experience, as, for example,
in watching the phases of an incident which stirs our
feelings.   That there is this transitional relation of
movement from the one element to the other, is shown
by the familiar fact that when one member of a series
of mental states is repeated in experience the others
also are revived in their time-order.

We have thus to make a distinction, which will
prove important also in the sequel in another connection,[1] between two kinds of process enjoyed in mental
space-time, which corresponds to the distinction between
'substantive' and 'transitive' states.   First, we have
the process intrinsically belonging to any mental act
independently of others, for instance, the process of
sensing a colour.   No matter what the underlying and
corresponding neural movements may be, we have, as
was mentioned before, the mental process of the
dawning of the sensing to its maximum and the subsequent evanescence.   Thus to be aware of any
particular sensum is to enjoy a mental movement

Perspec-
tive
mental
space-time.

---

[1] See the distinction drawn later between the intrinsic and the
extrinsic extension of a sensory quality.   Bk. III. ch. vi.

appropriate to it. But besides this intrinsic movement, there is also the movement from one sensing to another of a different (or to a repetition of the same) sort, as when a colour sensation is succeeded by one of sound. A mental process of one direction (that is compresent with an object of one quality) is linked by a movement of transition, apprehended as such, to a movement with another direction, that is compresent with an object of another quality; or in other words, there is a change in the quality of the experience. Thus while there are two independent lines of advance in the mental space-time corresponding to the two different qualities, there is also a line of advance which connects these two lines, the neural path being, from the purpose which it subsequently serves, known as an association-path (or fibre).

Even when two mental events occur simultaneously, as when I hear a voice and touch a hand at the same moment, this is not bare juxtaposition in space, if that word implies accidental or disconnected occurrence. On a subsequent occasion the image of the voice may recall the touch or *vice versa*. We have here a case of two different perspectives where events contemporaneous in the one perspective become successive in the other. Though the original relation appeared to be purely spatial, the mental events occurring side by side, a later perspective shows it to be also temporal. The two events belong to the same date, or the time was repeated at the two different points at which they occurred. They are connected in the mental space-time. This is our enjoyment of the relation of 'and,' corresponding to the contemplated relation of 'and' between the objects. A subsequent experience reveals that the two events are somehow connected in mental space-time by lines of advance. We may bring our awareness of 'and' into coherence with the relation of transition by passing from one object to the other in either order.

Among mental events which are simultaneous are those which belong together as part and parcel of one complex occurrence. Every mental event is spread out in fact. (It has even been suggested that a more intense act of sensing means a greater spatial extension of it.)   The best instance is derived from ordinary perceiving.   There is the sensory excitement and the ideal qualification of it.   These belong together in mental space, but they do not in general occupy the same parts of space ; for example, the sight of the marble qualified by the ideal feeling of cold.   We have here a mental act with a structure ; that is, parts of it are inherently in mental space at the same moment, or the mental instant is repeated in space.

In the same way, as we have seen abundantly in dealing with memory of mental states, we have mental space repeated in time ; that is, several events of the same sort occurring at different times but belonging to the same space ; that is, we have time coming back to its old place.   And we may repeat a remark like one made before in Chapter I. of physical Space-Time, that the repetition of time in space, which is the fact of the broad (not the deep) present, and of space in time, which is the fact of memory, are of the essence of mind as something with a structure and persistence.

We have thus found from simple inspection of our minds, and bringing to bear on the question the most commonplace kind of psychological observation, that space and time in mind are in experienced fact related in the same way as we have seen them to be related in physical Space and Time.   Space and time in the mind are indissolubly one.   For myself it is easier to be satisfied of this relation between the two, and all the details which enter into it—repetition, variation in the perspective whereby the contemporary becomes successive, and the like—in the case of mind, than in the case of external Space and Time, and to use this result as a clue to interpreting external or physical Space-time.   But I have explained already[1] why I have not adopted what for me is the more natural order.

We may now approach the more difficult question, in what sense it is possible, as it was in the case of

[1] Ch. iii. p. 93.

physical Space-Time, to make a selection from all the perspectives which the mind enjoys of its own space-time and treat the whole of mental space as occurring at the present and the whole of mental time as occupying one point of mental space. In the case of physical Space-Time we saw that an all-comprehensive observer whom we ourselves follow in thought could make such a selection, and we arrived thus at the ordinary notions of a Space in which at a given moment some event or other was occupying every point—Space as the frame-work of Time ; and of Time as the framework in which Space occurred, that is of a Time the whole of which streamed through every point of Space. In mental space-time such results are obtainable, but only approximately and with a qualification.

At first sight it might appear that there was no difficulty in taking a present 'section' through the whole of our mental space. We have only to identify the neural space, say the brain, with the mental space, and then it would seem that at any instant of our life every point in that space was occupied by some event or other that occurred in our history. But mental space enjoyed in any mental state is not merely neural space, but that neural space which is correlated with the mental action. There may be events going on say in the occipital region which happen there but which are not of that particular sort which is correlated with vision, or, as I shall often express it, which *carry* vision. Though the whole contemplated space within which mental action takes place may be considered by proper selection from all the moments of its history as occupied by some present event or other contemporary with the present, they will not necessarily be mental events. They may be unconscious.

When we consider mental events as such and neural processes only so far as they carry mind, we cannot find a section of mental space-time which is either the whole mental space occupied by contemporary events or the whole mental time streaming through one point. In our own experience it is clear we get no such thing.

Our enjoyed space in a moment of experience may on occasion be so limited that it contains neither memory nor expectation but is wholly present. For example, we may be absorbed in perception. We are then entirely present, for the ideal features in perception are, as we have seen, not expectations or memories, but are merely qualifications of the present, which are there indeed as the result of past experience, but have not the mark of the past nor even of the future. But though in such a perspective our mental space is all present, it is not the whole of our mental space, but only a part of it. Or again I may be seeing a man and also remembering something about him. The one place in the mental space which is common to the perception and the memory may belong both to the perception and to the memory. But it does not belong to them both at the same time, and is alternately part of the present perceiving and the past remembering.

This is as far as I can get by actual acquaintance. Even the angelic outsider, though he will go farther, and though we may anticipate him by thought, will not get a complete section. He cannot see the whole of our mental space occupied by the present moment. He can realise that any neural process which at this moment of my mind is for me a memory might have been occupied by a mental event contemporary with my present. But it is not certain that he can find such events. Potentially the places now occupied in my perspective by memories or expectations may be occupied in other perspectives by perceptions of the present date. But the selection is only a possibility and nothing more. In the same way he may think that the place of my present mental act may potentially be the scene of some mental event at every moment of my history. But again this is only a remote possibility.

The reason for this difference between mental space-time and physical Space-Time is that the second is infinite and the first finite. We are finite beings, and part of that finitude is that our neural space performs only specific functions. Hearing does not occur in the occipital, nor vision in the temporal region. But in physical Space-Time the reason why in the summation of perspectives a selection could be made of events filling the whole of Space at one moment, or the whole of Time at one place, is that the quality of the events was indifferent in the infinite whole. In one perspective a point of space is past, but in some other perspective a quite different sort of event might occupy that point in the present, that is at a moment identical with the point of reference. I see in front of me a point in a tree where a bird alighted a quarter of a second past. But a quarter of a second later, that is at the same moment as my act of seeing the bird, a bud sprouts on the tree at that point. That event is future for me, but for you, the onlooker, it occurs at the same moment as my act of sight, that is, you see them both as contemporary. There is thus always in some perspective or other some event or other at any point of space contemporary with my present. But places in mental space-time are, because of the specific character of the events which happen there, only occupied when there are events of the same sort. Now I am not every moment using my eyes, still less seeing a particular colour, such as red, at every moment of my history. We cannot, therefore, have a section of our whole history in which our whole space is occupied at each moment with some event or other ; nor one in which each point is occupied by some event or other through the whole of our time.

Except for this failure to find corresponding artificial sections in mind, the microcosm, to infinite Space-Time, the macrocosm, a failure founded on the finitude of mental space time, the relations of Space and Time to one another are identical in the two. It is obvious that the exception would apply equally to any limited piece of Space-Time which is occupied by the life of a finite thing, whether that thing is mental or not, provided it has specific qualities.

Mr. Berg-
n
Time and
Space. In Mr. Bergson's conception of Time or *duree* which is mental or psychological and is real Time which is the moving spirit of the universe, the past is said to penetrate

the present. Upon our analysis of memory there is a very good meaning to be attached to the penetration of the present by the past. It has been illustrated more than once by the qualification of the sensory present of perception by ideal elements which are an inheritance from the past. The past here leaves its traces in the conscious present. Other illustrations are the persistence of past experience in the form of dispositions which affect the present experience ; which may favour the emergence of one thought in our minds rather than another, or which may break in on the course of our thoughts and determine them, as for example a latent prejudice against a person. Whether these dispositions are properly psychical in all cases, or may not sometimes be physical traces which can condition and affect what is strictly psychical, we may leave undetermined. But in all these cases the inheritance from the past has the date of that which it conditions and into which it is merged.

Such present deposit in the mind of traces of the past are not, however, peculiar to mind, but are found in physical, to say nothing of organic, bodies. A storm blows and a tree or chimney leans out of the straight. The ground subsides and a tower leans. The storm and the subsidence belong to the past of these bodies, but the past persists in its effects, in the altered inclination, and this inclination is a factor in the response which is made to a fresh shock. Now to the outside observer these present conditions are traces of the past. So, too, the outside observer, knowing that I have seen a man already, may see in my recognition of him as a man that I am experiencing the traces of the past. But I should not myself experience them as past, for there is no true memory in my mind. Per contra, if we endow the tower with a mind and true memory it would perhaps remember the subsidence of the ground which made it sink, but it would remember this event as belonging to its past, and would not be conscious of it merely in the present effects left behind by the past.

But if there is real consciousness of the past, whether in the mere form of a past retained as such or in the form of true memory, the enjoyment of the past has not the mark of the present but of the past. It is only from the outsider's point of view that, as we have seen, it is possible to describe a conscious past as present. Strangely enough Mr. Bergson, whose method is distinguished by its effort to take the inside view of things, fails, as it appears, to distinguish the act of remembering, of appropriation of the past, which is really present, from the remembered past itself.

Now if the remembered past is past, and only in that way have we memory of our past which was once present to us, then penetration by the past can, as it appears to me, have no significance which Space does not also share with Time. It means two things : first, that Time is continuous ; and secondly, that each event in time is affected by what went before. These are indeed the same thing from two different points of view. Now, in the first place, the parts of real Space penetrate as much as the parts of Time, and for the excellent reason that every part of Space is animated by Time which drives it on to merge continuously in the rest of Space. Further, if Space were not a penetrating continuum, Time, as we have seen, would be none either. It would be once more a moment which would not know itself to have a past.

Secondly, it is part of the continuity of Time that material events (and pure events as well) have a different meaning because of their preceding events. This is both true and important. But, again, it does not distinguish Time from Space. It confuses the value which elements have in their combination from their intrinsic nature. A man is the same man by himself or in a crowd, but he may be fired by a crowd into doing acts which he would not do alone. A sensation of white is not the same in all respects when it is experienced the second time as the first time ; it has become familiar. But the white is the same as before ; only it is modified by assimilation ; it is qualified by the trace of the past. We no longer have, as before, the bare sensation, but something more complex. So, again, if white and sweet are connected in a continuous whole, the white remains white and the sweet sweet. But the elements have a new value in this combination. The sweet is that of sugar. But equally it is true that a point has a different value as a point on a circle and as a point on a straight line, while it remains the same point. It lies on different lines of advance.

The main result of our discussion has been to show that Time is really laid out in Space, and is intrinsically spatial. The representation of Time as spatial, Mr. Bergson regards as depriving Time of its real character. What he regards as a habit founded upon the weakness of our imagination has now been shown to be vital to the nature of Time. But his antagonism is determined by his belief that the Space in which Time is so spread out is the abstract Space which he believes is the Space of mathematics; and the Time which is thus spatialised is therefore not real Time but only abstract Time. It is impossible to do justice to him without discussing what mathematical Space and Time are ; and to this task I shall now proceed.

CHAPTER V

MATHEMATICAL SPACE AND TIME

Are points
fictions? PHYSICAL Space and Time are thus one with mental space
and time, or, more strictly, portions of the one Space and
Time may be enjoyed and are identical with parts of the
one contemplated Space and Time. Space and Time as we
have regarded them are empirical or experienced extension
or duration, though as continua of moments or points
they have been described by help of conceptual terms.
Are Space and Time so regarded the Space and Time of
the mathematicians, and if so, what is the difference between the metaphysics and the mathematics of them ? Our
answer will be, that directly or indirectly mathematics is
concerned with empirical Space and Time, and that, however remote from them mathematics may seem and be, they
are never in mathematics torn away from their original.
But a difficulty meets us at the outset because of the
different conceptions of mathematics entertained by mathematicians themselves. According to some, Space and Time
are the absolute or total Space and Time consisting of entities called points or instants. According to others, and
they are the more philosophical mathematicians, Space and
Time are not extension or duration, not in any sense stuff
or substance,[1] as Descartes, to all intents and purposes,
conceived particular spaces to be, but relations between
material things which move in them. This is the relational conception ; as distinguished from the absolute conception, which is expressed by Newton in the sentence,

[1] See, for the qualification of the use of the word substance, Bk. II.
ch. x. p. 341 : Space-Time is not substance at all, but stuff.

"For times and spaces are as it were the places as well of themselves as of all other things" (*Princ.* Book I. Schol. iv.). The contrast of absolute and relational is as we have seen entirely different from that of absolute and relative. But the relational conception of Space and Time carries with it, especially in its more recent forms, consequences which make it seem almost impossible to affirm that there is only one Space and Time, namely, the empirical one, with which mathematics is concerned. Rather it would seem that empirical Space and Time are but particular examples of constructions of a much wider scope.

The Space and Time of the previous chapters are then empirical. In essentials they are absolute Space and Time, though, regarded merely as constituents of the one reality which is Space-Time, they are purged of the errors which attach to them when they are considered independently of one another. All Space in fact is full of Time and there is no such thing as empty Space; all Time occupies Space and there is no such thing as empty Time. I do not think that the ordinary geometry (Euclidean or other) assumes Space to be divorced from Time. It makes no assumption on this point at all. On the contrary, whenever its purpose is suited it conceives of a figure genetically as traced by movement in time. Nor does mathematics in dealing with Time assume it to exist by itself. It treats Time by itself, though for the most part Time enters as being an element of motion, and consequently so far in space. But to treat Space or Time by themselves is not to assume that they can exist apart from one another. There is nothing in the procedure of geometry (I say nothing of the views of geometers themselves in the history of the subject) which implies that Space is a system of resting points, or Time a uniform flow which has no habitat.

The entities called points, of which Space is composed (or the instants of Time), are, it is said, commonly regarded by mathematicians as fictions. Mathematicians are very prone, indeed, to regard the notions and the methods they employ as fictions, as if they were mere constructions of our minds. The famous writer, R. Dedekind, himself one of the authors of that movement which has made geometry by an immense generalisation a department of arithmetic, pronounces numbers to be "free creations of the human mind."[1]   Under these circumstances we may ask ourselves the preliminary question, When is a fiction fictitious ?   I adopt, for instance, a son who becomes my son by a legal fiction, by a generalisation or extension of the notion of son.   How much of this fiction is real and how much unreal ?   So far as I treat him as a son, exchange with him affection and care and perform certain legal and moral obligations to him, the adopted son is really in the place to me of a son.   There is no fiction here.   There is only fiction if I strain the relation : if I should, for instance, go on to pretend that he owes his height to me and his wit to my wife, that his colour-blindness is traceable to her and may be found in her brother, and a little pit in the skin beside his ear to my father.   Here the fiction becomes fictitious.   The legal and moral relation of sonship must not be interchanged with the natural one of inheritance.   But in other respects the fiction is a true description of the new facts initiated by the adoption.

Isolation of points corrected by conception of continu-   Now the assumption of points as elements of Space in a continuous series is an attempt to describe in ideal and partly conceptual terms the given or empirical fact of the continuity of Space, that any stretch of space however small is divisible, and that there is no smallest part.   So far as the point is thought to be a self-subsistent entity by aggregation of which with other points Space is constituted, the point is fictitious.   But such an assumption is not in fact, and never need be, made.   On the contrary, the idea of the separate point is a first approximation, which is corrected by the notion of its continuity with other points.   This happens even in the ordinary elementary geometry.   For more thorough-going or philosophical mathematical analysis the concept of continuity taken over from sensible continuity is deepened into the analysis of continuity, which then supersedes that merely

---

[1] *Was sind und was sollen die Zahlen.*   Preface, p. vii. (Brunswick, 1911, ed. 3).

sensible continuity. This analysis is a crowning achievement of mathematical speculation. It has been described recently by Mr. Russell.[1] Like infinity, which has been touched upon before, it is not a mere negative but a positive conception. It does not rely upon or refer to any mental incapacity in us, that we are unable to reach an end of the division, but upon a real characteristic of the continuous series. We can think of Space extended indefinitely, said Locke, but not of Space infinite, because, in the happy phrase which contains the substance of Kant's later and more famous discussion of the same problem, we cannot "adjust a standing measure to a growing bulk."[2] In reality, infinite Space precedes any finite space. In the same way Space is not merely infinitely divisible in the sense that its division admits no end, but is in itself infinitely divided in the sense that between any two elements there exists another element; so that no two elements—we may call them points—are next or adjacent. Thus, just as before with the infinite the finite meant defect and the infinite self-subsistence, so here the division into a finite number of parts implies selection from the infinite of parts in the real continuum.

In this way the point which is an unextended entity with a fictitious self-subsistence is brought into conformity with facts by the correction of the conception. The definition of continuity starting with separate points screws them, or squeezes them, up into that closeness which is needed to express the nature of Space. Even this degree of closeness is not enough for the perfect definition of the continuum. But the further criterion which ensures that the series of points shall be not merely 'compact,' according to the description given that no two points are next points, but 'dense,' is more technical than I can take upon me to reproduce here. The effect of it, however, may be illustrated from the old puzzle of Achilles and the tortoise. In that puzzle the steps taken by the two competitors form two series which do not reach in any number of

[1] B. Russell, *Our Knowledge of the External World* (Chicago and London, 1914), ch. v.

[2] *Essay*, Bk. II. ch. xvii. § 7.

steps the point at which as a matter of fact Achilles overtakes the tortoise. That point is the limit of the two series.
But though the limit is not reached, and is not the end or
any member of the two series, it is a point on the actual
line of the journey which both Achilles and the tortoise
make. The fact that Achilles does overta√e the tortoise is
the very mark that their course, which has been artificially
broken up into discrete lengths, is really continuous.

The mathematical notion of continuity contains no
dreaded infinite regress ; the infinitude is of the essence
of the datum and expresses no repetition of steps upon
our part. On the other hand, if it be asked what is there
in space-points which makes them continuous, we are
asking a different question from the question what is the
criterion of their continuity. The answer, if I am right,
must be that points are continuous because they are not
mere points but are instants as well. It is Time which
distinguishes one point from another, but it is Time also
which connects them. For the point is really never at
rest but only a transition in a motion. Now it is this
restlessness of the point which is expressed in terms of
Space itself by the criteria of continuity which the mathematician adopts in order to free his points from their
apparent isolation and self-dependence. We are brought
back to the conclusion that the mathematical notion of
continuity as applied to Space or Time is an attempt to
render in terms of points or instants their crude original
continuity, and carries with it the corrective to the apparent
isolation of points and instants. At the same time, it must
be insisted that the mere concept of continuity of either
points or instants is only adequate to the crude continuity
of actual Space or Time when the points are recognised
as being intrinsically instants and the instants points ; just
as the concept of dog can only be adequate to a particular
dog when it is embodied in individualising circumstance.

The spatial-
of
Time

We may pause, before passing on, to complete the
remarks which were made in the last chapter on Mr.
Bergson's repugnance to the spatialising of Time. Mental
time or *duree* was, we saw, laid out in space, where Space

was understood to be the Space common to both the physical world and the mind. Thus the spatialising of mind or Time, which Mr. Bergson regarded as a common and natural vice, is in fact of the essence of Time and mental life. But the Space which Mr. Bergson fears and regards as the bare form of externality, the dead body into which the world resolves when Time is arrested, is what he supposes the Space of the geometer to be. Now if mathematics understood by Space or Time the Space of absolute rest, or its counterpart and mirror in mere undifferentiated, and inert, inefficacious, Time (and this is what Mr. Bergson is contending against), his fears would be justified. Such Space and Time are abstractions and correspond to nothing real. But, as we have seen, the Space and Time of the mathematician are not such, or at least are not necessarily such, and we are assured that they are not in fact so treated. Space is legitimately considered by itself and Time likewise. But they are not considered as made up of separate parts but as continuous, and their continuity is defined. In like manner motion is not for the mathematician made up of separate positions, but of separate positions corrected by continuity. Mr. Bergson's main concern is with motion, and he rightly insists that motion is a whole and continuous, having in his mind the original continuity which is given empirically and is antecedent to the conceptualisation of it in mathematics. This conceptualisation he mistakes apparently for destruction, and supposes that Space has been reduced to a series of separate points, and Time with it to a series of separate moments. It is true, moreover, that since geometry omits Time from Space there is a certain artificiality in the reconstruction of continuity within Space in purely spatial terms, and there is a corresponding artificiality in the continuity of Time without reference to Space. This arises from the nature of the case, and indicates that mathematics is not, like metaphysics, an ultimate treatment of its subject matter—on which topic more anon. What Mr. Bergson appears to forget is that this science works within its limits, but in doing so does do justice to that very continuity and wholeness of Space and Time, and with them motion, for which he himself is pleading.

The consequence of this misapprehension is visible through the twilight which envelops Mr. Bergson's conception of the relation of Time to Space and, with Space, to matter. No one has rendered such service to metaphysics as he has done in maintaining the claims of Time to be considered an ultimate reality. Moreover, Space is for him generated along with Time. The movement of Time, the swing and impulse of the world, the *élan vital*, is also a creation of matter. The two mutually involved processes remind us of the roads upward and downward of his prototype Heraclitus. But with his forerunner this relation is conceived quite naively : we are told that the unity of opposites means nothing more with Heraclitus than that opposites were two sides of one and the same process, so that day and night were but oscillations of the "measures" of fire and water.[1] With Mr. Bergson, on the other hand, Space is a sort of shadow or foil to Time, and not co-equal. It implies degradation and unreality, relatively to Time. Time remains the unique and ultimate reality. We have seen reason to regard them as so implicated in each other that each is vital to the other's existence. But whether this feature of his doctrine, at once the most interesting for the metaphysician and the most obscure and tantalising, is the outcome of his apparent misapprehension of the purpose and legitimacy of geometry, or the latter misapprehension a consequence of his incomplete analysis of the true relation of Space and Time, I leave undetermined, my aim being not to offer criticism of current or past philosophies, but to indicate where the analysis here maintained differs, whether to my misfortune or not, from a deservedly influential system of thought.

Mathematical and empirical Space.

The points of space and instants of time when interpreted aright are no fictions, in the sense of being fictitious, but the elementary constituents of Space and Time, as arrived at by a process which we have described already

[1] J. Burnet, *Early Greek Philosophy* (London, 1908, ed. 2), p. 186.

as being partly imaginative and partly conceptual. That is, we suppose the process of division continued without end, and we think of any space as integrated out of points so as to be a continuum, and thus we use the concept of point. But points though in this way ideal are none the less real. They are not made by our thought but discovered by it. To repeat what has been said before, reality is not limited to sensible constituents but contains ideal and conceptual ones. The back of a solid object which we see in front, the taste of an orange which we feel or see are ideal, but they belong none the less to the real solid and the real orange. Likewise the concept or thought of a dog is as real a constituent of the dog as what makes him a singular thing. It is its structural plan. Like all the objects of our experience, any part of Space contains the two aspects of singularity and universality. It is itself and it follows a law of structure. Points are singular, but they have such structure as becomes a point and are so far universal. In like manner, the figures of the mathematician, straight lines, triangles, conic sections, etc., are discovered by a process of idealisation, by an act of selection from the whole of Space. It is easy enough to recognise that this is the case with the geometrical figures taken apart from Time. For from Space we may select, by an ideal act, what Mr. Bradley calls an ideal experiment, the various geometrical figures. We do so whenever we draw them, and disregard the sensuous or sensible irregularities of our draughtsmanship, idealising these irregularities away. The construction of a parabola is an ideal drawing, or rather an ideal selection of points from Space in conformity with a certain law, expressed in the definition of the parabola. Such construction is in no sense a mere result of abstraction from sensible figures, but a discovery by thought that Space contains the geometrical figures which are thus dissected out of Space. Accordingly, in the history of the subject, geometry has proceeded from very simple figures like triangles to the discovery of more and more complex ones.

In maintaining that geometrical figures are ideal selections from Space, but really parts of that Space, I

may be thought guilty of inconsistency with my own
principles. Experienced reality I have said is not Space,
but Space-Time, of which the constituents are not spaces
or times but motions. The geometer himself, it will be
urged, treats his figures as the locus of motions. Now
in physical reality we find no perfectly triangular or
parabolic motions ; there can be no meaning in the attempt
to select such perfect movements from the motions which
actually exist. Something might indeed be said in
defence of the attempt : that where we have three intersecting directions we have the triangle. In the end,
however, it will be seen that the notion of a direction
prolonged into a straight line is incapable of defence if it
is supposed to exist in the real world of motions. But
in fact the objection taken is not relevant. The mathematician's Space is that Space which we have identified as
the framework of real motions. It is within this Space,
whose reality has been already maintained as essentially
involved in Space-Time, that the mathematician draws
his lines and circles and parabolas by an ideal selection.
In this sense the figures of the geometer are real constructions, and geometry (and the same thing is true of the
numbers of arithmetic) is a basal science of reality. When
such figures are thought, the geometer can then proceed to treat his figures as the locus of points moving
according to a certain law. But such conceptions in no
way commit us to the belief that these movements,
elaborated as it were by an afterthought, claim to be
selected from the real world of motions.

Not differ-
ent as con-
ceptual and
perceptual ;

We can now ask ourselves the question, what is the
relation of empirical Space to geometrical Space, and
answer it by saying that they are the same, but that
geometry treats Space differently from ordinary experience.
Mathematical Space and Time are sometimes contrasted
as conceptual or intelligible with empirical Space and
Time as perceptual. The contrast, in the first place, is not
strictly correct.[1] For Spaces and Times are not objects

---

[1] In an article, 'What do we mean by the question : Is our Space
Euclidean ?' in *Mind*, N.S. vol. xxiv. p. 472, Mr. C. D. Broad remarks
similarly upon this distinction ; though not to the same purpose.

of perception as trees or houses are. We have no sense for Space or Time, nor even in the proper meaning of sensation, for movement ; they are apprehended *through* the objects of perception, the things which fill spaces and times, but not *by* sense. They are more elementary than percepts. Half our difficulties have arisen from attempting to regard Space as given to us by touch or sight instead of only through touch and sight. Hence it is that some have entertained the naive and impossible notion that geometrical figures are got from material objects by a process of abstraction. They are got, as we have seen, by a selection from Space, which is always an ideal discovery. The only resemblance between figures of empirical Space and percepts is that they are individual or singular. Let us, however, overlook the inaccuracy of holding Space to be sensible at all, because the question is not ripe for our discussion in spite of the danger which such a notion involves that Space may be thought dependent on us in much the same way as colours and touches are supposed to be. It still remains true that the distinction of perceptual and conceptual is not sufficient to distinguish the Space of things from that of geometry, For empirical spaces besides being singular (and perceptual) are also conceptual. Each point is distinct from the other, because it is a point-instant and its time discriminates it ; but empirical Space involves also the concept point or point-instant. Its point-instants have a universal character or structure. Like material or sensible empirical things, spaces (and times) are saturated with concepts. On the other hand, the Space of geometry also consists of points, and the figures which it deals with are different instances of figures of one and the same kind. There are various triangles and parabolas. These are the so-called ' mathematicals ' of Plato, which he regarded (mistakenly as we shall see later) as intermediate between sensible things and universals. There are individual parabolas as well as the universal parabola. Thus empirical Space contains concepts and mathematical Space contains percepts. I am speaking here of the Space of elementary geometry, and am not considering as yet the speculative or arithmetised form of that science.

but differ-
n t
treated.

The difference lies not in there being a difference of empirical and geometrical Space but in the treatment of it. Geometry treats it wholly conceptually. Though there are many triangles and parabolas and points it considers the universal parabola or circle or point. It deals not with circles but with the circle or any circle. And it is able to do so, and is justified in doing so, because it abstracts from the Time of Space, though it does not as we have so often said exclude it. Conceiving the point without its time, it regards one point as the same as another. But that, even so, it does not exclude the real individuality of the point is evident from the fact that though its parabola has no definite place in space but may be anywhere, yet there is a relative individuality. For supposing the axis and the focus of the parabola fixed, all the other points of the curve are fixed in relation to it.

Geometry
deals with
figures, not
Space.

This leads us on to a more significant point of difference which in the end is identical with the one we have mentioned. Geometry omits Time from its Space, or introduces it again by a quasi-spatial artifice in the use of a fourth co-ordinate, the time co-ordinate, and consequently it treats its Space conceptually. But geometry is in strictness not concerned with Space as such at all ; that is the office of metaphysics. Geometry is concerned with figures in Space ; its subject matter is the various empirical or varying determinations of that *a priori* material, Space. It is the empirical science of such figures which are its data, which accordingly, like any other empirical science, it attempts to weave into a consistent system. Metaphysics, on the other hand, is not a science of empirical figures in Space. But one of its problems is what is the nature of Space and how there are figures within it. In like manner, arithmetic is not concerned with number as such, but with the empirical numbers (of all kinds) which are discoverable within the region of number, as empirical or varying determinations of that *a priori* material. The mathematician is not as a mathematician concerned with these ultimate questions ; he is only concerned with them, by the interchange of friendly offices between metaphysics and the special sciences, by which the special sciences have been enabled to contribute so helpfully to metaphysics ; because the student of a special department may also, if he has the eye for its ultimate questions, approach them with a fulness of knowledge. He may at the same time view these ultimate problems for his own purposes in a different light from the metaphysician, and this we shall see to be the case with the mathematician.[1] Now, just because the metaphysician deals with Space and number as such, it is of prime importance for him that individual points and circles are different from each other. But geometry not dealing with the problem of the individuality of its points and circles concerns itself with points and circles as such, and thus becomes wholly conceptual.

There are thus not two Spaces, the Space of elementary geometry and empirical Space, but one Space considered in metaphysics and mathematics with a different interest. The interest of mathematics is in the figures which are the empirical variations of the *a priori* Space ; the interest of metaphysics is in the nature of Space itself. The question may be asked, How can a point or rather a point-instant be individual, each one different from all others, as metaphysics insists, and yet a point-instant be a universal ? What makes the difference between the universal and its particulars ? We have not yet reached the stage at which this inquiry can be answered. We shall see that the very difference of universal and particular depends on the fact that each point-instant is itself, and yet of the same character as others. At present it is enough to observe that the elementary universal, point-instant, is comparable to a proper name like John Smith, the whole meaning of which, as Mr. Bosanquet has said, is to indicate any particular individual ; so that while any number of persons have that name, the name does not so much imply properties which are common to them all, but merely designates in each instance of its use a single individual, and is thus used in a different sense with each. I need hardly stop to reject the supposition

[1] The possible helpfulness of metaphysics, within its limitations, to the special sciences has not so generally been recognised by them.

that a point-instant is as it were the meeting-place of two concepts, point and instant, as if a combination of two concepts could confer individuality. For, firstly, no combination of concepts makes an individual. Secondly, point and instant are not concepts combined to make that of point-instant, as hard and yellow are combined in gold. For point and instant are not separable from one another, but each implies the other, and the concepts point and instant are merely elements distinguished in the concept point-instant. But all these matters belong strictly to a later stage of our inquiry. They are mentioned here only to anticipate difficulty.

Space and geometries of it.

The starting-point of geometry is then empirical Space presented in experience as what can only be described in conceptual terms as a continuum of points. The elaborate analysis of continuity by the speculative mathematicians does but explain what is given in this empirical form. But when I go on to ask what more precisely geometry does, and have regard to the history of the various geometries and to the most recent reduction of geometry to the status of an illustration of algebra, I find myself in danger of the fate which is said to overtake those who speak of mathematics without being mathematicians.[1] I have to do what I can, and I hope without presumption, with such information as is open to me. My object is the modest one of setting the empirical method of metaphysics as occupied with spaces and numbers in its relation first to elementary geometry of three dimensions, and next to the more generalised conceptions of mathematical procedure for which geometry is but a special application of arithmetic, or rather both geometry and arithmetic fall under one science of order.

Starting then with empirical Space, geometry, like

[1] " On the other hand," says Mr. A. N. Whitehead (*Introduction to Mathematics*, p. 113), "it must be said that, with hardly any exception, all the remarks on mathematics made by those philosophers who have possessed but a slight or hasty and late-acquired knowledge of it are entirely worthless, being either trivial or wrong." He is pointing the contrast with Descartes.

any other science, proceeds by means of axioms, definitions, and postulates, to discover what may be learnt about figures in space and, in general, about spatial relations. Thus Euclid from his premisses arrives at properties of triangles. The axioms and postulates of geometry are its hypotheses. Even the assumption of points when they are given a semi-independent existence in order to give support to the imagination is hypothetical. But Euclid's axioms are not the only ones out of which a body of geometrical truths can be constructed which still are applicable to empirical Space. There are many geometries though there is but one Space. Strictly speaking, it is only by a mistake of language that we speak of non-Euclidean Space or even of Euclidean Space; we have only Euclidean or non-Euclidean geometry. In the first place, while Euclidean geometry is metrical and involves magnitude and measurement, there is the more abstract geometry of position, or projective geometry, "which involves only the intersectional properties of points, lines, planes, etc.,"[1] and in metric geometry there are the modern systems which introduce notions of order or motion. But besides these there are the geometries, still three-dimensional, which are not Euclidean at all. The late H. Poincare, as is well known, thought that it was impossible and indeed meaningless to ask whether Euclid or these other geometries were true. They differ not in respect of truth but of practical convenience. Euclid's is the most convenient. It is by no means involved in empirical Space that a straight line should be the shortest between two points. Poincare imagines a spherical world where the temperature changes from centre to circumference, and bodies shrink or grow with the fall or rise of the temperature. Apparently such a geometry (in which the shortest lines are circles) would apply to empirical Space "within the possible error of observation."[2] In other words, the difference of its

---

[1] *Fundamental Concepts of Algebra and Geometry*, by J. Wesley Young, p. 135 (New York, 1911), to which I am deeply indebted in what follows for information.

[2] J. W. Young, *loc. cit.* p. 23.

conclusions from those of Euclidean geometry would not be capable of detection by our instruments.

This also, I understand, applies to the non-Euclidean geometries of Lobatchewsky and others, the so-called hyperbolic and elliptic geometries. Now, in the case of these geometries, the question does not arise whether they take us into a world different from our experienced Space. They are merely different systems of explaining, not the ultimate nature of Space, but its behaviour in detail. They employ different postulates. At the same time they introduce us to another feature of geometry and of mathematics generally, its method of generalisation. Euclidean geometry is only one instance of geometry of empirical Space. In it, a parallel may be drawn through any point outside a straight line to that line, and only one. In hyperbolic geometry there are two parallels; in elliptic geometry none. Or we may put the matter differently by reference to what is called the space-constant, or to what is less accurately spoken of as the 'curvature' of the Space. This constant has a finite value, positive or negative, in the other two geometries; in Euclidean geometry it tends to infinity. In the less accurate language the curvature of Euclidean space is zero, in the other two cases it is positive or negative. Now it is the generalising tendency of mathematics which has led ultimately to the reduction of geometry to arithmetic, and it raises the question in what sense the world of mathematical entities so conceived is real, whether it is not a neutral world, and empirical geometry only an application of its laws to sensible material.[1]

Generalised 'Space.' The simplest though not the most important example of such generalisation is found in geometries of more than three dimensions. Dimensionality, as Mr. Young

---

[1] "The geometrical system constructed upon these foundations (*i.e.* those of Lobatchewsky and Bolyai) is as consistent as that of Euclid. Not only so, but by a proper choice of a parameter entering into it, this system can be made to describe and agree with the external relations of things" (H. S. Carslaw, *Elements of Non-Euclidean Plane Geometry and Trigonometry*, London, 1916).

points out,[1] is an idea of order. A point by its motion generates a straight line, a line a plane, a plane solid Space, and this exhausts all the points of Space. We may think then of Space as a class of points arranged in three orders or dimensions. But this notion, once drawn from empirical Space, may be extended or generalised ; and we may think of a class of any number of dimensions which will have its geometry or be a new so-called 'Space.' We have taken a notion and generalised it, cutting it loose as it were from its attachments to the one empirical Space. Such generalisation is of the very life of mathematics, and its most important example is the process by which the notion of number has been extended. The study of numbers begins with the integral numbers, however they are conceived ; but the notion of number has been extended by successive steps, so that there have been included in the number-system fractions as well as integral rational numbers, negative as well as positive numbers, irrationals, imaginary numbers, complex numbers consisting of a rational combined with an irrational number, and now the class of infinite or transfinite numbers. All these symbols have been so defined as to preserve the general laws of ordinary numbers, and great advances in the understanding of numbers have been marked by successful definitions, like the famous definition of an irrational number by R. Dedekind. To a certain extent it may be sufficient to describe these numbers as conventional, but that they are not mere conventions is shown partly by their having been suggested in some cases by geometry (as incommensurable numbers, for example, by the relation of magnitude between the side and the diagonal of a square) ; partly by the possibility of interpreting them geometrically. Mr. Young quotes a saying of Prof. Klein, that it looks as though the algebraical symbols were more reasonable than the men who employed them.[2]

Now I assume that the notion of an n-dimensional geometry is fruitful and profitable as a topic of inquiry. And if so, it seems to me to be as unreasonable to deny

[1] *Loc. cit.* p. 170.　　　[2] P. 112.

the value of it, which some philosophers are inclined to do, as it would be to reject imaginaries because there are no imaginary points in real Space. What we have in both cases alike is the investigation of certain notions for their own sakes when taken apart from their attachments ; and the question rather is not whether they are legitimate, for I do not see how their legitimacy can be questioned, but the much more interesting question of whether they ever lose their original connection with the empirical so as to constitute a ' neutral ' world of thought which is neither physical nor mental.

A product
of art. This question, so far as it is raised, even at this stage appears to admit of an answer. The idea of dimensionality taken by itself is combined with that of number, and a system is constructed by thought of elements in an n-dimensional total, and the consequences are worked out of this assumption. The systems are not, properly speaking, Spaces at all, nor their elements points in the empirical sense, but three-dimensional Space may be treated as derived from such a ' Space,' e.g. from four-dimensional ' Space,' on the analogy of the derivation of two-dimensional Space (which after all is an abstraction) from three-dimensional Space. Now if we may assume for the moment what will appear later,[1] that integral number itself is but a conception founded in empirical Space-Time, what we have here is nothing more in kind than the imagination of a gold mountain or any other work of imagination, only that in imagination the elements are sensory and found in the sensory world, whereas thought liberates itself from this condition. If the notions of dimensionality and number are rooted in Space-Time, the construction of a more than three-dimensional ' Space ' does not lead us into a neutral world but takes notions which are empirical at bottom and combines them by an act of our minds. But just as the arbitrary act of imagination by which

---

[1] It is a great disadvantage for me that I cannot anticipate the discussion of this point. Without it my assertion may appear to be dogma. See Book II. where number is described (as well as order) along with the other categories in its place.

we construct a chimaera leaves us still dealing with physical features, though combined in a way which is not verified in physical fact, so in these thought constructions we are dealing all the time with ideas belonging to the empirical world. No new or neutral world is established, but the freedom of thought gives rise to fresh combinations.

No one would admit that a chimaera belongs to a neutral world ; but rather so far as it claims to be real its claims are a pretence. The question then we have to ask is, are such intellectual constructions as many-dimensional 'Spaces,' or imaginary numbers, merely imaginary or are they true. A chimaera is not true, though it may have its place in a world of art as a work of pure imagination ; and it is not true because it does not follow the lines of nature in the organic world. But a concept which is founded in the nature of Space-Time may admit of extensions or generalisations which are the work of pure thought, and discovered by it, and yet being on the lines of nature in the empirical world of Space-Time may be coherent with the spatial or numerical system and, at whatever degree of remoteness, be applicable again to the nature from which it sprang. Thus, to take an instance which supposes very little acquaintance with geometry, the idea that all circles pass through the same two imaginary points at infinity is a pure construction of thought. It is founded on the general proposition that two curves of the second degree intersect each other in four points. Two intersecting circles also intersect at these circular points at infinity. But by the use of this intellectual construction we can pass by projection from properties of the circle to properties of the ellipse. Such intellectual constructs are thus not mere exercises of thought, like a chimaera, but are coherent with the system of thoughts which have correspondents in real Space. They have therefore a double value, first in themselves, and secondly in the application of them.

Now as to the various kinds of numbers which have been discovered and introduced into arithmetic in virtue of the tendency towards that generality which, Mr. Whitehead says, the mathematician is always seeking,[1] their connection with the integral numbers has been observed above, where I have mentioned the fact that they admit of spatial interpretation. As to the usefulness of the extensions of the notion of dimensionality, I can but quote the words of Mr. Young (p. 174): " It may be stated without fear of contradiction that the study of such spaces has been of the greatest practical value, both in pure mathematics and in the applications of mathematics to the physical sciences."

Thus in one respect the extensions in which geometry deserts empirical Space and creates new 'Spaces,' or the constructions within the system of number, are, it would seem, comparable to the scaffoldings by the help of which we build great buildings or ships. They allow us to raise the structure with which we are concerned, and to come indirectly into contact with it. Sometimes, as in the scaffolding of a building, parts of the scaffolding may be inserted into the building itself which is being raised. Sometimes they may be detached like the great framework of steel within which a ship is built, such as one sees as one steams down the river at Belfast or other great dockyard. These are still material structures, and belong to the same world as the ships or buildings. In higher geometry or arithmetic we have in like manner works of art whose materials are derived from experienced Space - Time, however intricately combined by thought, and they also have their utility in their application. But in another respect the comparison is faulty. For the scaffoldings of houses and ships exist only in order to build houses or ships. But the mathematician's constructions are made for their own sakes and are discoveries within geometry and arithmetic itself; like all scientific constructions they have a value irrespective of utility. Still, also like them, they are based upon and draw their life from the empirical material with which they are in organic connection.

[1] *Introduction to Mathematics*, p. 82.

I am far from supposing that the notion of many-dimensional 'Spaces' is comparable in importance philosophically with the numerical constructions which have given us in arithmetic the irrational, imaginary, or transfinite, numbers. I am not able to judge. But it seems fairly clear that the intimacy of connection between the first set of constructions and the empirical world is much less than in the case of the second set. A four-dimensional 'Space' is not a Space at all, and it appears to be rather a means for discovery in three-dimensional Space than itself the discovery of something in the world of Space; rather a work of art than a discovery. But the numbers are discoveries within the system of numbers. My object, however, has not been to assign to these different constructions their grades of value; it has been no more than to indicate that they do not take us into a neutral world of thought but keep us still in contact with the one Space and Time which we apprehend in experience, and seek to understand in mathematics in their empirical determinations by the selective analysis and intellectual construction employed in mathematics. In other words, we are not entitled to say, because by generalisation we arrive at a world of thoughts, that that world of thought is for metaphysics a neutral world of which our empirical world is the manifestation under certain conditions of sensible experience; that empirical Space, for instance, is a particular example of a system of complex numbers. We have in fact started from the empirical world itself, in particular from empirical Space and Time, extended by thought the conceptions derived from it, and descended again to empirical Space. The procedure is legitimate, but it does not establish the primacy of a neutral world. Metaphysically, empirical Space and Time are themselves the foundation of this neutral world. There is however another problem set to us, which belongs to the theory of knowledge, that is to that chapter of metaphysics. We have to ask what kind of reality belongs to such thought-constructions, and this runs into the general question, what reality belongs to ideas and to hypotheses

Relation of the generalisations to empirical pac and Time

and all assumptions and to mere imaginations and illusions, and ideas which are commonly called unreal, like a round square, which still remain objects of thought or we could not speak about them. Now it is only one solution that there is a world of neutral being simpler than the world of physical or mental things which exist. There may be the world of truth and error or art (suggested above) which is not to be characterised as neither physical nor mental but as both physical and mental.[1] For our present purpose it is enough to insist that metaphysically all these constructions are rooted in the empirical world of existence, and ultimately in empirical Space and Time.

But in order properly to understand what is implied in the generalisation by which geometry and arithmetic become one science, we must go further and discuss a fundamental question which has been reserved. Dimensionality is an idea of order and order is connected with relation. I have assumed provisionally that for empirical metaphysics order and number can be exhibited as derived from Space-Time and dependent on it. But we can only satisfy ourselves that the concepts of mathematics are still attached to empirical Space-Time by examining the view that Space and Time are relations and not as we have supposed a stuff. We shall then see that the concepts in which mathematics appears to move away from Space-Time are in the end saturated with the notion of Space-Time. We have thus to ask ourselves, what are relations in Space and Time, and under what conditions Space and Time can be treated as systems of relations.

[1] See later, Bk. III. ch. ix. A.

CHAPTER VI

RELATIONS IN SPACE AND TIME

THAT was a profound maxim of Hume, when inquiring Spatial into the value or the real existence of an idea to seek for relations the impression to which the idea corresponded. In more Space itself. general language it is the maxim to seek the empirical basis of our ideas. It is true that Hume himself overlooked in experience facts which were in the language of Plato's *Republic* rolling about before his feet ; and hence failing to find in experience any impression of the self or of causality, he was compelled to refer the ideas of self or causality to the imagination, though in the case of self, for instance, we can see that while he noticed the substantive conditions he overlooked the transitive ones, and missed the essential continuity of mind against which the perceptions are merely standing out in relief. A thorough‑going empiricism accepts his formula, but having no prejudice in favour of the separate and distinct existences which attract our attention, insists that in surveying experience no items shall be omitted from the inventory.

Following this maxim, if we ask what are relations in Space and Time the answer is not doubtful. They are themselves spaces and times. "Years ago," says James in one of the chapters of his book, *The Meaning of Truth* (chap. vi. ' A Word more about Truth,' pp. 138 ff.), " when T. H. Green's ideas were most influential, I was much troubled by his criticisms of English sensationalism. One of his disciples in particular would always say to me, ' Yes ! *terms* may indeed be possibly sensational in origin ; but *relations*, what are they but pure acts of the intellect coming upon the sensations from above, and of a higher nature?' I well remember the sudden relief it gave me to perceive one day that *space*-relations at any rate were homogeneous with the terms between which they mediated. The terms were spaces and the relations were other intervening spaces." The same kind of feeling of relief may have been felt by many besides myself who were nursed in the teaching of Green and remember their training with gratitude, when they read the chapter in James's *Psychology* (vol. ii. pp. 148–53) where this truth was first stated by him ; for example in the words, " The relation of direction of two points toward each other is the sensation of the line that joins the two points together." Other topics are raised by the form of the statement, whether the alternative is merely between relations conceived as the work of the mind or as given in experience, and whether the relation which is a space is really a sensation. These matters do not concern us, at any rate at present. Nor have we yet to ask whether what is said of spatial is not true of all relations, namely that they are of the same stuff as their terms. What does concern us is that relations between bits of Space are also spaces. The same answer applies plainly to Time. If the bits of Space are points they are connected by the points which intervene. A relation of space or time is a transaction into which the two terms, the points or lines or planes or whatever they may be, enter ; and that transaction is itself spatial. Relations in space are possible because Space is itself a connected whole, and there are no parts of it which are disconnected from the rest. The relation of continuity itself between the points of space is the original datum that the points are empirically continuous, and the conceptual relation translates into conceptual terms this original continuity, first regarding the points as provisionally distinct and then correcting that provisional distinctness. The " impression"—the empirical fact—to which the idea of continuity corresponds is this given character of Space which we describe by the sophisticated and reflective name of continuity. Relations in space or spatial relations are thus not mere concepts, still less mere words by which somehow we connect bits of space together. They are the concrete connections of these bits of space, and simple as Space is, it is (at least when taken along with its Time) as concrete as a rock or tree. Moreover, when we introduce into Space the element of Time which is intrinsic to it, relations of space become literally *transactions* between the spatial terms. All Space is process, and hence the spatial relation has what belongs to all relations, sense, so that the relation of a to b differs from the relation of b to a. Thus if a and b are points, the relation is the line between them, but that line is full of Time, and though it is the same space whether it relates a to b or b to a, it is not the same space-time or motion. The transaction has a different direction.

All relations which are spatial or temporal are thus contained within the Space and Time to which the terms belong. Space and Time, though absolute in the sense we have described, namely that spaces and times are in .Newton's words their own places, are relational through and through, because it is one extension and it is one duration in which parts are distinguishable and are distinguished, not merely by us but intrinsically and of themselves : as we have seen through the action of Space and Time upon each other. Whether we call Space and Time a system of points and instants or of relations is therefore indifferent. Moreover, in any given case the relation may be of more interest than its terms. James has pointed out that while in general the relations between terms form fringes to the terms in our experience, so that the terms are substantive and the relations transitive, yet on occasion it may be the transition which is in the foreground—it may become substantival and the terms become its fringes. For instance the plot of a play may be distinct and impressive, and the persons shadowy, points of attachment to the plot. In a constitutional monarchy it is the relations of king and subjects which are substantive, the person of the king or of his subjects are merely the dim suggestions of things which the constitution unites.

Thus Space as extension and Time as duration are internally orderly, and they are orders, the one of co-existence and the other of succession, because order is a relation, and a comprehensive one, within extension and duration ; or rather it is a relation within Space-Time, for it implies sense, and neither Space alone nor Time alone possesses sense. In other words, given empirical Space-Time, order of the parts of Space-Time is a relation, in the meaning of transition from part to part. Just as conceptual continuity corresponds to empirical or apprehended continuity, so conceptual order determined by some law or principle corresponds, as a relation between points or other bits of space and time themselves, to the empirical transitions between those bits. These empirical transitions in virtue of which one part of space and time is between others are the "impressions" which are the originals of the conceptual order.

How far a science of order could be founded on this bare conception of ordered parts of Space-Time I do not know. But at any rate the more comprehensive theorems of speculative mathematics at the present time do not thus proceed. They appear to use the conception of Space and Time not as being stuffs, as we have taken them to be, within which there are relations of the parts of Space and Time themselves, but as relational in the sense that they are relations between *things* or entities. This is the antithesis between absolute and relational Space and Time.

Absolute and relational Space and Time. In the one philosophical view, the one which I have adopted, Space and Time are themselves entities, or rather there is one entity, Space-Time, and there are relations spatio-temporal within it. In the other, Space and Time are nothing but systems of relations between entities which are not themselves intrinsically spatio-temporal. In the simplest form of the doctrine they are relations between material points. They may be, as in some sense with Leibniz, relations between monads. But in every case the presupposition is of entities, which when the relations are introduced may then be said to be in Space and Time. We are, it seems, at once transported into a logical world of entities and their relations which subsist, but do not belong in themselves to either physical or mental empirical existence. For it must be admitted, I think, that it would be impossible to take Space and Time as relations between, say, material bodies, and at the same time to postulate an absolute Space and Time in which the bodies exist. The physical bodies, besides standing in spatial and temporal relations to one another, must then stand in a new relation to the places they occupy. But this offers an insuperable difficulty. Space and Time cannot at once be entities in their own right and at the same time merely be relations between entities ; and the relation supposed between the place which is an entity and the physical body at that place is either a mere verbal convenience or it stands for nothing. All we can do is to define the place by means of relations between physical entities ; and this it is which has been attempted by Messrs. Whitehead and Russell in a construction of extraordinary ingenuity, expounded in Mr. Russell's recent book on *Our Knowledge of the External World.* There the elements of the construction of a point are various perspectives of a thing, which is usually said to be *at* that point, arranged in a certain order, these perspectives being themselves physical objects.

Not to enter minutely into details for which I am not competent, I may illustrate the character of this mathematical method by reference to the number system, which shows how completely the method takes its start from assumed entities. Cardinal numbers are defined by the independent investigation of Messrs. Frege and Russell as the class of classes similar to a given class. The number 2 is the class of all groups of two things, which may be ordered in a one-to-one correspondence with each other. From this definition of number in neutral terms, for entity is any object of thought whatever, we can proceed to define the whole system of real numbers ; first the fractions and then the surds, finally arriving at a purely logical definition of the system of real numbers, involving entities, certain relations of order, and certain operations.[1] But once arrived at this point we may go farther. " It is possible, starting with the assumptions characterising the algebra of real numbers, to define a system of things which is abstractly equivalent to metric Euclidean geometry."[2] So that real algebra and ordinary geometry become abstractly identical. This is one stage in the arithmetisation of geometry which is the outstanding feature of recent mathematics. In the end, as I understand, there is but one science, arithmetic, and geometry is a special case of it.

It is no part of my purpose to question the legitimacy of this method. On the contrary, I take for granted that it is legitimate. Our question is whether it really does leave empirical Space behind it, and what light it throws on the difference, if any, between metaphysics and mathematics. For, as we have seen, in the simpler theory of mathematics which takes absolute Space and Time for granted, even if as fictions, geometry was concerned with the properties of figures and their relation to the principles adopted for convenience in the science, and the metaphysics of Space was an analysis of empirical Space ; and the demarcation of the two sciences was fairly clear. But if it is claimed that mathematics at its best is not concerned with empirical Space at all, but with relations between entities, then we are threatened with one of two results. Either our metaphysics in dealing with empirical Space is concerned with a totally different subject from geometry, not merely treating the same topic in a different way or with a different interest, or else we must revise our conception of metaphysics and identify it in effect with mathematics or logic.

Assump-
n   f
relational
theory.

We may most clearly realise the contrast of this method with the empirical method of metaphysics if we recur to the importunate question, What then is a relation if Space and Time are relations ? Empirical metaphysics explains what relations are.[3] But the mathematical method can clearly not avail itself of the same answer. Relation is

---

[1] Young, *loc. cit.* p. 98.   [2] *Loc. cit.* p. 182.
[3] See later, Bk. II. ch. iv.

indeed the vaguest word in the philosophical vocabulary, and it is often a mere word or symbol indicating some connection or other which is left perfectly undefined ; that is, relation is used as a mere thought, for which its equivalent in experience is not indicated.   For Leibniz there is still an attachment left between the relations which are spatial and the Space we see.   For empirical Space is but the confused perception by the senses of these intelligible relations. He never explains what the intelligible relations are.   But our mathematical metaphysicians leave us in no doubt. "A relation," says Mr. Russell (*Principles of Mathematics*, p. 95), "is a concept which occurs in a proposition in which there are two terms not occurring as concepts, and in which the interchange of the two terms gives a different proposition."   This is however a description of relation by its function in a proposition, and is a purely logical generalisation ; it does not profess to say what relations are in themselves.   To do this, we must have recourse to the method used in defining numbers, which gives us constructions of thought, in terms of empirical things, that are a substitute for the so-called things or relations of our empirical world.   An admirable statement of the spirit of this method has been supplied by Mr. Russell himself in an article in *Scientia*.[1]   Thus, for instance, if we define a point, *e.g.* the point at which a penny is, by an order among perspectives of the penny, we are in fact

[1] "*Wherever possible, logical constructions are to be substituted for inferred entities* [*e.g.*, the cardinal number of two equally numerous collections]. . . . The method by which the construction proceeds is closely analogous in these and all similar cases.   Given a set of propositions nominally dealing with the supposed inferred entities, we observe the properties which are required of the supposed entities in order to make these propositions true.   By dint of a little logical ingenuity, we then construct some logical function of less hypothetical entities which has the requisite properties.   This constructed function we substitute for the supposed inferred entities, and thereby obtain a new and less doubtful interpretation of the body of propositions in question " ('The Relation of Sense-data to Physics,' Sec. vi. *Scientia*, 1914.   The article is now reprinted in *Mysticism and Logic* (London, 1918) ; the reference is to pp. 155-6.

What I imply in the text is that number, thing, relation, are directly experienced, and that metaphysics has to describe what is thus directly experienced.   This is attempted in Bk. II.

substituting for the empirical point an intelligible construction which, as it is maintained, can take its place in science. When a thing is defined as the class of its perspectives, a construction is supplied which serves all the purposes of the loose idea of an empirical thing which we carry about with us. A relation is defined upon the same method.[1] We are moving here in a highly generalised region of thoughts, used to indicate the empirical, but removed by thought from the empirical. The Humian question, What is the impression to which the idea of a relation (or that of a thing) corresponds, has lost its meaning. A thing or a relation such as we commonly suppose ourselves to apprehend empirically is replaced by a device of thought which enables us to handle them more effectively. Such constructions describe their object indirectly, and are quite unlike a hypothesis such as that of the ether, which however much an invention of thought professes to describe its object directly. As in the case of the theory of number, we seem to be in a logical or neutral world.

But we have cut our moorings to the empirical stuff of Space and Time only in appearance, and by an assumption the legitimacy of which is not in question, but which remains an assumption. The starting-point is entities or things which have being, and in the end this notion is a generalisation from material things or events. Now such things are supposed, on the relational doctrine, to be distinct from the Space and Time in which they are ordered. But there is an alternative hypothesis, the one which we have more than once suggested as involved with the empirical method here expounded. The hypothesis is that the simplest being is Space-Time itself, and that material things are but modes of this one simple being, finite complexes of Space-Time or motion, dowered with the qualities which are familiar to us in sensible experience. That hypothesis must justify itself in the sequel by its metaphysical success. But at least it is an alternative that cannot be overlooked. The neglect of it is traceable to the belief that we must choose

[1] *Principia Mathematica*, i. p. 211.

between an absolute Space and Time, which are alike the places of themselves and the places of material things, and, on the other hand, a spatial and temporal world which is a system of relations between things. As we have seen, we cannot combine these notions. But if things are bits of Space-Time, they are not entities with mere thought relations which correspond to empirical Space and Time ; rather, we only proceed to speak of relations between them because they are from the beginning spatio-temporal and in spatio-temporal relations to one another.

I am not contending that this hypothesis, which is no Contrast new one but as old as the *Timaeus* of Plato with its with construction of things out of elementary triangles, and theory. has been revived in physics in our own day in a different form,[1] is established ; but only that it is inevitable to an empirical metaphysics of Space and Time. Order is, as we have seen, a relation amongst these finite complexes within Space-Time. When we begin with developed material things, later in metaphysical (and actual) sequence than Space-Time itself, we are by an act of thought separating things from the matrix in which they are generated. When we do so we forget their origin, generalise them into entities, construct relations in thought between them, transport ourselves into a kind of neutral world by our thought, and elaborate complexes of neutral elements by which we can descend again to the spatio-temporal entities of sense. We can legitimately cut ourselves adrift from Space and Time because our data are themselves in their origin and ultimate being spatio-temporal, and the relations between them in their origin equally spatio-temporal. Thus we construct substitutes for Space and Time because our materials are thoughts of things and events in space and time. We appear to leave Space and Time behind us

[1] The reference is to the physical theory of the late Osborne Reynolds, according to which the universe is Space, and matter is comparable to a strain or a geological fault in this homogeneous medium. See his Rede Lecture, *On an Inversion of Ideas as to the Structure of the Universe*, Cambridge, 1903. Reynolds's theory that Space is granular in structure does not concern us here, but concerns the physicist.

and we do so ; but our attachments are still to Space
and Time, just as they were in extending the idea of
dimensionality. Only here our contact is less direct.
For dimensionality or order is implied in Space and
Time, but in this later method we are basing ourselves
on entities which are not implied *in* Space and Time but
which do presuppose it. Indirect as the attachment is,
yet it persists. Consequently, though we construct a
thought of order or of an operation and interpret Space
and Time in terms of order, we are but connecting
thought entities by a relation which those entities in
their real attachments already contain or imply. If our
hypothesis is sound, order is as much a datum of Space-
Time apprehension as continuity is, and in the same
sense.

Thus the answer to the question, are Space and Time
relations between things, must be that they may be so
treated for certain purposes ; but that they are so, really
and metaphysically, only in a secondary sense, for that
notion refers us back to the nature of the things between
which they are said to be relations, and that nature
already involves Space and Time. Until we discover
what reality it is for which the word relation stands and
in that sense define it, the notion of relation is a mere
word or symbol. It is an invention of our thought,
not something which we discover. The only account we
can give of it is that relation is what obtains between a
king and his subjects or a town and a village a mile away
or a father and his son. But such an account suffers
from a double weakness. By using the word ' between '
it introduces a relation into the account of relation ; and
it substitutes for definition illustration. We may legitimately use the unanalysed conception of relation and
of entity as the starting-point of a special science. But
there still remains for another science the question what
relation and entity are, and that science is metaphysics.
So examined, we find that relations of space and time are
intrinsically for metaphysics relations within Space and
Time, that is within extension and duration. Accordingly
the relational view as opposed to the absolute view of

Space and Time, whatever value it possesses for scientific purposes, is not intrinsically metaphysical.

We are now, however, in a position to contrast the metaphysical method with the mathematical. The method of metaphysics is analytical. It takes experience, that is, what is experienced (whether by way of contemplation or enjoyment), and dissects it into its constituents and discovers the relations of parts of experience to one another in the manner I have attempted to describe in the Introduction. But mathematics is essentially a method of generalisation. Partly that generalising spirit is evidenced by the extension of its concepts beyond their first illustrations. This has been noted already. But more than this, it is busy in discussing what may be learned about the simplest features of things. Mathematics as a science, says Mr. Whitehead, " commenced when first some one, probably a Greek, proved propositions about *any* things or about *some* things without specification of particular things. These propositions were first enunciated by the Greeks for geometry ; and accordingly geometry was the great Greek mathematical science." [1] This is an admirable statement of the spirit of the science and of why it outgrew the limits of geometry. It also indicates why when mathematics is pushed to its farthest limits it becomes indistinguishable from logic. On this conception our starting-point is things, and we discuss their simplest and most general characters. They have being, are entities ; they have number, order, and relation, and form classes. These are wide generalities about things. Accordingly geometry turns out in the end to be a specification of properties of number. In treating its subject mathematics proceeds analytically in the sense of any other science : it finds the simplest principles from which to proceed to the propositions it is concerned with. But it is not analytical to the death as metaphysics is. Existence, number and the like are for it simply general characters of things, categories of things, if the technical word be preferred. Now an analysis of

[1] *Introduction to Mathematics*, p. 14.

things in the metaphysical sense would seek to show if it can what the nature of relation or quantity or number is, and in what sense it enters into the constitution of things. But here in mathematics things are taken as the ultimates under their generalised name of beings or entities. They are then designated by descriptions. What can be said about things in their character of being the elements of number? Hence we have a definition of number by things and their correspondences. But metaphysics does not generalise about things but merely analyses them to discover their constituents. The categories become constituents of things for it, not names of systems into which things enter. Its method is a method not so much of description as of acquaintance.

Mathe-

deals with
extension;
meta-
physics
with
intension.

The same point may be expressed usefully in a different way by reference to the familiar distinction in logic between the extension and the intension of names. Mathematics is concerned with the extension of its terms, while metaphysics is concerned with their intension, and of course with the connection between the two. The most general description of thing is entity, the most general description of their behaviour to each other is relation. Things are grouped extensionally into classes; intensionally they are connected by their common nature. Number is therefore for the mathematician described in its extensional aspect; so is relation.[1] Now for metaphysics intension is prior to extension. When the science of extensional characters is completed, there still remains a science of intensional characters. It is not necessarily a greater or more important science. It is only ultimate.

The spirit by which mathematics has passed the limits of being merely the science of space and number, till it assumes the highly generalised form we have described, carries it still further, till in the end it becomes identical with formal logic. For logic also is concerned not with the analysis of things but with the forms of propositions

[1] Whitehead and Russell, *Princ. Math.*, Introduction, vol. i. p. 27. "Relations, like classes, are to be taken in *extension*, *i.e.* if R and S are relations which hold between the same pairs of terms, R and S are to be identical." Compare *ibid.* p. 211.

in which the connections of things are expressed. Hence
at the end pure mathematics is defined by one of its
most eminent exponents as the class of all propositions of
the form '*p* implies *q*,' where *p* and *q* are themselves
propositions.[1]

Mathematics is a term which clearly has different
meanings, and the speculative conception of it endeavours
to include the other meanings. But it is remarkable
that as the science becomes more and more advanced, its
affinity to empirical metaphysics becomes not closer but
less intimate. The simple geometry and arithmetic which
purported to deal with Space and quantity were very near
to empirical metaphysics, for Space and Time of which they
described the properties are for metaphysics the simplest
characters of things. But in the more generalised conception, the two sciences drift apart. It is true that still
mathematics deals with some of the most general
properties of things, their categories. And so far it
is in the same position towards metaphysics as before.
But Space and Time have now been victoriously reduced
to relations, while experiential metaphysics regards them
as constituents and the simplest constituents of things.
Hence it was that we were obliged to show that in cutting
itself loose from Space and Time mathematics was like a
captive balloon. It gained the advantage of its altitude
and comprehensive view and discovered much that was
hidden from the dweller upon the earth. But it needed
to be reminded of the rope which held it to the earth
from which it rose. Without that reminder either
mathematics parts company from experiential metaphysics
or metaphysics must give up the claim to be purely
analytical of the given world.

Now it is this last calamity with which metaphysics
is threatened, and I add some remarks upon the point
in order to illustrate further the conception of experiential metaphysics. For the mathematical philosopher,
mathematics and logic and metaphysics become in the
end, except for minor qualifications, identical. Hence
philosophy has been described by Mr. Russell as the

*Is meta-
p y s)
the possible
or the
actual?*

---

[1] Russell, *Principles of Mathematics*, p. 3.

science of the possible.[1]   This is the inevitable outcome
of beginning with things or entities and generalising
on that basis.   Our empirical world is one of many
possible worlds, as Leibniz thought in his time.   But
all possible worlds conform to metaphysics.   For us,
on the contrary, metaphysics is the science of the actual
world, though only of the *a priori* features of it.   The conception of possible worlds is an extension from the
actual world in which something vital has been left out
by an abstraction.   That vital element is Space-Time.
For Space-Time is one, and when you cut things from
their anchors in the one sea, and regard the sea as
relations between the vessels which ride in it and without
which they would not serve the office of ships, you
may learn much and of the last value about the relations
of things, but it will not be metaphysics.   Thus the
possible world, in the sense in which there can be many
such, is not something to which we must add something
in order to get the actual world.   I am not sure whether
Kant was not guilty of a mere pun when he said that
any addition to the possible would be outside the possible
and thus impossible.   But at any rate the added element
must be a foreign one, not already subsumed within
the possible.   And once more we encounter the difficulty,
which if my interest here were critical or polemical it
might be profitable to expound, of descending from the
possible to the actual, when you have cut the rope of
the balloon.

The need
for meta-
physics.

Nothing that I have written is intended to suggest
any suspicion of the legitimacy or usefulness of the
speculative method in mathematics.   On the contrary
I have been careful to say the opposite.   Once more,
as in the case of many-dimensional ' Space,' it would seem
to me not only presumptuous on my part but idle on
the part of any philosopher to question these achieve-
ments.   Where I have been able to follow these speculations I have found them, as for instance in the famous
definition of cardinal number and its consequences,

[1] "On Scientific Method in Philosophy" (Herbert Spencer Lecture), Oxford, 1914, p. 17.   Reprinted in *Mysticism and Logic*, p. 111.

illuminating.   My business has consisted merely in indicating where the mathematical method in the treatment of such topics differs from that of empirical metaphysics ; and in particular that the neutral world of number and logic is only provisionally neutral and is in truth still tied to the empirical stuff of Space-Time.   Suppose it to be true that number is in its essence, as I believe, dependent on Space-Time, is the conception, we may ask, of Messrs. Frege and Russell to be regarded as a fiction ?   We may revert once more to the previous question, when a fiction is fictitious. If this doctrine is substituted for the analysis of number as performed by metaphysics as a complete and final analysis of that conception it would doubtless contain a fictitious element.   Or, as this topic has not yet been explained, if the conception of Space as relations between things is intended not merely as supplying a working scientific substitute for the ordinary notion of extension but to displace empirical Space with its internal relations, the conception is fictitious.   But if not, and if it serves within its own domain and for its own purpose to acquire knowledge not otherwise attainable, how can it be fictitious ?   I venture to add as regards the construction of points in space and time and physical things out of relations between sensibles proposed recently by Messrs. Whitehead and Russell, that if it bears out the hopes of its inventors and provides a fruitful instrument of discovery it will have irrespectively of its metaphysical soundness or sufficiency established its claim to acceptance.   " Any method," we may be reminded, " which leads to true knowledge must be called a scientific method." [1]   Only, till its metaphysical sufficiency is proved it would needs have to be content with the name of science.   For Space and Time may be considered as relations between things without distortion of fact.   Now the sciences exist by selecting certain departments or features of reality for investigation, and this applies to metaphysics among the rest.   They are only subject to correction so far as their subject matter

[1] A. Schuster, Presidential Address to British Association, 1916.

is distorted by the selection. But to omit is not necessarily to distort.

On the other hand, if a method proper to a particular science is converted into a metaphysical method it may be defective or false. This is why I ventured to say of Minkowski's Space-Time,[1] as a four-dimensional whole which admitted of infinite Spaces, that it was a mathematical representation of facts, but that it did not justly imply that the Universe was a four-dimensional one, because it overlooked the mutual implication of Space and Time with each other. If it were so understood it would contain a fictitious element. As it is, it contains an element which is not fictitious but only scientifically artificial.

Summary.

We may then sum up this long inquiry in the brief statement that whether in physics, in psychology, or in mathematics, we are dealing in different degrees of directness with one and the same Space and Time ; and that these two, Space and Time, are in reality one : that they are the same reality considered under different attributes. What is contemplated as physical Space-Time is enjoyed as mental space-time. And however much the more generalised mathematics may seem to take us away from this empirical Space-Time, its neutral world is filled with the characters of Space-Time, which for its own purposes it does not discuss. To parody a famous saying, a little mathematics leaves us still in direct contact with Space-Time which it conceptualises. A great deal more takes us away from it. But reviewed by metaphysics it brings us back to Space-Time again, even apart from its success in application. Thus if we are asked the question what do you mean by Space and Time ? Do you mean by it physical Space and Time, extension and duration, or mental space and time which you experience in your mind (if Space be allowed so to be experienced), or do you mean by it the orders of relations which mathematics investigates ? The answer is, that we mean all these things indifferently, for in the end they are one.

[1] Above, Bk. I. ch. i. p. 59.

BOOK II

THE CATEGORIES

CHAPTER I

NATURE OF THE CATEGORIES

SPACE-TIME then is in Kantian language an infinite Categories id Qualities given whole, that is to say, it is experienced as such, where the term experience includes thought as well as sensible experience. Its elements are represented conceptually as point-instants or bare events ; and we have added the hypothesis that other empirical things or existents are groupings of such events, whirlpools within that ocean, or they are crystals in that matrix. Only whereas a crystal may be separated from its matrix, existents never can ; they remain swimming in the medium of Space-Time. Their very being is continuity ; they are themselves continuously connected groupings of motions, and they are connected through the circum-ambient Space-Time with other such groupings or complexes. In less metaphorical language, they are complexes of motion differentiated within the one all-containing and all-encompassing system of motion. Primarily, therefore, empirical existents are spatio-temporal and remain so to the end. But with certain groupings of motion, certain spatio-temporal complexes, there are correlated what we call qualities, such as materiality, life, colour, consciousness. What the exact relation is between the quality and its spatio-temporal basis is to be the subject matter of a part of the next Book. We shall have to ask there whether it is fitly to be described as mere correlation or is still more intimate. The brief description contained in the name correlation is sufficient for our present purposes. Finite existents so understood, with their correlated qualities, are the things and

events of our ordinary experience, moving about or
happening in Space-Time, and endowed with qualities
the laws of which it is the office of the special sciences
to discover and co-ordinate. So much by way of
explanation of our hypothesis as to empirical existence.

Unlike the hypothesis of the Introduction, (that the
world of things might be treated as existing in its own
right and not dependent on the mind,) which is a hypothesis of method ; it is a hypothesis as to the nature
of things, or, in ordinary language, one of substance, not
merely of method. In order to avoid the constant use
of the long phrase empirical existents, I shall speak
simply of existents. These include not only ordinary
finites but also point-instants which are the limiting cases
at which we arrive in infinite division, and infinites like
infinite lines or numbers, which are the limiting cases in
the other direction ; and for this reason, in order to
include these two classes of existents which involve the
notion of infinitude, I speak of existents rather than of
finites. But while there will be much to say of point-
instants, I shall for the most part disregard infinites till
a later stage, and then touch upon them only briefly.[1]

Now amongst the characters of empirical existents
there is a clear distinction between those which are
variable and those which are pervasive. Some things
possess life, others not. Some things are red, others
green or yellow ; some are sweet, others sour. Some
have colour but no taste. Matter has mass but is not
conscious. These characters are what have been called
above qualities, and because they vary from thing to
thing they may be called empirical characters. But
there are other characters which are pervasive and
belong in some form to all existents whatever. Such
are identity (numerical identity for example), substance,
diversity, magnitude, even number. Moreover, not
only are these characters of what we commonly call
things, but they are characters of all existents whatever,
that is to say of everything, where the word thing is

<hr>

[1] Bk. IV. ch. i.   Some remarks upon point-instants and infinites
will be found in ch. ix. of Bk. II. pp. 324 ff.

equivalent to any finite object of experience. Thus not only is a living thing an extended substance of a certain magnitude and number of parts ; but a life itself, if you consider it, or so far as you can consider it, without direct reference to its body whose life it is, is extended, a substance, and possessed of magnitude, and moreover it is spread out into a multiplicity of parts and therefore contains number. Even mind, now that we have satisfied ourselves of its extended character in its enjoyment of itself, possesses these characters.

It is true the pervasive characters also undergo variation according to the empirical circumstances. The wax is always extended, but its particular magnitude and shape change when it is melted. Still, it retains some extension and magnitude and shape in all its empirical transformations. An earthquake may last a long or short time, an illumination may be constant or intermittent. But they are never without temporal character. Such empirical variations of the pervasive characters of things may be called primary qualities in distinction from the secondary qualities, where the phrase covers not only the traditional secondary qualities of matter but qualities like life or consciousness. These qualities may be present in one thing and absent from another, and differ in this respect from the empirical variations of the pervasive characters.

The pervasive characters of existents are what are known from Kant's usage as the categories of experience, and I shall call them, in distinction from the empirical ones or qualities, categorial characters. They may also be called the *a priori* or non-empirical characters. But the contrast must be taken at its face value as a distinction within the characters of experienced things. It does not imply that *a priori* or categorial characters, because not empirical, are not experienced. On the contrary, they are the essential and universal constituents of whatever is experienced, and in the wider sense of that term are therefore empirical. It was in this wider sense that philosophy was described as the empirical (or experiential) study of the non-empirical. The word categorial is not so much exposed to misunderstanding as non-empirical or in consequence of its history *a priori* ; and I shall most frequently employ it. At any rate the two classes of characters are distinguished within experience itself.

These categories then are the prerogative characters of things which run through all the rest as the warp on which the others are woven. Or, to vary the metaphor, they are the grey or neutral-coloured canvas on which the bright colours of the universe are embroidered. The primary 'qualities' are variations of them in empirical circumstance. The secondary qualities are correlated with complexities in the primary qualities themselves. Life is correlated with physical and chemical movements, themselves reducible to complexities of more elementary movements. Mind is correlated in turn with vital movements of a certain sort. Colour (whether it is partly dependent upon mind or not) corresponds, it is thought, to vibrations in a hypothetical medium, the ether, which hypothetically (and there is reason to think, superfluously) fills all Space. The categories are thus the groundwork of all empirical reality ; what Plato called the highest kinds of beings ($\mu\acute{\epsilon}\gamma\iota\sigma\tau a$ $\gamma\acute{\epsilon}\nu\eta$ $\tau\omega\nu$ $o\nu\tau\omega\nu$). According to his latest interpreter, the interest of these highest kinds displaced in his latest writings that of the Forms of sensible things ; and justly. For the Forms for all their eternal nature are, as compared with the categories, empirical—the form of dog in which individual dogs participate or which they imitate, but which trees do not ; the form of tree, or the form of justice, and the like. These are empirical universals. But the categories are not only universals, but, though I do not know if Plato would have said so, are truly universal in the sense that all existents partake of them.

Why the
categories
are per-
vasive : not
because
they are
due to
mind
The most remarkable feature of the categories which 's disclosed to inspection is that they are common to mind and to physical and generally non-mental things. Consider mind as it is known by direct acquaintance, that is by enjoyment, without the addition of indirect knowledge from any source, whether from reflective experience about

mind, or from speculative theory. It has identity, is a
substance, exhibits causality, etc. Something has been said
of this in the introductory chapter and need not be
repeated. What is the meaning of this presence of
the categories not only in the contemplated but the
enjoyed ?

One way of solving this problem is to say that the
mind is aware of the categories in its experience of itself,
and then imputes them to its objects. Whether this
answer has ever been attempted on a thorough-going scale,
I do not know. But it has often been attempted in
respect of the categories of causality and substance in
particular. We find these characters in ourselves, and we
interpret things, it is said, in our own likeness and find
that the interpretation is successful. Now it is certain
that experience of our own minds and experience of
external things play upon each other reciprocally, reinforce and elucidate each other. When we have learned
in ourselves the continuity, of a decision with its motives,
of the issue of a train of thought with its premisses, of the
mere unfolding of an idea in its details with the vague
and implicit apprehension of the same idea, and particularly the continuity of our performances with our inten-
tions ; we can then look to external things and events to
see whether there is not such continuity also there, the
same definite order of succession. Or, again, whether in
things there is not the like permanence in change that
we can so easily detect in our enjoyment of ourselves.
We speak then of causality or substance in external things,
of physical causality and physical substances ; and having
these conceptions we come back to our own minds and
ask whether we ourselves are not subject to physical
causation, or are not substances in the same sense as
external things, and we may thus raise problems which
seem to us of great difficulty. Out of this interplay of
mind and things it follows that while, on the one hand, we
speak of force or power in physical things in language
borrowed from our own wills ; on the other hand,
psychological terminology, as in such terms as apprehension
or comprehension or conception, is largely derived from

experience of physical things or of the action of our bodies on physical things.

But the mutual interplay of our experience of mind and things, which is an indisputable fact, is very far from the imputation by the mind of its own characters to external things. One simple consideration is enough to show that we do not merely construe things on the analogy of ourselves. For there must be something in the things which makes the analogy valid, or which gives a handle to the alleged imputation. If all we observe in external events is uniform succession, to impute to one of them a power to produce the other is a fiction, the fiction which Hume set himself to discredit. It may be serviceable anthropomorphism, but it is not science nor philosophy. If there is no power traceable in things, then there is none ; if the number of things is due to our counting, then there is no number in the things. The world then becomes indebted for its pervasive and prerogative characters to mind. Such a result is only satisfactory if the process is carried further, and if every character in things is attributed to mind, otherwise we could not understand how things should offer a reason to us to construe them so. I do not say this result is not true merely because it disagrees with our hypothesis of method, that we may treat mind as merely one of the many things in the universe. Yet at any rate we are bound before accepting it to see whether an explanation is not possible consistent with that hypothesis.

But now if there is something in the things which gives colour to the imputation, if for instance there is something in external things which is identical with the causal or substantial continuity which we find in mind, *when we do not take that experience to be more than it really is*, the imputation is unnecessary. Things may be numbered because they already contain number, not because they can be counted. On the contrary, they can be counted because they are countable and numerical. All the profit then that we can derive from the interplay of mind and things in becoming aware of the categories is that we may more easily derive from the enjoyed than from the contemplated the nature of the categories ; which categories they share in common. Of this liberty we shall avail ourselves.

Are we then to be content with the bare fact that the categories are unlike empirical characters in belonging to all things, and in particular in belonging to minds as well as to external things ? Such a coincidence would be sufficiently remarkable, but it clamours for the discovery of a reason. The reason is that the categories prove upon examination to be fundamental properties or determinations of Space-Time itself, not taken as a whole, but in every portion of it. They belong to all existents because, if our hypothesis is sound, existents are in the end, and in their simplest terms, differentiations of Space-Time, the complexes of events generated within that matrix. If that hypothesis be sound we should expect to find the pervasive features of things in the characters of their ultimate foundation. Or to put the same thing in another way, when and if it is seen that the categorial characters of things are features of any bit of Space-Time as such, merely so far as it is spatio-temporal, we are forced to the further conclusion that the empirical characters of things, their qualities, are correlated with the empirical groupings in Space-Time, and that things with their qualities are, as our hypothesis supposes, complexes within Space-Time. The categories are, as it were, begotten by Time on Space. It will be our business to exhibit this proposition in some detail with respect to the various categories.

The gist of the formula will perhaps be understood best by meeting in advance a possible misunderstanding, to the danger of which I shall recur more than once as the inquiry proceeds. Spaces or times it will be said have, it is true, magnitude, have identity, have a universal character, have existence. The categories, or at least some of them, are indeed applicable to spaces and times or, if you will, bits of Space-Time. These are instances which fall under these various categories, just as trees and dogs and tables do. But since they are but instances

but because they are fundamental properties of Space-Time.

of the categories, the source of these categories must be found elsewhere. Now the clue to the understanding of our thesis is that the categories are not applicable as it were *ab extra* to spaces and times, but that they are applicable to things (including minds) because they flow from the nature of the space-times which they occupy or which they are. Applicability to space-times has no meaning for the categories, which are the features or determinations of the space-times themselves. I do not wish to anticipate too much, but a single instance may suffice. My mind exists at this moment because it occupies a certain portion of Space-Time, and that bare occupation is existence. Moreover, it is so far universal, that I remain in broad outlines the same mind whether I am here in Glasgow or there in Florence. That transplantation does not affect my identity. *Caelum non animum mutant qui trans mare currunt.*

Kant's
re ment
of the
Categories.

In making this inquiry into the categories I have the good fortune to be able to make use for my own purposes, first, of the great later dialogues of Plato and, next, of Kant's work in the 'Schematism of the Categories' and above all in the 'Principles of the Understanding,' the most significant and fruitful chapter of the *Critique of Pure Reason*. But it would be at once tedious to the reader and an interruption to the argument to indicate in detail where I have been helped by Kant. Indeed it would seem at first sight as if little help were to be derived from him in this matter. For the drawbacks and deficiencies of Kant's doctrine of knowledge in general and of the categories in particular are obvious enough. The categories are referred, like the forms of Space and Time, to the mind, because it is thought that what Hutchison Stirling called the "empirical instruction" does not contain them already. They are universal and *a priori* and belong therefore to the understanding, and are sharply separated from sense and its forms. Nevertheless, Kant is far removed from the notion that we manufacture or work up objects of knowledge by means of the categories, still less that we impute these forms to objects. They are for him veritable elements in objective knowledge, though they are the contribution of objective mind and not of the empirical instruction. And of still more importance and value is his effort to supply what he calls a " proof " of the principles of the understanding. In essentials the " proof " is this,[1] that objective external experience contains the categories in correspondence with the features which the experience of Time possesses as given in the inner sense,—such as that it has duration, determinate order, permanence, is fuller or less full [2] and the like. Since the form of external experience is Space, it is not so far a cry from this reasoning to the present doctrine, founded not on any pretence of proof or reasoning but on empirical inspection, that the categories are begotten by Time on Space, or are fundamental features of any space-time. For Space and Time are for Kant also forms of the mind, though the categories belong to understanding and they to sense.

Unfortunately the separation of the forms of sense or intuition from those of the understanding, and of both from the empirical instruction, gives to Kant's analysis an air of artificiality and unresolved miracle, and perhaps it is not to be wondered at that those who have regarded his formal procedure rather than the spirit of it have represented the forms as if they were instruments used in working up knowledge, as planes or chisels are used in carpentering wood. The artificial separation does not arise for us. For the categories are for us expressions of the nature of Space-Time itself, and on the other hand the empirical instruction consists of nothing but complexes of this same space-time stuff. All the elements of things we know are ultimately of the same stuff. But in spite of these difficulties I cannot think that this part of Kant's doctrine is so innocently inadequate as is often believed. And I am making these remarks not in order to fortify myself by his authority, which I certainly could

[1] At least this is one of the lines of thought Kant pursues in his proof.
[2] To which corresponds the category of intensive quantity.

not invoke, but to record a grateful conviction that with or after Plato there is nothing comparable in importance upon this subject with what may be learned from him, even by one who believes that mind which is Kant's source of categories has nothing whatever to do with the matter, and that mind is only a name for minds which are empirical things like other empirical things, and like them possess categorial characters and for the same reason as other things possess them, that they are all alike empirical complexes of space-time stuff. Leave out from Kant the objective mind with all the dependencies of that conception ; and what he teaches us is mainly sound. It is true that the omission produces a considerable transformation, so considerable that the result would hardly be recognised as related to his doctrine by any affiliation of descent. But it is to be remembered that for a man of Kant's age the only method open to a philosopher, whether it was Kant or Reid, of indicating that the world of experience contains pervasive features as well as variable ones, was to refer this part of experience to mind in its objective character. Be this as it may, it is not always those who teach us most truth from whom we learn most, but those who best point the way to truth.

There are one or two questions of a general character about the categories which, to avoid repetition, will best be deferred till we have reviewed the categories in detail. For instance, whether at all, and if so in what sense, Space and Time themselves are to be called categories. Categorial they plainly are, and equally plainly Space-Time itself, which is the infinite matrix of all finites, is not a category. Again, it is plain from our description of the relation of empirical quality to Space-Time (that it is correlated with a certain complexity within Space-Time) that if our account be correct quality is not a category, and is no more than a comprehensive name for all the empirical qualities, and does not follow from the characters of Space-Time as such. Even for Kant, who regarded quality as a category, it only anticipates experience in respect of the intensity of the quality. It is in fact only another name for the empirical element in things.   But to avoid repetition at a later stage or imperfect discussion now, I omit these matters for the present.

We proceed then to describe the categories in order. The reader will bear in mind that they enter as constituent factors or as constitutive characters into every existent, whatever its quality.   He needs only, in order to help himself in the abstract (that is elementary) inquiry, to think of empirical things, divest them of their qualitative colouring, and single out the categorial foundations of what the colouring is correlated with. While he may, if he chooses, regard also the embroidery he will be pleased to think only of the canvas.

CHAPTER II

IDENTITY, DIVERSITY, AND EXISTENCE

Numerical identity and diversity. THERE are more senses than one of identity. There is, in the first place, bare or numerical identity, which is the identity of a thing with itself. Next, there is identity of kind, which is universality or generic identity. A dog is as dog generically identical with another dog. Thirdly, there is individual identity, which implies the blending of numerical and generic identity ; an individual is a particular of a certain sort. Lastly, there is substantial identity, which, besides individuality as just described, contains the element of substance. Such substantial identity is what is commonly understood by a numerically identical individual. But it is really more complex as we shall see than merely being an individual. One of its instances is personal identity.

We are concerned at present with bare numerical identity, or self-identity. Any point-instant or group of them is as such self-identical, and the self-identity of anything is its occupation of a space-time. Diversity is the occupation of another space - time, that is another place with its time. One thing is diverse from another in so far as it occupies a different point-instant from another thing or more generally a different portion of space-time. The occupation of any space-time, that is self-identity, in distinction from any other space-time is existence or determinate being. Owing to the empirical continuity of Space-Time, any piece of Space-Time and consequently any self-identity is distinct from some other self-identity, that is, it possesses an other, and is thus an existent or has existence. Existence or determinate being is therefore identity in its relation to the other. It is, as Plato taught in the *Timaeus* through the mouth of his Pythagorean speaker, the union of the same and the other. Identity, diversity, and existence arise out of the intrinsic nature of Space-Time as a continuum of its parts which are space-times, or rather it arises out of the nature of any space-time, as being a part of Space-Time and therefore connected with other space-times.

Such union calls for no explanation ; it is given with Space-Time itself. For Time makes Space distinct and Space makes Time distinct. We have in fact noted already that either of the two, Space and Time, may be regarded as supplying the element of diversity to the element of identity supplied by the other.[1] Any point-instant, or group of them, is therefore intrinsically itself, and other than some other, and indeed than every other, point-instant or group of them. It follows that existence is distinct from identity only in this reference or relation to the other. It therefore, to use another Platonic conception, " communicates " with the category of relation.

There is much in this if not brief yet abstract statement which calls for comment. Being is the occupation of space-time which also excludes other occupancy of space-time. This seems at first sight to be a flagrant piece of circular reasoning. When it is said that a point-instant is identical with itself and different from another, same or identical and other or different appear to be prior denominations of which point-instants are particular instances. Is not the point-instant declared to be the same as itself and other than a different point-instant ? Though I have entered a warning against such a misapprehension in the preceding chapter, I must, at the risk of repetition, renew the warning here and perhaps later again. It is not because there is sameness and there is difference, and still less because we have the notion of sameness and difference, that a point-instant is the same (as itself) and different (from another), but because there are point-instants or

Defence
t
objection

[1] See above, Bk I. ch. i. p. 60.

groups of them which are the parts of Space-Time that there is sameness and difference in existents. I am not starting from the world in which man exists with his clear-cut and reflective thoughts which he thinks to apply to particular things, but from the bare elements of the world, its primary stuff out of which things are made ; and am accounting for the notions we possess, or rather verifying them, by reference to this stuff. In the skeleton universe of Space-Time we are attempting to detect what are the primitive features of pieces of that skeleton which appear in our experience clothed in the flesh and blood of what we call empirical things, with all their richness and complexity of qualities. It is not our human conceptions of things which metaphysics seeks to exhibit but the constitution of the world itself.

Even if we avoid the mistake of supposing that such categories as same and different are supplied by the mind, and urge the old objection in the form that same and different though not conceptions made by us are yet objective universals, are the highest forms of things, and point-instants or groups of them do but participate in these ; the answer is that same and different (that is numerical sameness and difference) are indeed not only categorial characters intrinsic to any space-time but also universal, but that this consideration is at present irrelevant. The reason why same and different are categories is not that they are universals, but that they are characters which belong to any space-time and therefore to the existent which occupies it. We are concerned here with the specific nature of same and different, not with their universality. It is true that they are like all categories universal. Just as same and different communicate with relation, so also they communicate with the category of universality. There is a good sense in which a particular point-instant may be called a case of identity, that is of generic identity. An existent or being is a particular case of existence as a generic universal. The " this " in Mr. Bradley's language is a case of " thisness." We have yet to see what constitutes universality or generic identity, and we shall find that it too is founded in the nature of Space-Time. But though existence is universal, a point-instant is not a mere case of the universal 'existence'; but it exists because it is a point-instant, and its existence is identical generically with the existence of other point-instants for a different reason. In other words, existents exist or are subject to the category of existence because they occupy space-times, and on our hypothesis are in their simplest determination spatio-temporal complexes; the occupation of their own space-time is a non-empirical or *a priori* determination of the very Space-Time of which things are made; their existence is another name for this occupancy, that is to say for being a piece of Space-Time. That existence may be resolved into its two elements of identity and difference, because a point-instant or group of them is in the first place what it is, and in the next place is not a mere isolated point of space or instant of time, but is saturated with Time or Space respectively, and driven thereby out of its isolation into relation with point-instants other than itself. The point-instants are so far from being merely instances of identity, difference, or existence, that these categories are but the conceptual shapes of real concrete determinations of things in their spatio-temporal character. We shall find this to be true of all the categories. They are not as it were adjectives or predicates of things; they stand for the simplest and most fundamental features (in the sense in which red is a feature of this rose) of things, and have the concreteness of Space-Time. Existence and numerical sameness and difference are the most elementary of these determinations. Consider the spatio-temporal structure which underlies any thing whatever, even if that thing be no more than a point-instant itself; and going to the direct experience of it, as clarified by re-flection, you realise that the self-identity of the thing is nothing more nor less than the experienced fact that it is the bit of space-time which it is.

Existence, or determinate being, or being itself (for we shall see there is no being but determinate being), is the union of identity and difference. But this designation of union must be received with caution. It is not properly a blending or mixture of identity and difference ; nor on the other hand are identity and difference to be regarded as in reality one. The splendid image of the *Timaeus* in which the Demiurge is represented as pouring the Same and the Other into a bowl and creating Being (Ousia) from their mixture is not by us to be understood literally, if it was so understood by Timaeus. Being is an occupation of a space-time. It does not contain within itself the exclusion of other space-times. It contains of course within itself, when it is more than a point-instant, internal difference. But the exclusion of the other which makes identity into being is its relation not within itself but within Space-Time to other space-times. As in this relation identity is being. Being is not something new made up of the two, but is the same taken along with its relation of otherness. Neither is its otherness to be conceived as one with its identity. Its otherness is its relation to the other, and that relation is what we shall call later an intrinsic relation, without which the same would not be the same. But its sameness is one character and its otherness another. It would not be different without the other, and the other is external to it, and something new ; not extrinsic to it (because of the nature of Space-Time) but yet not identical with it. Its identity is so far from being identical or one with its otherness that it would have no otherness except there were an other, and it is other than the other, not the same as the other. But the completer understanding of this, if it needs further elucidation, belongs to the inquiry into the category of relation.

Being and not-being.

Being it was said is the same as determinate being or existence. This means there is no such category as bare or neutral being to which some further determination must be added to make existence. When such neutral being is examined it will be found to stand for something different from real or categorial being, either for the relation of things to thought, or as a compendious name for the relations between terms in a proposition.

We might indeed distinguish bare being from determinate being by substituting in our exposition being for identity, and not-being for difference, and describing determinate being or existence as the union of being and not-being, that is as being in relation to other being. Bare being is then simple occupancy of a space-time. But over and above the loss of the phrase numerical identity, we gain nothing for clearness. For occupancy of a space-time is *ipso facto* exclusion of other space-times. There are no beings (occupants of space-times) which are not existents.

But the idea of bare being leads on conveniently to the subject of not-being, which is not the bare absence of being, not in the language of the logicians a privative conception, but is equivalent to other-being, that is occupation of a different space-time. It may be the occupation of any different portion in the whole remainder of Space-Time, as when we distinguish red from what is not-red and include under not-red anything whatever whether coloured or not which is not red. Or it may be and generally is the occupation of a different portion of Space-Time within the same 'universe of discourse,' as when not-red means any colour which excludes red. The subject more properly comes under the head of identity and difference of sort or kind (generic). But not-being whether numerical or generic is always different being, and remains being. If we try to think of not-being as if it were something wholly disparate from being, we are surreptitiously imagining or thinking some world which has being, that is, is within Space-Time, but of a different kind. A mere blank negation is nothing at all. The nothing we can think of and experience is not nothing-at-all but is an object of some kind and is a department of being. These are ancient considerations, derived from Plato's *Sophistes*. They have been revived in our day to much purpose by Mr. Bergson in an admirable passage of the *Creative Evolution*,[1] where he interprets disorder as a different order from what we call order, and repudiates the notion of nothing

---

[1] *Évolution créatrice*, ch. iv. pp. 297 ff.   Eng. tr. pp. 232 ff.

except as something different from the something which constitutes the circle of our experience.

I may add that negation as a category is equivalent to not-being. Negation is not merely a subjective attitude of mind. That is only an instance of negation, in the region of mental acts. Negation or negativity is a real character of things, which means exclusion or rejection. Not-white is the character which excludes or is different from white. In this sense it is true that all determination is negation. For all definite occupation of space-time is other than other such occupation and excludes it.

Neutral being.

There is no category then of being other than that of determinate being or the existent. Since existence is occupancy of a space-time in exclusion of other occupancy, and since such occupation is always temporal, existence must not be limited to present existence but includes past and future. But various attempts might be or have been made to find a being which is wider or more comprehensive than existence. Such being may be called neutral being, but in no case is such neutral being a category, of which determinate being is a species, or closer determination.

Thus it may be said that there is neutral being which corresponds to the copula in judgment, and is what is meant whenever we say 'is.' But, in fact, the linguistic copula 'is' is appropriate only to certain propositions, those, namely, in which the terms are in the relation of subject and attribute. In some propositions, as Mr. Bradley has pointed out, it does not occur at all (interjectional ones) ; in others the relation of the terms as Mr. Russell insists is not expressed by the copula at all, but may be, for example, a relation of quantity, as in 'A exceeds B in intellect,' or of causality, as in 'Brutus killed Caesar.' A special importance has come to be attached to 'is' because with more or less ingenuity any proposition may be tortured artificially into the subject-attribute form. There is indeed in every proposition something implied which happens to be expressed by the copula in ordinary categorical propositions ; but that something is not 'being' but the reality of whatever relation the proposition expresses between its terms. For a proposition is the explicit analysis of a complex, and asserts the reality of the relation thus exhibited, whether it is the relation of substance and attribute, or causality, or the like.[1] What corresponds to the copula is thus not being but reality, and reality is at least existence or determinate being ; it may be and is much more, but at any rate it is not less and wider than existence. It is not something simpler of which existence is a specialisation. The attempt to look for a category more pervasive than other categories is in truth vain, for categories as such are all alike pervasive, and belong to all things. There is much however to be said before the statement can be accepted that all propositions deal with existents ; in particular, we have yet to consider how propositions which involve universals can be so described.

Being, *i.e.* neutral being, may be understood in a different sense as the object of thought. Whatever the mind thinks of has being or is 'formally objective.' A recent writer [2] proposes to say, accordingly, that there is a world or *summum genus* of 'subsistence,' of which what exists in space and time is a part. Determinate being would, according to this, be a special determination of 'subsistence' or being in the widest sense. The reason for introducing this notion is that besides true propositions there are errors and mere imaginations and

---

[1] Even the existential proposition, *e.g.* King George exists, means that the subject is a part of the whole reality of existence. For further remarks on the assertion of reality in the proposition, see later, Bk. III. ch. x. B.

[2] W. P. Montague, in *The New Realism* (New York, 1912) ; essay on 'A Theory of Truth and Error,' p. 253. I have borrowed the name 'neutral being' from Mr. Holt (see his essay in the same book, and his *Concept of Consciousness*), who uses it in a different sense. His neutral being is a being which is neither mental nor physical, the simplest form of which appears to be categories such as identity and difference. Also Mr. Montague, to whom I refer here, does not use the phrase neutral being at all, and he does not call his subsistence being, and perhaps would not do so (see his account of 'isness' on p. 263). Both his doctrine and Mr. Holt's seem to me, however, in the end to imply what I call neutral or bare being, the idea of something simpler than the world of Space-Time. I stand in many respects so close to them that I am the more anxious to make the real differences clear.

there are also what are now known, since Prof. Meinong's work on the subject,[1] as supposals, where there is neither truth nor error, since no belief is entertained ; for example, 'that the Earth is flat is still maintained by certain persons' ; 'it is reported that a victory has been gained,' in neither of which cases is the included proposition a belief, but a supposal.   The consideration of this notion must be delayed till we have reached that special kind of empirical existent, the mind, and inquire into the relation of the subject of knowledge to the object.   My contention against any being other than spatio-temporal is in fact that we begin at the wrong end if we start with the fact of errors or supposals which appear undoubtedly to be and yet not to be existent, so that we are led to conceive a being which is less, and wider, than existence.   Whereas if we begin not with ourselves and what we think, but with what the world is in its simplest terms, of which world we are a part, we arrive at a different and less perplexing result.   We shall find reason if we pursue this method to reject the notion that existence in Space and Time is something added to some more formal reality, call it being, call it subsistence, call it what corresponds to the 'is' of propositions ; and to conclude on the contrary that such being is real or determinate being with something left out, that it implies the interference of the subject or the empirical mind with the real world in Space and Time ; that it is not prior in analysis to reality but, rather, subsequent to it ; and that error does not give us a new and more shadowy being than the spatio-temporal reality, but is the world of determinate being misread.   Here for the present it is enough to note that being as the mere formal object of thought is a conception derived from the relation of the world to an empirical part of itself, the mind.

The use of the term subsistence in the above statement to describe bare being inclusive of being in space and time, is not in itself a matter of much consequence, but it is unfortunate because 'subsistence' is used by

---

[1] *Über Annahmen* (Leipzig, 1910, ed. 2).   The notion of neutral being discussed in this paragraph is not imputed to Mr. Meinong.

Mr. Meinong (and the usage has become established through him) to describe not being as such or bare being, but that kind of being which contrasts with particular existence. Subsistence is, it is thought, timeless or eternal being, and it belongs to universals and to supposals. For instance, I may say that A exists ; but it is urged that the proposition 'that A exists' does not itself exist. The battle of Waterloo was fought in 1815 ; but it is said, the fact that it was fought then is something independent of the time of the actual battle. The issue which is here raised is a different one ; are universals or supposals or ' facts that ' out of Time and Space ? There is no doubt of the reality of these things ; but have they or not being within Space-Time, or determinate being ? We are about to show in the following chapter that universals are not timeless. But at any rate the word subsistence marks a distinction between two classes of objects of thought, two groups of reality, for which it is important to have a distinctive designation.

It may throw light on the denial here made of any being which is less than determinate being, as well as upon other matters, if I stop to consider briefly the famous doctrine with which Hegel's logic opens, that being is the same as not-being, and the two are merged into the category of becoming. If being were concrete being, something which has a place in the world of reality and not in the inventions of abstract thinking, the one thing which is more obviously true about it than another is that it is not identical with not-being, but different from it, that is, that it is not identical with the other but other than it. But being is not on this doctrine concrete. It stands for the least that can be said about anything, namely, that it is, and it is quite true that such being is indistinguishable from nothing. Instead of concluding that neither of them is anything at all, Hegel proceeds to declare their synthesis to be 'becoming,' which as he himself maintains is the first concrete notion. But how can bare abstract thoughts, abstractions as he allows them to be, combine or be combined to produce a concrete

The Hegelian identity of being and not-being.

one ? or how could they be combined if they were
identical and not different ? Or if we suppose that we
treat them as a mere analysis of becoming, how could
a concrete real thought be analysed into two abstractions ?
Such an analysis is not comparable to our own analysis of
Space-Time into the two elements of Space and Time.
For each of these elements is concrete, and is only an
abstraction when it is supposed to exclude the other.
They are as concrete as body and life are in the organism.
Had becoming, which is in fact motion or Space-Time in
its simplest conceptual form, been analysed into being and
non-being as different but mutually involved elements
with becoming, becoming would have been equivalent to
what we have called existence, for the existent is nothing
but motion (that is Space-Time). But it would not be
the thoughts themselves which produced their own
unification, but the character of the concrete of which the
concept becoming is the concept. It would indeed be a
gross misreading of Hegel to suppose that he " manufactured the world out of categories." He is a perfectly
concrete thinker, and to each thought corresponds a
reality. But the inadequacy of his conception of the
relation of thought to nature betrays itself at the outset
of his triumphant procession of thoughts. Instead of
conceiving the thoughts as the concepts of what is given
in nature, he treats nature as a falling off from thought.
But all true or concrete thought is tied down to nature ;
all its balloons are captive ones. The transitions from
thought to thought are not made by thought itself, for
transition is only possible to thoughts which are alive.
The thoughts owe their connection not to thought but to
the motions of which they are the thoughts. And when
once the glamour is gone from the first transition from
thesis (being) through antithesis (nothing) to synthesis
(becoming) the principle of the whole series of logical
forms which is founded on this principle, and really uses
the contrast and identity of being and not-being, becomes
suspect. No wonder that to some like Mr. Bradley these
logical concepts appear to be shadows. Realities they are
not, for they live in a region of thought divorced from its

material, which in the end is nothing but Space-Time. There is no way from logic to nature in Hegel, as his critics have often observed, except through a metaphor.[1]

The so-called Laws of Thought, regarded as meta-physical laws, follow at once from these considerations. The most important of them is the law of contradiction. Ultimately that law means that occupation of one piece of Space-Time is not occupation of a different one. A thing cannot be both A and not-A at once, for if so it would occupy two different space-times. Or more shortly the meaning is that one space-time is not another. I have not yet spoken of generic identity nor of sub-stantial identity; but even now it is plain why the law is true where we speak of attributes and not of numerical identity or difference. For if a thing has the attribute A, that attribute is, as in the thing, a numerically distinct individual. The red of this rose is generically identical with other reds, but it is as in this rose individual. This rose cannot be both red and not-red, for otherwise it would in respect of its red be at once in a piece of Space-Time, and in a piece of Space-Time which the first piece excludes. Considered on the other hand as a law of our thinking, the law of contradiction means that the thinking of one object and the thinking of its contradictory occupy mutually exclusive places in the mental space-time.

The law of contra-

The law of identity means that to occupy Space-Time is to occupy it, that a thing is itself. The law of excluded middle means in its metaphysical interpretation that given a special occupation of Space-Time, every occupation of

---

[1] It will be plain from the sequel why for me Hegel's conception of an evolution in thought of logical categories is mistaken. There is only an evolution in time of empirical existences which occupy space-times. Hegel's categories are in fact not categories at all, as they are understood here, the *a priori* constituents of all existences. They are rather the concepts of the various phases of natural existence : *e.g.* they include 'mechanism' and 'chemism' and 'life.' Or perhaps it is truer to say that the two notions of categories as *a priori* features, and categories as concepts of phases, of existence, are not clearly separated. Hence the apparent movement in thought is only artificial.

Space-Time is either that or belongs to the rest of Space-Time, and is another way of expressing the relation of any being to not-being.

These conclusions are obvious from the premisses, but they lead to another which will be unwelcome to a method of thought which has predominating influence at the present time. The criterion of reality (or truth) has been found in self-contradiction; what is self-contradictory cannot be ultimately real but only apparent. The principle is valid, if it means that what is self-contradictory is neither ultimately nor derivately real but downright false ; it derives its validity however not from any self-evidence, but from the experiential or empirical nature of Space-Time. The reason why nothing can be real which contradicts itself is not that this is an axiom of our thought, but that reality since it occupies a space-time does not occupy a different one. Deriving its validity then from Space-Time itself, it cannot be employed to undermine the reality of Space and Time and reduce them to appearances of an ultimate reality which is neither, but accounts for both. If Space-Time is the ground on which the criterion of contradiction is based, Space and Time are not themselves contradictory. To suppose so would be like invoking the authority of law to break law, or sinning against the conscience conscientiously.

To find out what is contradictory we must therefore have reference to experience itself, of which the principle of contradiction is the statement of the simplest feature. As reflected in our thinking, the test is that of internal self-contradiction or verbal inconsistency. Accordingly, the only way in which the test of contradiction can be successfully applied in the hands of Mr. Bradley to show that the categories, or even such notions as the self, which have been put forward as real in their own right are not so, is to show that they are inherently inconsistent. But this as has been pointed out [1] is not what has been

---

[1] See in particular a paper of Mr. G. F. Stout's, *Proceedings of the Aristotelian Society*, N.S. vol. ii., 'Alleged self-contradictions in the concept of relation,' especially section 2.

done.   And if it could be done, the pretenders would not
have even possessed a secondary reality but would be false.
As a matter of fact what has been done is to show that
these conceptions present great difficulties and the appearance of inconsistency to the understanding.   But perhaps
it is their inconsistency which is apparent and not they
themselves.   If we are right and all the categories are
derived from the nature of Space-Time in any part of
it, they are all real in their own right and ultimately,
because Space-Time is the stuff of which all things are
made and the categories are its simplest characters.

If such an answer were intended as a short way with
absolute idealism, it would seem to the defenders of that
method merely cavalier, because it starts from Space-Time
as a given experience.   The only way which is either
possible or respectful is the long way.   We have first to
verify in detail the assertion that categories are properties
of any space-time.   Even then it will be urged that
Space and Time are riddled with intolerable difficulties,
although these difficulties may not amount to inherent
self-contradiction.   These difficulties must be examined
and if possible removed.   I am persuaded that the
alleged inconsistencies of Space and Time arise from the
separation of either of them from the other : from
neglecting the temporal character of Space and the spatial
character of Time ; and that consequently the Space and
Time which are thought to be inconsistent are not Space
and Time at all, as Space and Time enter into real
experience.   But as the arguments against their reality
turn on the ultimate unreality of relation, any further
discussion is best deferred until we reach that category.

CHAPTER III

UNIVERSAL, PARTICULAR, AND INDIVIDUAL

Intro-
duc ory. EXISTENCE is identity of place and time, or numerical
identity, and distinct from other such identities. Universality is identity of kind. It is the existence or subsistence
of a universal or concept which unites its particulars,
which they imitate or in which they participate, or however
else we may provisionally and traditionally describe the
relation between the universal and its particulars—the
transaction in which they are engaged. An individual is
a particular as determined by its universal. Strictly
speaking, there is no such thing as a particular or a universal. All things are individuals. But every individual
possesses particularity which separates it from others of
the same kind, or under the same universal ; and it
possesses universality which converts its bare particularity
into individuality. Universality is thus a categorial
character of all things. Such a thing need not be a thing
with continued existence in time. It may be a sensory
object, a flash of colour, or of sweetness, which is
momentary and yet as being of a certain kind, red or
sweet, is individual. A bare event or point-instant is
particular as distinct from other events, but as qualified
by the universal character of existence, its particularity is
determined in total Space-Time and it is individual
though from the nature of the case momentary and
punctual. Can we discover in Space-Time any fundamental feature in virtue of which the empirical complexes
within it possess universality and hence are individualised
so that throughout the world we have existents embody-
ing laws of construction ?

Let us begin with an individual of a low type or organisation, for example a marble ball whose particularity may be supposed secured by its markings of colour. Let us suppose for simplicity that these do not change in colour, and let us disregard the intramolecular movements of the ball, confining our attention to its spherical form. The ball changes its place in space and time as the earth moves, and may also be displaced on the relatively resting earth. Its universality is that in all these changes it is unaffected in form ; that wherever it is, it undergoes no distortion, and this arises from the uniformity of Space-Time or, as it may be expressed equivalently, from the constant 'curvature'[1] of Space. The same account applies obviously to balls which are turned out from one machine, so that they differ from one another, let us say, only in their place and time. They are identical in kind because owing to the constant curvature of Space their form is unaffected, and so far as form goes one can take the place of the other. A round ball does not become in another place elliptic or crooked.

We may next take a more highly organised individual, say a person whose life may be regarded as arranged on a certain plan. This is the best instance of the singular universal. Lotze compares it to the structure of a melody. It is such a plan of a man's personality which an artistic portrait endeavours to express, whereas a photograph gives only a picture of the man at a passing moment, unless by artistry of technique the hardness of the momentary outlines may be softened and the photograph

---

[1] This phrase, as I have had occasion to remark before, is inaccurate (see D. M. Y. Sommerville, *The Elements of Non-Euclidean Geometry*, London, 1914, ch. vi.). It is of course not used here with the assumption which the author imputes to many philosophers that three-dimensional geometry implies Space of four dimensions. That has been seen (Bk. I. ch. v.) in the first place not to be Space at all, in the next place to owe what reality it possesses to the work of thought. But the phrase is a convenient one. For the most part, however, I shall speak of the uniformity of Space. This is to be distinguished carefully from the supposed homogeneity or indifference of Space, which is declared to be characteristic of 'conceptual' in contrast with 'perceptual' Space. See before, Bk. I. ch. v. p. 152, and below, p. 216 n.

approximate to a portrait.[1] This individual person contains indeed besides universality the category of substantiality, or substantial identity, a category not yet to be
investigated. He is highly complex, and the parts are
in those conditions of motion to which, as I here assume,
qualities are correlated. Yet in all his changes of space
and time a certain plan of construction is preserved. It
is preserved in his internal changes of body or mind, so
that for instance he does not alter the colour of his skin
from hour to hour like certain crustaceans ; and so that
a certain balance of actions is maintained. But it is also
preserved not only in these subtle changes of space and
time within his bodily outlines, but also in the grosser
external transferences from position to position in space
or time. I shall call a grouping or complex of point-
instants or pure events a configuration of space-time or of
motion. Now the universality of this highly complex
person (as distinct from his substantiality) means as in
the simpler case of the ball, that though at each particular
moment of his life his configuration varies and is particular,
the configuration follows a certain plan and remains within
the limits of that plan. In other words, his configuration
remains relatively unaltered while he changes in his place
or time or both. However much he be transferred or
otherwise more subtly changed internally in space-time
he preserves a certain proportion of his parts and is undistorted. When he is so distorted as to forsake the plan
he becomes (as happens for instance in double personality)
a different individual. Once more, in this more difficult
case, he being himself a highly intricate complex of space-
time owes his universality to the uniformity of his
medium, that is to the constant curvature of Space.

Generic
universals.
     Now the identification of universality with this
uniformity was easy enough with our single ball, or our
identical balls, for here the configuration was repeated
exactly. But with the person the actual configuration

---

[1] Doubtless this comparison has often been made, but it seems to
me as suggestive and true now as when I first heard it from the late
Hermann Grimm at Berlin more than thirty years ago.

changes from moment to moment and only the plan of it persists. This difficulty which was slurred over above is still more pressing, when we come to the ordinary generic universal, like tree or dog or justice. Dogs vary in size and shape and disposition. How then can we speak of the universality of dog as a plan or form of configuration of space-time, since the spatio-temporal patterns of no two dogs can be superposed and fit into each other?

Let us follow our usual prescription and turn to our own minds which we know more intimately than external things. There, in our minds, we find habits which are dispositions of response to situations of a certain kind. On each occasion the response, let it be an act of will like telling the truth when we are asked a question, or the simpler instinctive response to a perception like holding our hands to catch a ball which is thrown to us—on each occasion the response is particular or rather individual, but it obeys a plan or uniform method. It varies on each occasion by modifications particular to that instance. It may be swift or slow, eager or reluctant, slight or intense; the hands move to one side or another with nicely adapted changes of direction according to the motion of the ball; the words are adjusted not merely to the subject of the question, but to the requirements, which vary in each case, of exactitude and sincerity or of that tactfulness in telling the truth which takes account of the mental condition of the questioner, and regards his intelligence and his feelings and susceptibilities, so that there is a fine art of truth-telling as there is of catching a cricket ball. But however great or fine the variations in conduct, they have their limits within the plan of the response which is uniform. The response proceeds with these allowances for modification, or rather with these necessities of modification, on established and constant mental lines which are also constant plans of direction within the neural space. We may tell the truth facing a person or with our back to him, but within that neural space which we enjoy in mind the configuration of the response follows a certain plan. In all the variations of particular response there is no distortion of the pattern of response.

What mental dispositions in general are, in distinction from their effective realisation in actual conduct, I need not inquire too minutely. I am content to regard them as psychophysical, indicating by that word that being themselves physical they are ready upon occasion to start up into mental life. It may be that, as some think, there is a perpetual process of fainter actual functioning along the neural lines. It is at least certain that the disposition is not a bare physical one, but at least physiological. It is not represented merely by purely anatomical patterns and is something more than a mere physical arrangement, such as is supposed to exist in a permanently magnetised steel bar through the tilting of the molecules in one direction. It is more than this, because the elements which are tilted in our neural lines are living cells. This important question I must leave. But at any rate besides those mental habits which are purely psychophysical, or latent, we can detect conditions of mind which are actually conscious, and though not definite and individual but vaguely defined have a more special claim to be considered *mental* dispositions or schemes of response. The underlying psychophysical disposition may not be actualised in an individual mental response, but in a mental outline or scheme of one, which is a diagram of response, but yet is mental. It may betray or reveal itself in shoots of consciousness which are not so individual as if I were actually performing the action, but are of a specific sort or on a recognisable plan. I mean by the term specific, to take an illustration, that the vague premonitory shoots of consciousness which anticipate at times the actual winding up of my watch at night are recognisably different (I should say in 'direction') from the premonitory shoots of consciousness connected with some other habit, like turning off the electric light in my study before I go to bed. These attitudes, rather than actions, of mind can be verified most easily in the uneasiness which warns us to perform the action or reminds us that we have failed to do so. In each case the uneasiness is of a different sort, and has a vaguely specific direction.

The clearest instances, perhaps the only ones, of these

mental schemes in the proper sense, are afforded by the action of conceiving, of which concepts or universals are the compresent objects. Observation conducted first under ordinary conditions and then under the conditions of the laboratory [1] has convinced us of the existence of 'imageless thinking,' which seemed so inconceivable to some earlier psychologists. Though our thinking does not proceed without attachment to some particular of sense, it may be to a word, it may be to the button which we twist while we think, or the lock of hair which we pull to the distraction of our companions, it may be to some mere external circumstance contained in the conditions of the experiment ; yet it may proceed without any individual embodiment or illustration of the thought itself :

> By the pricking of my thumbs
> Something wicked this way comes.

The witch is a true psychologist. The pricking of her thumbs is the particular sensory experience to which the thought of something wicked (observe the conceptual expression) is attached though it is no image of wickedness.

Turn now from mental habits or universals to the non-mental universals which are found in external things. They are 'habits' of Space-Time, and empirical universals like dog or tree or justice are possible because Space-Time is uniform and behaves therefore on plans which are undistorted by difference of place and time. There is only one respect in which the transition from mental habits to habits of Space-Time appears to limp. Mental habits occur in assignable neural places, though the limits of these areas are extensible. But the habits of Space-Time are localised indifferently all over Space-Time. Given the appropriate empirical conditions a triangle or a dog may be drawn anywhere according to their universal plan of configuration. We have indicated in a previous chapter the reason for this difference

Habits of [ ] e-Time.

---

[1] There is now a large literature on imageless thinking. I may cite in particular the earlier work of Mr. Stout in *Analytical Psychology*, vol. i. Bk. I. ch. iv., and the researches by Messrs. Ach, Buehler, H. J. Watt of the Wurzburg School of the late O. Kulpe.

between mind and Space-Time.[1] The mind is not like Space-Time an infinite but a finite whole. Moreover its consciousness of things is awaked through the senses with their highly specialised machinery of nerve endings and nerve centres and paths. For specific objects specific means of apprehension are necessary, and vision, taste and the other senses, and still more the complex patterns for apprehending complex objects have their specific lodgings in the brain. What is said here of mind or consciousness applies of course with proper qualifications to all kinds of finites, so far as these have specific methods of response to their surroundings. Such habits are localised in specific portions of the spatio-temporal structure; as will be clearer in the sequel. Further it follows as a consequence of the want of localisation of the habits of Space-Time to definite portions of it, that different habits may have certain parts of Space-Time in common, though not at the same time. Thus the same point may be the beginning of a circle or a parabola; though the point-instant will have different values in the different cases, because it will be the beginning of different lines of advance.

I may add that the comparison of universals with habits is not made for the first time by me, though I do not know that the comparison has been made with the same implications.[2]

Universality is therefore a category or determination of Space-Time. Every finite possesses universality or identity of kind in so far as it admits without distortion of repetition in Space-Time, that is, can itself undergo change of place or time or both without alteration, or can be replaced by some other finite. Empirical universals are plans of configuration of particulars which are identical in kind. They may be called patterns of con-

---

[1] Bk. I. ch. iv. pp. 139 f.

[2] Thus Mr. Bosanquet writes (*Principle of Individuality*, p. 40, note 3): "The universal is essentially a system or habit of self-adjusting response or reaction." My difference from him lies in the phrase "system or habit." A habit is for me not a system of its acts but the plan, or in extensional terms, the class of them. See below, pp. 233 ff.

figuration or, to use the old Greek word, 'forms' of
Space-Time.   They are essentially in their simplest terms
spatio-temporal forms or shapes.

If this is true of empirical universals like dog or
plant or triangle it is still more obviously true of the
most comprehensive of all universals, the categories
themselves, which are *a priori* plans of configuration.   I
am anticipating the complete verification that they all of
them are fundamental determinations of any space-time.
In so far as relation or substance or existence, etc., is
an *a priori* determination of Space-Time, these are forms
or plans or patterns of configuration of Space-Time or
motion.   They are the key plans of all plans of empirical
determination.   The rest of them excluding universality
communicate with universality, and universality itself
stands for the fact that everything has its form.   We
cannot say that universality itself is a universal any more
than we can say that the empirical universal dog is a dog.
Universality is the category in virtue of which there are
universals, whether empirical or *a priori* ones.

Universality is thus the name of the constancy of
any existent in Space-Time, so far as it is constant, that
is, its freedom from distortion wherever it is in Space-
Time, and this is equivalent to the uniformity of Space
(or what is the same thing, Space-Time).   Just as existence
is the name for occupation of a space-time in relation to
other occupation.

If it be objected that the uniformity of Space and with
it Space-Time is after all only an empirical character and
that there need not be such constancy, I can only answer
that Space-Time though itself categorial or *a priori* is empirical in the sense of being presented in experience with
certain characters.   I should be content with this simple
fact.   It is true that a geometry may be imagined whose
'Space' is not uniform.   But our Space is not such, whether
the Euclidean or some other geometry be the closest
approximation to the description of it.   For I am not
assuming Space to be flat, with zero curvature, but merely
to have a constant curvature.   In a 'Space' which is not
uniform I do not see how there should be universals,

Why Space
is uniform.

for each plan would suffer distortion as it was transferred.[1]
The world would consist of nothing but particulars, not
even of individuals, for there would be no meaning in the
contrast of individual and particular without the idea of a
plan of configuration. But if we seek to understand the
deeper meaning of the constancy of Space and Space-Time
we may refer to the relations set out in a previous chapter
between Space and Time, though with the same feeling of
modesty in our assurance as beset us there. Time as we
saw was not an addition to Space, but the characters of
Space were conformable to those of Time. It is the conformity of Space to the one-dimensional Time, which is
uniform—flows uniformly as Newton said—that involves
with it the uniformity of Space. Universality is thus, in

---

[1] More than one friendly critic has urged that if we can think
of a Space of varying curvature, there must be at least one universal, that is the concept of the class of such curvatures; and consequently my contention that there are universals because there is
uniformity or constant curvature breaks down in this instance. The
answer which will be clearer from the 'objections and elucidations'
which follow is from my point of view fairly clear. The notion of a
variable curvature of Space is got from experience of Space with a
constant one by a construction of thought, like four-dimensional Space.
Because, being familiar with universals, we can universalise Space-
curvature in thought, we are not therefore free to deny that universality as we know it in experience depends on constancy of curvature.
Moreover, while there is a good meaning in the universal contained in
the varying curvatures of curves in our Space, it is difficult to see what
is the universal element in the varying curvatures of the supposed Space
which itself varies in curvature. The supposed universal is rather
comparable to colour in relation to the various colours, red, green, etc.
There is no element colour in these of which red and green are variations. Colour is a collective name rather than a class one or a
universal. Such a universal curvature is nothing then, as before, but
a bare thought; and no conclusion can be drawn from the supposition
of my critics. But, whether this last comparison be valid or not, I
recall their attention to the real problem, which is how there can be
sameness or generic identity at all. You may take these different
entities, space-curvatures, however measured, and construct a new so-
called 'Space' from them. But their generic identity is of your
making. Unless they are the same in themselves there is no real
universal of them. You may consider them as forming a class with
the sameness called curvature. But you have still to ask the prior
question how there can be classes of things at all. Sameness has
to be accounted for before things can form a class. It is this fundamental question that the text endeavours to answer.

our drastic metaphor, begotten like the other categories by Time on Space.   In all this the constancy or uniformity of Space-Time or Space is carefully to be separated from the notion of the bare homogeneity of Space or Time, in the sense that there is imagined to be no real difference between one part of Space or Time and another.   This notion is justly the bugbear of philosophers ; though some have thought to retain it by distinguishing between conceptual and perceptual Space or Time.   I need not now revert to the errors which underlie this distinction, which would make conceptual Space a falsification of perceptual Space.   But in fact we have seen that Space and Time differentiate each other : that every point differs from any other by its instant and every instant by its point.   Point-instants are concepts but singular ones, and each point-instant is an individual.   As Mr. Russell has observed, points seem all alike to us only because we have no interest in discriminating them.   The uniformity of Space or Time or Space-Time does not mean this supposed conceptual indifference of point-instants but merely that a given plan of configuration is repeated in any part of Space-Time where it occurs without distortion.

We have first to enter a caveat against the old possibility of misunderstanding which has been noted from the beginning.   Plans, it may be thought, of space-time are nothing but the universals of different patches of Space-Time, the circular plan, for example, the universal of all circular patches.   They are but particular applications of a conceptual universal which is prior to Space and Time and is supplied from understanding or thought, it matters not how.   Universality belongs to Space-Time but comes down upon it, either it may be imagined from mind or from some eternal region as the Forms are supposed to enter into Space by Timaeus.   Our answer is the old one. It is not because there are universals that any space-time has a plan, but because Space-Time is uniform, or constant in curvature, and admits a plan that existents which are patches of space-time possess universality.   Or the misunderstanding may take another form.   A constant

Objections
nd el ci-
dations

curvature means that the curvature is the same, and there is a prior notion of generic sameness. I answer that the constancy of curvature is an experienced or empirical fact or character of Space-Time, and that it is this which makes particulars of a sort the same in different positions. Sameness (generic identity) follows from the constant curvature ; the logical denomination of things follows from or expresses the real nature of Space-Time.

These are misunderstandings. There is however a different objection to meet which has much better pretensions to be heard. The very name of plan or pattern or form or law implies, it will be said, the idea of universality ; and the problem is concealed by a word. For a plan is something of which many copies are possible. If only a definite configuration of space-time were concerned, like a right angle or a definite loudness of the note C, we might be content with a reference to the constancy of Space-Time. But when you allege that an acute angle at A and an obtuse angle at B are instances of one and the same plan or habit, the angular habit, you are really under the protection of a name introducing the universal ' angle.' For there is no one configuration of space-time which can be called an angle. Thus to account for the generic identity of angles you are introducing between the constancy of Space to which you appeal and the particular angles a universal under the name of a plan, which is the condition under which that constancy can be applied to individual angles of such great variation. The universal you say belongs to Space-Time as such, but a new universal is needed on your own showing to mediate between the particulars and Space-Time. This objection is highly relevant, and it is analogous to one of the kinds of objection taken in ancient Greece to the Forms under the name of the argument of the ' third man.' [1] Besides the individual men and the form Man there is a third man.

---

[1] There is a very instructive critical account of the various forms of the third man argument in a paper by Mr. A. E. Taylor on ' Parmenides, Zeno and Socrates,' in *Proceedings Arist. Soc.*, 1915-16, N.S. vol. xvi. I do not enter into the question, which among these arguments the above objection corresponds to. I think it is the argument from infinite regress used in the *Parmenides*.

But it is in truth groundless as directed against the present conception of universals. It arises only from the latitude of the universal in question. Angle means a configuration formed by two straight lines of divergent directions in a plane. The habit of Space-Time to which it is equivalent is the possibility of the existence of such a configuration at any point. The magnitude of the angle does not enter into the plan. If the universal were the limited one of an angle of 60°, there would be no variation of magnitude in the copies. The plan triangle allows for variation in the magnitude of angles and sides within the limits fixed by triangularity. The four-sided figure with equal sides is similarly a plan or pattern which is satisfied by the rhombus or the square.

What is true of the empirical universals of geometry, which have been chosen in these examples, is true in like manner of ordinary 'qualitied' universals, like dog or tree or justice. The relation between the universal and the particulars is the same in these cases as the relation between the universal triangle or circle and the particular triangles or circles, which Plato called mathematical objects. For a particular dog is in the end a spatio-temporal configuration, where the groupings of motion are such as to have sensible qualities correlative with them. So regarded a particular dog differs from a particular triangle only in its much greater complexity. It too is spatially considered a geometrical figure, but of an order which is too complicated to be treated by the geometry of simpler figures. Particular triangles are perfectly rectilinear because the triangle is a figure ideally constructed within Space, or selected from it. But irregular as the contours of a dog may be, he is none the less a geometrical figure. Mathematical particulars are therefore not as Plato thought intermediate between sensible figures and universals. Sensible figures are only less simple mathematical ones. This is the whole of the difference. In any case whether it is with a mathematical or a qualitied universal that we are concerned, there is no question of any plan mediating between the particular and the uniformity of Space-Time ; the plan is an embodiment of that uniformity. The universality of the plan is the capacity of Space-Time to respond on each occasion according to that plan.

Thus the universal is related to its particulars as the equation of a curve is related to the instances of it which may be obtained by varying the so-called constants in the equation. For example the equation to the parabola $(y^2 = 4ax)$ is universal as the formula which applies to all curves described by the formula, where the element a varies.[1] A more satisfactory statement still is that the equation of the second degree $Ax^2 + By^2 + Cxy + Dx + Ey + F = O$ is the universal of all conic sections which can be obtained by appropriate values in the capital letters. This brings out most clearly how the universal or plan is the key to the utmost range of variation not merely in magnitude but in configuration within the limits of the pattern configuration. For it includes under its formula such different configurations as the ellipse and the parabola and the hyperbola which yet are subject to the one more comprehensive pattern or habit of Space-Time. The formula of the circle whose centre is the origin $x^2 + y^2 = r^2$ has a much smaller limit of variation in the magnitude of its one constant, while the equation $x^2 + y^2 = 36$ is limited to the one definite kind of configuration.

It will be observed that I do not call the equation to the circle or the parabola the universal of the points of which the circle or parabola consists, the significance of which reservation will appear in another context.[2]

It has not seemed to me necessary to insist that the universals of physical things are non-mental ; for this is the only statement which is consistent with the whole spirit of our hypothesis, even if the mentality of Forms had not been summarily disposed of by Plato himself.[3] But what kind of reality, it may be asked, do universals possess? Half the difficulty, or perhaps all of it, disappears when once it is admitted that particulars are complexes of

[1] Cp. Lotze, *Logic*, § 117.   [2] Below, p. 235.
[3] *Parmenides*, 132 b. The argument is discussed fully in Mr. Taylor's paper just cited.

space - time and belong therefore to the same order or are of the same stuff as the universals which are plans of space-time.   The objections taken to the conception that the particulars participate in the universals or imitate them, a conception which plays so great a part in the history of the theory of universals, vanish upon this doctrine.   The argument of the 'third man' arose from the apparent separation of the form from its particulars because the particulars were sensible.   But if sensibles are made of space-time stuff they follow their spatio-temporal pattern, and whether we call the relation one of imitation or participation, either designation is valid and true.   Of the two, participation is to be preferred because imitation suggests a separate independent reality of the universal, and participation means that the plan is not copied but modified to suit the special circumstances of time and place.

To say with Aristotle in his mood of antagonism to his master that the universal is predicable of the particulars converts the universal into a simple predicate and risks confusion with the notion of the inherence of a quality in its substance, a very different relation, the discussion of which belongs to the head of substance.   For the proposition 'this is yellow or sweet' has an entirely different meaning from the proposition ' this is a dog ' or ' this is a yellow or a sweet.'   Taken in extension this last pro-position means that this is one of a class, but that class is itself defined and designated (denoted) by its constitutive universal.   Taken in intension the predicate here is not a quality at all but a plan of construction.   The universal is never therefore something which we assert of its particulars or which merely obtains of its particulars, and the universal does not depend on the predication but the predication on the universal.

On the other hand to call the universal an independent reality appears to give it a unique position from which as it were it should descend upon its particulars and inform them with its spirit.   It seems to transfer universals into a neutral world, whereas their stuff is the same as the stuff of their particulars.   The same objection applies to the notion that the universal is the limit towards which the particulars are a progression. For the limit of a series is never itself a member of that series but outside it.[1] Thus the series, $1, 1 + \frac{1}{2}, 1 + _2 + _4$, etc. approaches to 2 as its limit, but 2 is not a member of the series. It is true that the limit of a series is of the same order as the series, the limit of a series of numbers is itself a number, and this is what makes the conception of universals as limits enlightening. But the limit is constitutive of the series only to the afterthought which recognises that the series has the limit. What corresponds in the series to the universal is the law of its formation and this is not outside but ' within ' the series, though it is not of course a particular member of the series.

The universal exists therefore only so far as it is realised in its particulars and it has such reality as, to use a phrase of Mr. Bosanquet, is possible to it. It may be said to have that reality of existence which is called subsistence. For it is free from limitation to one particular space and time. But subsistence must not be understood to imply a neutral being which is distinct from the world of spatio-temporal existence. The universal subsists in so far as its particulars exist and is spatio-temporal though not particular. The universal is nowhere and nowhen in particular but anywhere and anywhen, and in Hume's language is in readiness to start into being (which is existence) when the occasion calls. It is not timeless or eternal as being out of time, but as being free from limitation to a particular time.

Moreover not only does the universal exist in this qualified sense which is called subsistence, but we must add, extreme as the statement may sound, the universals are spatio-temporal, physical, biological, mental, according to the level of existence to which their individuals belong. Universals are not necessarily like triangle or square merely spatio-temporal. When we reach rocks or plants or minds, we have plans or habits of Space-Time which include plans to which various qualities are correlated and which are a plan of the combination of such plans. In this sense we must

---

[1] Cp. T. P. Nunn, *The Teaching of Algebra*, London, 1914, p. 542.

say, though the full meaning cannot be developed at present, that universals of physical things are physical, and that the universal man though it is not a man is man or human.   A physical universal is a physical subsistent and a mental one a mental subsistent.   This does not interfere with their being ultimately all alike spatio - temporal, for all things no matter what their qualities are bits of Space-Time.

In order to realise more clearly the meaning of the subsistence of universals we may first revert to mental dispositions.   Such a disposition is either experienced consciously in imageless thought (by what may be called a diagrammatic process of mind) or else we can conceive it as a neural (psychophysical) disposition, or physical tilt of cells.   Now our habits as we saw are localised. But there is nothing lower than Space-Time in which to locate a disposition of it.   What then is this disposition ? It is certainly not something which we who think can say, *apres coup*, about Space and Time, merely because upon occasion we have particulars of a certain kind which we put into classes.   On the contrary, only because of the universal and at its guidance can we arrange in a class. It is itself something spatio-temporal.   Nor is it a bare potentiality.   When a part of Space-Time is not occupied by a real dog, it is occupied by something else, if not by something material, then by Space-Time.   For Space-Time is always full ; there are no vacua in that matrix of things.   It differs only at one moment and another (and the difference may be enormous) by the different configuration of its motions.   Thus there may be no dog or chalk triangle at this moment here in the space before me—those are not the lines of advance within that space—yet when the occasion comes the dog may be there, because the actual grouping of movements has been replaced by that grouping of movements, with their correlative qualities, which is a dog.   Provided of course the empirical circumstances do not impede ; for no dog can replace a stone wall which is not removed. To take a more obvious instance, which is suggested to me by an interruption to my writing, a volume of space-time filled by wind may be displaced by that highly complex grouping of qualities, my body, as I walk. We may make the matter easier for imagination by saying that any space contains actually all geometrical patterns as soon as the time comes to draw them.

Such instances do nothing more than illustrate the feature of Space-Time that within any part of it the distribution of point-instants may take any plan permitted or required by the empirical conditions. It is only in this sense that the plan of a universal is potential; its potentiality is a reality consisting in the readiness of Space-Time to adopt it, because Space-Time is built up of point-instants whose place and time are perpetually changing their distribution. This is the general potentiality of Space-Time. Its specific potentiality, as when an acorn is said to be potentially an oak, is describable in more specific real terms. But all potentiality is real though it is not an existence in particular. And in fact can anything be more real, a more concrete (though elementary and not specific) determination than the constancy to which all universality has been traced? From the point of view of this question, perhaps our labour to give a more definite meaning to subsistence is labour lost.

Universals then though they have not existence in particular have subsistence in so far as Space-Time suffers or allows existence according to the plan of the universal. They are the formulae according to which Time brings forth particulars in a Space which can receive this plan. Time is not therefore the moving image of eternity as Plato or Timaeus said, holding the forms to be eternal. The forms are not imposed on Space. But the Time which is the life of Space brings to birth particulars in their image.

Universals are not more real than their particulars but have greater significance, as the general equation to a circle is of greater significance than the same equation with a numerical magnitude assigned to its radius. They are concrete in the sense that they are not abstract general ideas such as Berkeley directed his invective upon. They are the constitutive plans of things. They are spatio-temporal and have all the concrete reality of Space-Time. For the matrix and its determinations are as concrete as the crystals deposited from it.

It has been thought that extramental universals, owing nothing to thought save that they are compresent with thinking and owe to thinking that they are known or thought *of*, must be lifeless—' petrified ' is the word used.[1] Nothing can be farther from the truth. Universals do not move or act ; it is their particulars which do this. But they are the plans of motion and action, to which all action conforms. Like the cockles and mussels of the fishergirl's song they are " alive, alive, O ! " But they do not owe their life to mind. On the contrary, the life which universals possess in mind is but an example of the spatio-temporal vitality of all universals. Mental universals are mental habits, and it is in virtue of the dispositional character which they realise that particular mental acts work their effects. The best known instance of this is found in ordinary association of ideas. One particular idea having been united with a second in an interesting experience, another idea which is like the first calls up an idea like the second. For an idea is never repeated identically. What is repeated is its disposition. The new idea which sets this disposition going, set in action the connected disposition which is actualised in a particular. The original experience was a_1b_1. The new experience is a_2b_2. The two a's are particulars of the mental habit A, the two b's of the habit B. The variation of b produced by experiencing a_2 rather than a_1, leads to the reinstatement of B in the form b_2 rather than b_1, by the operation of what Mr. Stout calls relative suggestion, which is in fact an instance of the organic character of mind. All this has now become the common possession of psychologists. Nothing in it except what is biological is peculiar to mind, and what is biological is shared by mind with life. The plants also exhibit the working of relative suggestion in adapting themselves

[1] Mr. Bosanquet's *Distinction of Mind from its Objects*, p. 36, Manchester, 1913.

within settled lines to changing circumstances. In the end the character of all action physical or mental depends on universals, and in the end all universals, mental as well as physical, are spatio-temporal habits, though they are patterns of other qualities as well.

It is in fact the cardinal defect of universals as conceived by Plato or the Pythagoreans that they were changeless and immoveable and eternal. For not even the mind of Plato could be free from the habits of his age, one of whose tendencies was to seek the highest ideals of perfection in gravity of action and statuesque repose rather than in restless motion.[1] Hence to account for motion he had to look for another source which he found in soul. It is claiming no great credit that for us universals should have from the beginning the form of motion,[2] should be not merely spatial but spatio-temporal. They are not particular motions but the plans of motion and they are actualised in particular motions. As the empirical universals vary from bare geometrical patterns to the universals of material and living and thinking things they become plans of motions which are correlated with qualities. They are plans of configuration of qualities or configurations of matter or mental action. But they are never dead or petrified, because in the end they are spatio-temporal plans and instinct with Time. And above all they are never bare potentialities, the creatures of abstract thinking, but possess such actuality as they can possess, which is not particular actuality or

[1] In a very interesting conversation, reported by M. Paul Gzell (*Art*, by Auguste Rodin, translated from the French by Mrs. Romilly Fedden, London, 1912), Rodin points out how the Greek statues, *e.g.* the Venus of Milo, or the Tanagra statuettes, secured the impression of repose by the opposite inclinations of the lines of the shoulders and the hips, so as to produce a balance of the body. Whereas in later art, as in the David of Michael Angelo, the lines are in the same direction, and the result is the impression of motion.

[2] I can accept with equanimity the laughing charge of Aristophanes against one of the sophists of his time that "Vortex has expelled Zeus and reigns in his place." Empirical things are vortices or eddies in the stuff of Space-Time, and universals are the laws of their construction. But I hope to show in the end how Vortex reintroduces Zeus in a more considered and worthier guise and to a securer throne.

existence.   The laws of the construction of things and those of the relations of things to one another are not therefore inventions of the mind imputed to nature, but part and parcel of the constitution of nature, and far more important parts than the particular facts from which they are supposed to be merely derived by our human thought, as if thought could make anything real which it does not find.[1]

Whatever difficulty there may be in conceiving the nature of a universal and its relation to its particulars, Universals n repetition

[1] I have made no attempt in the above to consider the bearing of the result on the teaching of Plato and the Pythagoreans ; partly because it would be a matter of great length but mostly because I have not the required scholarship.   I imagine that it is more in keeping with Pythagoreanism than with Plato himself.   On the other hand, in describing universals as patterns of motion I do not go the length of one of the later Pythagoreans, Eurytus, of whom Mr. Burnet tells us that he represented the form of man (supposed identical with the number 250) by sticking pebbles to that number into wet plaster along the outlines of a human shape.   This makes the form of man not merely a pattern of matter but actually a material thing.   But exaggerated as the procedure is, the spirit of it is sound, and I delight in Eurytus.   The Platonic doctrine of forms as numbers, that they are composed of limit and the unlimited or indeterminate dyad, represents within the world of forms what I am trying to say without any division of form from sensible things, allowance always being made for the absence of Time from Plato's conception of numbers or forms.   But the separation of forms from sense which is common to Plato and the Pythagoreans disappears, as remarked above, when sensibles are regarded as spatio-temporal complexes.   I have thought it best to use Plato for my purposes as a guide to my own inquiry without nice discussion of him for his own sake.   For the same reason I do not enter into the question of how much in the above is in agreement with Aristotle's teaching when he is constructive and not merely critical of Plato. For Plato (with qualifications) as for him the forms were constructive laws.   His doctrine that the species is the genus in energy or actualised appears to me of the greatest significance.   On the other hand, what he adds to Plato in the matter is not very satisfying and certainly does not bridge the gap between sense and thought.   For the actualisation of the species demands a prior individual of the same species : " man begets man."   But Aristotle though an evolutionist was necessarily only a logical and not a biological evolutionist—like Hegel after him.   The whole controversy as to whether forms are beside particulars or in them loses its importance, as I have observed before, when both form and particulars are spatio-temporal.

one thing can at least be affirmed, that without repetition or the possibility of it there would be no universality. The idea of a plan contains two features which must be distinguished. A plan is a complex of parts, and accordingly all universals imply such complexity, except in the limiting case of bare existence or point-instants where there is simplicity ; though even here an instant is intrinsically (not merely empirically or as a matter of fact) repeated in space and a point in time ; point-instants being the bare conceptual elements of Space-Time. A plan or universal involves, outside this case, relations of parts, or when it is a 'law of nature' it involves relations of things to one another. The relation within such plan or law is preserved under all instances, though with indefinite scope for variation so long as the relation is preserved. What these limits are is a purely empirical matter. There is no categorial reason why there should not be human beings two miles high. The reason is found in the empirical conditions, the difficulty of obtaining food enough, the extreme difference in the temperature of the atmosphere at the head and the feet, and the like. The experiment has been tried on a modest scale with mammoths and dinosaurs and has failed.

But the internal complexity or systematic character of a plan is not its universality; and because of the ambiguity of the word plan, law, which means universality, is preferable. To a universal, whether the law of construction of a thing or of relation to other things, repetition or the possibility of it is vital. A generic universal may as a matter of fact never be repeated empirically. There may be only one instance of the generic universal 'a Napoleon.' But as a universal and not merely a plan it implies repetition. The singular universal, *e.g.* Napoleon, is repeated in its moments of actual existence. Apart from possible repetition a plan would be only the plan of a particular, and would be in fact not a plan or law but an actual particular, not even an individual. This is in fact only to say again that a universal is a habit.

Why certain universals should occur only once and others repeated in varying numbers, why there should be actual repetition of complexes of events, is for the moment greatly dark.   It again concerns the empirical order of things, of which we know so little and of which philosophers can say even less.   There are multitudes of atoms of gold, and multitudes of electrons from which a selection is made to constitute atoms, and many trees and dogs.   The inorganic world spawns, like fishes in the organic world.   The universe in its lower levels behaves apparently (does it do so really ?) as if endowed with life.   Knowledge of this kind we have, but what more have we?   We accept repetition of things in their kinds as an empirical fact.   To do so presents, it must be confessed, a problem of the gravest difficulty, which is only mitigated and not removed by the consideration that the multiplicity of individuals of one type, or that of types which fall under higher types, is not bare repetition, that the many specimens differ from one another however slightly, that even an atom is only a statistical conception, the conception of an average of individuals all varying about a mean.   The fact of multiplicity remains.   Supposing it to be true that no reason can be found in the nature of Space-Time itself why types should repeat themselves in many instances, we should have succeeded in overcoming the difficulty of how universals can be realised in particulars, only to be left with the problem, apparently insoluble, of how there come to be particulars at all.   Later we shall see that quality is the distinctive empirical element in things, as contrasted with their *a priori* or categorial characters and with the relations of empirical things which arise from their being complexes of Space-Time.   It may be that we must regard the multiplicity of nature in instances as something equally empirical.   It may be that the problem though not now soluble, and I cannot see at present the solution of it, may ultimately admit solution, as I hope. I shall return to the matter at a later stage.[1]   At present we must insist that if there were no universals which as

The problem of multiplicity.

[1] Bk. III. ch. ix. F, 'On values in general.'

a matter of fact were repeated in their instances, we should not have reached the conception of universals. And more than that, if there were not the categorial possibility (that is the *a priori* possibility) of empirical repetition, not only would universality not be known (which after all concerns only human beings) but there would be no universality.

The distrust of repetition.

Several reasons exist which account for the tendency on the part of certain writers to push too far their reaction against the teaching of sheer empiricism which, not being empirical enough, disallows the reality of the non-empirical. They neglect the claims of repetition to be regarded as vital to universality and to be distinguished from the systematic nature of a universal. One reason is the fear of bare repetition, of instances which are not variations of a plan, but manufactured articles which exactly reproduce each other. If such repetition existed the use of instances would lie merely in their number. But as Mr. Bosanquet has so impressively taught us, the value of instances is that by their differences of character, not by their number, we are able to control one case by another and render precise the fundamental law which is involved and which may be masked by irrelevant circumstances or counteracted by others, " to purify " the law " by exceptions and finally limit it by negations." [1] When a single instance is of the right character it may be sufficient to establish a law ; and the business of the logician is to define that rightness of character. On the other hand, mere number of instances which we roughly call the same is only useful when analysis is impotent, and it can serve us because we can reason backwards from the relations between the number of various groups of instances to the probable character of the causes which are at work.

Now our conception of repetition renders this fear groundless ; it means that repetition brings not exact identity but modifications within limits of an identical plan of construction. The more comprehensive is the plan, the greater the room left for variations which may

[1] *Logic*, vol. ii. ch. iv. p. 117, eds. i. and ii.

themselves be specific variations of kind.   Bare repetition
it may be affirmed does not even exist.   Manufactured
articles are not identical though they may be identical
within certain limits of precision.   It is, however, true
that the more closely instances reproduce each other the
less useful they are for scientific discovery.   But the mere
difference of place and time which makes an instance
numerically distinct may supply empirical conditions
sufficient to lead to variation utilisable for scientific
method.

A second reason is the fear lest laws or universals
should be mistaken for the abstract generalities or
generalisations which Berkeley demolished, which are
derived or are supposed to be derived from their
particulars by a process of omission.   The specific
features of individuals which give to things their ordered
variety and richness of colouring are omitted ; their
common features are retained, and it is the business of
thought to discover and arrange these generalities.   Such
abstractions are often spoken of, by those who justly
repudiate them, as ' class-concepts.'   Correspondingly, laws
of nature have sometimes been conceived as abstractions
of the common elements in the relations of things to the
neglect of the variations of those relations.   Now it is
evident enough that useful as such abstractions may be
and are for artificial or provisional purposes, they have
nothing in common with universals as plans or laws of
construction, for these so far from neglecting the wealth
and variety of their particular instances are the formulae
which hold the instances together, not merely in our
thinking but in fact.   But I cannot see from such
acquaintance as I possess with science that these abstractions represent its practice.   A class in the actual
practice of the sciences is not a bare collection of particulars which happen to agree in certain important
respects, but a group determined by their constitutive
formula.   Witness the displacement in biology of the
artificial by the natural system of classification.   Even
the artificial system was inspired by a true scientific
instinct, for all its faults.   For the sexual parts on which

the classification is founded are of the last importance in organic life, and supply a clue to, or in Mill's phrase are an index of, a vast number of other important properties. The constant effort of the physicist or chemist is to discover characters which are index characters to the real constitution of things. The atomic weights were a first approximation to this end. At present we are witnessing the attempt to resolve the atom into a planetary system of electrons in motion round their central nucleus. Where would it be possible to find a more flagrant example of the real striving of physical science after constitutive plans ? It is true that so eminent a logician as Jevons has represented scientific procedure as founded on the ideal of perfect enumeration of instances. But it is hardly just that the sciences should be saddled with the errors of their interpreters. The most elementary acquaintance with simple mathematics is enough to show in them the same endeavour after systematising their facts that is verifiable in the less ' abstract ' sciences. The idea that mathematical propositions are mere generalisa- tions could only be entertained by the misunderstanding of empirical method to which Mill fell a victim. He attempted to set geometry on the level of the inductive sciences by regarding geometry and arithmetic as con- cerned not with Space and Time themselves but with the physical things which occupy them. Geometry is indeed an empirical and experimental science ; but its empirical subject-matter is not the things which fill Space, but their spaces. It observes the behaviour of Space, and the variety of its empirical material supplied by complexes within Space are the figures whose properties it discovers and connects into a system. It is thus not the sciences themselves which in their spirit and purpose worship the idol of abstract generalities. A spectre has been conjured up by the fears of philosophers which is called the mechanical method of science. But so far as I can see, it is the offspring of mistaken philo- sophers, or of science playing the part, as it often rightly does, of a spectator of its own procedure, but failing to do it justice.

A profounder reason for the distrust of universals, The described as laws which are repeated in particular instances, 'concrete' ur is connected with the previous one.   They seem to some to remove us from reality, whereas the aim of all thought and science is to preserve the most intimate contact with reality, and with reality in its sensible form.   Such an aim is more surely, say they, embodied in a work of art where every part of the work is vivified by its meaning, which as it were penetrates into every corner of the statue or the picture or the poem.   Laws are infected with the repetitive disease ; and the infection is conveyed by Space and Time, which are for these thinkers the beau-ideal of endlessness without purpose, the splintering of things into dissipated elements without the stability of real existence.   The duty of thought is to be organic, and even if there is something which can never be reduced to terms of thought, if a person for instance can never be exhausted in his personality by any organisation of predicates, yet thought aspires to be individual and in its own sphere to mirror reality so far as thought can.   All thinking tends thus to the concrete, defining itself into complex individuality.   The 'mechanical principle' neglects this purpose and misses the true concreteness of thought.

It is such reasons which have led to the doctrine of the 'concrete universal,' a doctrine derived from Hegel and nowhere expounded with more effect and enthusiasm than by Mr. Bosanquet in the second chapter of his *Principle of Individuality and Value.*   For our hypothesis on which things are ultimately complexes of space-time, it seemed that thoughts, whose object is the plans of such configurations, never can be divorced from their particulars ; that Space and Time, so far from being the least self-subsistent of things, are in truth in their indissoluble union the ultimate reality in its simplest and barest terms ; that the plans which it admitted are therefore concrete.   But they do not aspire to be 'concrete universals' in distinction from the alleged abstract ones which do not and cannot exist.   The so-called 'concrete universal' is in fact not a universal but a universe.   It is not a law but a system. The relation of the universal to its particulars ceases to be that of a plan to its participants, but becomes that of a society to its members or a world to its parts. " The true embodiment of the logical universal," says Mr. Bosanquet, " takes the form of a world whose members are worlds." " The universal in the form of a world refers to diversity of content within every member as the universal in the form of a class neglects it." (The universal we have described has neither the form of a world nor of a so-called class, but of a plan or law.) In the end there can be but one true universal, and that is the world itself as a single individual. Hence the significance of the phrase " a world whose members are worlds." " The test of universality which it (the concrete universal) imposes is not the number of subjects " (granted at once !) " which share a common predicate, but rather than this, the number of predicates that can be attached to a single subject " (for instance, the name of a person).[1]

The recognition of this logical form as the true type of universality, Mr. Bosanquet says, " is the key to all sound philosophy." With all respect to the writer who defends it with such skill, I venture to think this doctrine combines into one two distinct notions. One is that of the union of different features into a plan or law which is realised with modifications in individual instances, the combination of many predicates which appears to be intended in the passage I have quoted. This is the universal as I have described it. But such a plan cannot be called a universe. The other notion is that of the union into a system of different individuals in or by or under such a plan. Such a union is indeed a universe, but its relation to its particulars is not that of an individual to its predicates, nor that of a plan to its embodiments. A universe of particulars is not the universal of them. It introduces in fact a different and important conception which it misnames universal, that of an individual substance or the totality of changing phases of an individual's life, every one of which follows a certain plan

[1] *Loc. cit.* pp. 37-40.

or universal. I find in the doctrine of the concrete universal these two notions intermixed.[1]

The distinction may be illustrated first from the case of an individual person, which is regarded as typical. Any fact as we have seen is universal in so far as it follows a plan of constitution and can be repeated according to that plan in time and space. As a particular determined according to a plan it is an individual. An individual substance or thing (to anticipate what belongs to a later chapter) is the continuum of these repeated instances of its universal plan. In a personality the various acts of the individual are highly organised, and in the phases of his life distinct activities become prominent, but always in subordination to the one plan. Thus when an individual follows the well-known rule of Sir William Jones :

> Six hours to law, to soothing slumbers seven,
> Ten to the world allot, and all to Heaven ;

dedication to Heaven describes the universal plan, the individual person is the continuum of different conditions of life which follow this plan. The theory of the concrete universal would make him the universal of his acts as well as the universe of them.

This case is that of an organised individual, and is of great complexity. A simpler case is that of a parabola whose equation is $y^2 = 4ax$, where a has some definite value. This individual parabola is the thing or substance composed of all the points which follow the plan so described, and is the universe of them. But their universal is not the parabola but what may be described by the phrase 'any point which satisfies this equation.' The parabola is not a universal. On the other hand, there is a universal parabola which is the plan of all such totalities of points, a plan symbolised by the same equation when the parameter a may vary from curve to curve. This universal parabola is not, however, the universe of all parabolas, and in fact there is no such individual or universe.

---

[1] Thus Mr. Bosanquet himself, as before noted, compares a universal in the mind to a habit, and so far I seem to be repeating his view of the universal. But a habit is surely not related to its realisations as a thing to its predicates.

This is still plainer when we pass to a species or genus, which can only be called the universal of its specimens as being their plan of construction. If it means their universe, where is such an individual whole to be found ? There is only the collection of individuals, which have not even that approach to organisation that can be found in a parabola. It may indeed happen that instances of a species (or, if we prefer to say so, species of a genus) are connected together into an organic whole which is more than a mere whole of parts. This is the case as I believe with human societies ; and wherever beings tend to communal life there is an approach to this state of things. The members of a society are instances of a type which is represented by the society as a whole, and the society is in fact a species which is itself an individual existence.[1] But we are not entitled on the strength of such special (and perhaps disputable cases) to identify a universal with an organised individual because the plan of the individual members happens in these cases to be in some way embodied in the whole. We still need the notion of a plan or law, and this is what commonly is called a universal.

In avoiding abstract universals, which not true science uses but a false logic of science imagines, the theory we are commenting upon assigns the name of universal to something which is not a universal in the traditional sense, but something different which is yet blended with the older meaning of universal. If the matter were one of nomenclature alone, it would not signify so much. Its importance lies in the metaphysical consequences. If universals (on the discovery of which all science turns) are really universes, and not merely laws, there is in the end only one universe or individual which is self-existent ; the minor universes are shadows. For if the universal is related to its particulars as a thing to its predicates they become "adjectival" to it, and in the end the minor universes are adjectival to the one universe or absolute individual. If on the other hand the reality is Space-

---

[1] H. Spencer has, I believe, a remark somewhere to this effect, where I cannot remember.

Time, individual things, and minor universes which are groupings of them, are real with the reality of their parent, which is then " the nurse and mother of all becoming," not the devouring maw which swallows all empirical things.

The 'concrete universal' then mistakes universality for system. It remains to add that the idea of system or organisation is of the highest value for understanding the problem of knowledge, and it is by this clue that Mr. Bosanquet himself has been able to render such service to logical theory. Organisation is a great empirical fact. It begins lower down than organic life and is perpetually overcoming the repetitive tendency which is equally empirical. As we ascend the scale of being in the order of time, aggregates are replaced by organic systems ; and the higher a thing is in the scale, the greater it seems is its ordered complexity. But system in general exists in every complex even in the least organised, all disorder has its own complex plan. System is the coherence of elements, and the notion of system represents the essential continuity of Space-Time which it retains while it breaks up into its parts. The parts remain within the whole and are coherent with one another. Science investigates the particular forms of such coherence, and organisms are a highly-developed instance of it. The nature of an organism and still more a work of art is rightly exemplary in the methods which reason follows. Thought, in following the clue of coherence amongst its data, as science always does, is thus bringing back the scattered members of the universe into the spatio-temporal continuity out of which, in spite of their disguises of qualities higher than mere motion, they ultimately sprang. These considerations belong properly to the theory of truth, and the methods by which it is attained in science. Those methods are empirical rules by which we seek to bring order into the empirical material ; and it may be surmised even at this stage that logic is an empirical science which deals with the interconnection of the isolated portions of our knowledge (that is, of reality) as presented in propositional form.[1]

---

[1] For this topic see later, Bk. III. ch. ix. B, ' Truth and Error.'

CHAPTER IV

RELATION

ALL existents are in relation because events or groups of
them are connected within Space-Time. Relation amongst
existents follows from the continuity of Space-Time. The
continuity of Space-Time is something primordial and
given in experience. When it is described in conceptual
terms as the continuous relation of point-instants it is
described in terms derived from finite complexes or things,
just in the same way as we apply the conception of
causality in physical events to mental events though we
are familiar with the causal experience first in mental life.
Thus there is no circularity, to anticipate the old misapprehension, in explaining relation by continuity of
Space-Time. It is a certain determination of Space-Time,
afterwards known as its continuity, in virtue of which
existents are related to one another. Not all relations of
existents are in their immediate character or quality
spatio-temporal ; but if our hypothesis is sound they are
always spatio-temporal in their simplest expression.
Relation is, as James has so constantly and rightly insisted,
as elementary a feature of the universe as 'substantive'
things. This is true not only of our mental states, where
it is apprehended in enjoyment, but of the external world,
where it is apprehended in contemplation. In the end it
depends upon and expresses the continuity of Space-Time.
Space and Time we have seen are not relations but they are
through and through relational. Neither are they mere
existence, but they contain all existence. They are the
stuff in which existences are related ; and the terms and
the relations between them are equally spatio-temporal.

Hence it is that relation is as vague a word in philosophy as being. It stands for any connection between things. Specific or empirical relations can be described, mostly by naming their terms. But relation itself, relation as such, is rarely defined or identified. The reason is apparent now. It is a category and can only be indicated by the finger as a characteristic of Space-Time or described by conceptual terms which are later in the order of reality than itself, just as we may describe red as the colour of blood.

What then are empirical relations? We have seen *Empirical* that empirical relations of space and time are themselves *relations.* spaces and times or are homogeneous with their terms, made of the same stuff. Following a distinction drawn by Mr. C. A. Strong, James classes them as "ambulatory" relations in distinction from "saltatory" ones.[1] For example, "difference is saltatory, jumping as it were immediately from one term to another, but distance in time or space is made out of intervening parts of experience through which we ambulate in succession." James goes on to describe the knowing relation as ambulatory, because in it we ambulate from idea to percept or thing, which is of the same stuff as idea, and we ambulate though a medium of the same stuff. With that we are not here concerned. However, the distinction of the two kinds of relation, happy and useful as it is, is not of more than secondary importance. Whether a relation is of the same stuff as the terms or not, it makes the terms into a connected whole, an integral situation. From this point of view all relations are ambulatory. Moreover, on our hypothesis it is clear that in the end all relation is reducible to spatio-temporal terms. Even apart from this ultimate reduction there can be no jump from term to term, for the relation, if it is to be concrete and not a mere thought about its terms, must be some specific bond between its

[1] W. James, *The Meaning of Truth*, New York, 1909. 'A word more about Truth,' p. 138. For the whole subject of relation see his Appendix A on 'The thing and its relations' in *A Pluralistic Universe*, New York, 1909.

terms which binds them into one continuous tissue. If it falls short of this, the relation fails to relate. Whether the relation is homogeneous with its terms or not is therefore a secondary matter.

Conceived in this concrete fashion a relation may be described as the whole situation into which its terms enter, in virtue of that relation. The qualification, 'in virtue of that relation,' is added because terms may have other characters which do not concern the relation in question. Thus a king may, like Saul, be taller than his subjects. But the relation of height does not concern the kingly situation but a different one ; or a mother may be more beautiful than her daughters, but this does not concern the maternal relation, but a relation of degree. The situation may be one of successive events as in the causal relation of the blow which fells an ox ; or of simultaneous things like the rivalry of two suitors. By the 'situation' is meant the concrete system of circumstances which brings the terms into connection with one another. It used to be said that a relation was based on a *fundamentum relationis*, and the distinction of the relation and its foundation is, as I suppose, merely that the relation itself is the concrete connection between the terms set up by the acts and events or circumstances which constitute the *fundamentum*. Mill has admirably described this *fundamentum* in his *Logic*,[1] though the reader must always discount Mill's metaphysical prepossessions. Take the relation of interval between two points or two moments. The interval is the connecting situation of the two terms, in the one case a line, in the other a duration ; that interval is the transaction into which two points or instants enter in virtue of their real nature as point-instants. The points or moments themselves do not belong to the connecting situation except as they are the beginnings of that transaction. (It is a subtlety to be mentioned hereafter that the interval, as the stretch of points between two positions, is not the same relation as

---

[1] *Logic*, Bk. III. ch. ii. sec. 7, and particularly ch. iii. sec. 10. I mean by Mill's prepossessions his leaning (1) to subjective idealism in metaphysics, and along with that (2) to atomism in psychology.

the interval which is the distance between them.[1]) The relation of maternity consists in like manner in the history of bearing the child and the whole set of actions and feelings in which the mother is engaged towards her child and correspondingly ('correlatively') the child is engaged towards its mother ; always with the proviso in so far as these actions and feelings on one side or the other establish a connection between the two partners, or initiate a transaction between them. For the actions and feelings are *prima facie* states of the mother or of the child, some of them actions, some passions ; services on one part, acceptance on the other of those services. The relation is the situation or connection or transaction set up between the two partners in virtue of these services and acceptances. Similarly the relation of knowing, the cognitive relation, is not the act of knowing or the existence of the object but the situation of connection between the two. To take a further example, the relation of king to subjects is the system of acts and capacities of them or passions and capacities of them in which the king as king is concerned with his subjects, in so far as these set up a certain situation or transaction between the two sides.

These examples illustrate the truth that, not merely in

[1] The distance between two points as distinguished from the stretch of points between them is their unlikeness in respect of position. [Cf. the distinction drawn by A. Meinong between 'difference or interval' (*Unterschied*) and 'unlikeness' (*Verschiedenheit*), used below in respect of intensity, in ch. vii. (*Über die Bedeutung des Weberschen Gesetzes.* Hamburg, Leipzig, 1896).] The points are identical as points but different in position. Now such unlikeness in position is the situation constituted by the interval, but that interval taken not as divisible into points but as the occupation of a space to a certain extent taken as a whole. It is a matter of subsequent experience that degrees of spatial unlikeness are themselves expressible by extensive measurement, so that one distance may be two feet and another three feet. Consequently, though distance of two points is as a matter of fact the spatial interval of the two points and can be resolved into parts and measured, it does not follow that any distance, as between the intensities of a quality, *e.g.* the sound C, or between qualitative units themselves like pitches of sound, is necessarily extensive, that is, is an extensive quantity. See later, ch. vii. on intensive quantity, pp. 307 ff.

bare Space or Time but in the empirical relations that subsist between things with qualities, the relation is just as concrete and just as much a reality (being ultimately spatio-temporal) as the terms and belongs to the same tissue with them. This is what James in the *Psychology* affirmed of spatial and temporal relations. The relation may in fact be on occasion the centre of importance and the terms, as it were, adjectival of it, instead of its being adjectival of them. The fringe may be central and the centre a fringe. Illustrations were given in a previous passage, and fresh ones may be added here. The two ends of a line may be merely its ends, the line itself, the relation between them, being central, or they may be thought of as the limits which bound the line, and, as it were, press it in—in which case the points are central. This difference of emphasis has been used by Th. Lipps to explain various illusions to which we are subject in the estimation of the interval between two points.[1] Again, in a Homeric battle, it is the personality of the champions which is central, the engagement is a fringe. But in a battle of the great war, what we thought of first was the swaying backwards and forwards, the advance and retreat of the combatants, while the combatants themselves were dim and confused masses.

Sense of relations.

Every relation is a situation or more properly a trans-action between its terms. If the terms are transposed they enter into a new relation which is of the same kind as before but differs from it in 'sense' or direction. Thus if A is the mother of B, B is a child born of A. Two such relations differing only in sense are said to be the one the converse of the other. This result might seem at first sight to be incompatible with the account we have given of relation. Since the situation of mother and child involves both parties, it would seem that the

---

[1] Th. Lipps : *Raumästhetik und geometrisch-optische Täuschungen.* (Schriften d. Ges. f. psych. Forschung (II. Leipzig, 1893–7, Section 3). Thus the empty horizontal distance between two points looks shorter than a horizontal line of the same length, because the points in the first case are more independent and seem to shut in their space interval.

maternal and the filial relation are not different but the
same. And so they are if the terms are merely interchanged and the terms themselves remain the same.
There is no difference in the situation or relation if the
terms are singular. The propositions, A is the mother
of B, and (the same) B is a child born of A, describe
precisely the same fact, but they describe it in the light
of the general relations of maternity or filial relation.
Now these two general relations differ in sense, and the
situations though the same in kind are different situations.
There is a real difference between the propositions A is
the mother of B and A is the child born of B. Actions
in the first case are replaced by passions in the second
and *vice versa*. The difference lies in the direction of
the connecting movements. Similarly as between A
precedes B and A succeeds B. The quality of the situation is the same but its direction is reversed. The
journey from Edinburgh to London is not the same
journey as that from London to Edinburgh, though it
covers the same interval of space. If A is the mother of
B and the child of C there are two sets of transactions
which are of the same sort but in a different sense, and
the situations are also different. It is only if the situation is treated as a resting one and not a transaction that
the real empirical difference in the situation is overlooked.
When the same situation is expressed in two different
senses by interchanging the terms (Edinburgh is north
of London, London is south of Edinburgh), the difference is not indeed a merely verbal one, though perilously
near to it, but a difference of aspect or description, what
Aristotle expressed by saying that the two things *are* the
same but not in their *being*.[1] The same actual situation
is interpreted differently according to the plan of the
general converse relation by interchanging the terms.

The above is what is meant by saying that a difference
of sense depends on the order of the terms.[2] It affords

---

[1] Ἔστι μὲν το αυτο, τὸ δε εἶναι ου τὸ αυτο. Aristotle's example is
the road from Peiraeus to Athens.

[2] In so-called logical conversion there is no difference of 'sense'
involved. There the relation or "pseudo-relation" as Mr. Russell

also another testimony to the truth that we do not have terms and relations but terms in relation. When terms are transposed the general relation alters with them in direction. Two conclusions follow. First, the difference of sense is not something of which no account can be given. If it cannot be defined, it can be described by indicating what it stands for, the real difference of spatio-temporal direction, that is of direction of motion, to which it corresponds ; just in the same way as relation itself is indicated by pointing to its crude primordial basis in Space-Time. Transactions are temporal as well as spatial and are motions with direction. Secondly, we are confirmed in the belief, hinted in a previous chapter, that order arises out of the spatio-temporal character of things, is founded upon Space-Time itself, and is not prior to Space and Time, except when legitimately so considered for artificial purposes.

Relation and other categories.

Primarily relations hold between individual things. But universals have a quasi-individual existence and we may with propriety speak of relations in which universals are concerned. The relation is, however, only indirect and through the particulars. Universality communicates with relation in the strict sense, in that the universal establishes a relation of identity between the particulars. It is doubtful whether we should admit relation between a universal and its particulars ; we can only do so, I think, by a substantiation of the universal. The relation between a universal and its particulars is more strictly one between the particulars themselves in respect of the universal. In the same way a thing or substance may be said to be related to a universal which is an adjective of it, though once again this is really a relation between the universal,

calls it is unaltered. Conversion alters or may alter the quantity of the terms. Here, too, the converse is not a mere verbal change.

I have not referred to the accidental matter that in some relations, symmetrical ones, the converse is the same as the original relation ; for example, equality. On the whole subject of the sense of relations see Mr. Russell's *Princ. of Math.* ch. ix. pp. 95, 96. My differences from him will be plain from the text.

e.g. sweet, as particularised in sugar, to the other particularised qualities and to the substantial permanence of
sugar—all which matters are to be investigated presently.[1]
Thus we may continue on this understanding to speak of
the relation of subject to predicate. What is important
is that we shall not confuse the relation of subject to
predicate in the ordinary categorical proposition which
expresses the relation of substance to attribute with
relations of space or time or quantity or quality, or the
like, which are specifically relational, or express relation
as such. No contortions of language, however ingeniously
successful, will overcome the difference between an
attribute which inheres in its substance and a relation
like that of quantity which does not inhere and cannot
therefore be regarded as an adjective in the proper sense.

Other categories, then, like universality or existence
or quantity or causality, communicate with relation.
Existence, *e.g.*, is diverse from other existence ; and the
like. Relation in its turn communicates with other
categories. Thus it exists as being itself a spatio-temporal
occupation, what we have called the situation connecting
its terms. Again it is either particular or universal : there
may be plans of relation as well as individual relations.
The relation of paternity or that of difference is universal,
though embodied like other universals in particulars.
Thus relations as universals are real and the objects of
thought ; though, in view of the abuse by which this
truth is transformed into the proposition that relations
are the special object or even product of thought, it is
almost more important to insist with James that relations
are perceived as well as thought and belong to the same
sensible reality as terms. And, above all, universal
relations are concrete, and relate terms, and they are not
to be floated off from terms as if they could be abstracted
from them, a danger not avoided as it seems by certain
conceptions of relation.

Relations, it hardly needs to say, are external realities Relations
when they are relations of external things, and mental ᵉ ʸ mental.

[1] Ch. vi. A, ‘Substance.’

ones when they belong to enjoyments or mental things. They are in no sense subjective or the work of the mind. Some relations like likeness and difference, identity, equality, greater or less, or those expressed by the words 'and' or 'but' or 'however,' might seem at first sight to be eminently mental, due to comparison. They have sometimes been referred to the experience of the attention which compares (likeness) or hesitates or is obstructed ('but') or rejects ('not'). Red and green are red and green; but it is we who feel them *different*. We might even think that one magnitude is greater than another because the act of attending has a felt excess in the one case to the other. But it is clear that the theory is circular and that the acts of attention are themselves compared (in enjoyment) in order to feel their likeness or difference or excess. These relations are, in fact, empirical variations of the category relation just as triangles and parabolas are empirical variations of Space, or the various integers or fractions are of the category number, and are felt in mind as well as contemplated outside it. Even 'but' and 'still,' though apprehended by mental acts of obstruction, are objective situations of opposition in the objects they connect. Negation is not mental only but exists in things as well, and is such difference as is asserted in contrary or contradictory propositions.

What then are the objective situations which constitute such relations as these? In the case of empirical relations, relations of a certain quality like paternity which connect things of empirical quality, the answer is plain. Since qualities are, we assume, correlated with spatio-temporal processes, the relations, however otherwise represented summarily or compendiously by their qualities, are in the end spatio-temporal, though it may be of great complexity. They are at least reducible without residue to such relations, which are themselves configurations of space-time. As to relations which arise out of categories themselves, we must leave the other categories for subsequent description. We have only hitherto dealt with existence and universality. All existence involves the relation of difference from other existence, and this we have seen is the exclusion of other existents from the occupation of its own space-time. The relation of particulars to one another under or by their universal is a more difficult matter. A convenient method is to adopt, like James,[1] a pragmatist criterion. The relation is that one particular may be substituted for the other. Likeness is partially successful and partially unsuccessful capacity of substitution. Such a criterion is not open to us, for it carries the relation back to a device of human thought, whereas the relation is in the things and not to be exhausted by a secondary criterion, which gives rather a symptom than the reality. Our previous inquiry supplies the answer. Things of the same sort are in the first place numerically different and exclude each other in Space-Time. But the transaction of conceptual identity[2] between them is their co-inclusion in the one Space-Time which, in virtue of its constancy, works at different places according to a plan which does not suffer distortion merely in virtue of the difference of place and time.

Likeness or unlikeness is a derivative relation, which is combined of the relation of sameness of kind with that of difference in kind. Two things are like each other only if they are different, and unlike each other only if they are identical. Hence both likeness and unlikeness are partial identity in kind. We may take as examples a white and a purple pansy, a red triangle and a red square, a tall or short man, a loud or a soft C. In all but the first case, the different kinds are empirical differences of categorial characters, extension, quantity, intensity, which are more than merely numerical differences. Space - Time provides us with likeness or difference in so far as two empirical universals overlap, or, in Plato's phrase, communicate with each other. Owing to the constancy of Space-Time it is possible for one configuration to be partially the same as

Likeness.

---

[1] *Some Problems of Philosophy* (London, 1911), p. 103.
[2] Cf. for the phrase Mr. G. E. Moore's paper on *Identity*, *Proc. Arist. Soc.* N.S. vol. i., 1900–1, pp. 103 ff.

one set of particulars and partially the same as another set.

The attempt has been made to explain identity as an extreme degree of likeness and thus to make 'like' the prior conception. Given a subject of reference A, we may arrange the similars to it in a scale of varying degrees of increasing likeness or decreasing difference. When the difference reaches its minimum or the likeness its maximum we have identity. This view was expounded by James as a psychological thesis and contested by Mr. Bradley.[1] Thus, for instance, we may have sounds of the same pitch but different intensity, where as the distance in the intensity from the standard diminishes the compared sensation becomes identical with the standard.

This would seem, however, metaphysically erroneous, for distance can only mean a greater or less degree of unlikeness in respect of something which remains constant or the same. The scale of unlike or like sensations postulates identity and diversity. Being metaphysically erroneous, the view is also psychologically so ; for nothing can be true for one science which is false for another. But James's doctrine admits of a different interpretation. It is true that we apprehend distinctly the shock of unlikeness or distance before we apprehend the underlying identity. And it is the series of diminishing distances ending in zero which forces on our minds the explicit identity of kind. Thus James is explaining how we become aware of identity as such and disentangle it from its concomitants. Still it remains the case psychologically (and not merely metaphysically) that the identity must be in our minds, our minds must be working in the same way and have the same sort of object, in order that we should apprehend likeness or unlikeness.[2] Thus identity is primordial and likeness derivative.

A more difficult question is whether likeness (or unlikeness) is an empirical relation, as I have implied above,

---

[1] W. James, *Psychology*, vol. i. p. 528 ff. For the controversy by the two writers see *Mind*, N.S. vol. ii. pp. 83, 208, 366, 509.

[2] Compare on this point F. H. Bradley, *Logic* (London, 1883), p. 422.

or is itself a category though a derived one. Though a relation of the most extreme generality, it must be declared to be empirical. There is nothing in Space-Time which requires (though Space-Time admits) the over-lapping of empirical universals. It might seem that one kind involved in itself relation to other kinds, in the same way as numerical identity is of itself the exclusion of other point-instants and is therefore different from other numerical identity. But the cases are not parallel. For universality is a relation of identity between its own individuals, but is not as such a relation to other universals. Hence there is no reason in Space-Time itself (no non-empirical reason) why two individuals identical in kind should be also different in kind. Plato himself was careful to distinguish the overlapping of empirical universals from the overlapping of categories as such.

Relations, then, are the spatio-temporal connections of things, these things themselves being also in the end spatio-temporal complexes. Since Space-Time is con-tinuous, the connecting situation which constitutes a relation is but spatio-temporal continuity in another form. The relations and the things they relate are equally elements in the one reality and so far are separate realities. But the business of a relation is to relate, and there is consequently no relation without things it relates, which are then called its terms. On the other hand, there are no things which are unrelated to others, which would imply spatio-temporal discontinuity. They must at least be connected in Space and Time, and it is plain that they must be connected by all the relations which arise out of the categories, seeing that categories are pervasive features of all things. Bearing these considerations in mind we can answer directly certain controversial questions about relations. Are re-lations internal or external?

Are relations external or internal to their terms ? We must answer that everything depends on what is meant by external and internal. If to be external means to have a recognisable existence as much as terms have, relations are external. If it means that relations can exist in separation from their terms or things, they do not so exist ; for if they did so they would not relate. The habit of describing relations by abstract terms instead of concrete ones, *e.g.* the relation of paternity, is partly responsible for this misapprehension. Substitute the phrase 'the paternal relation,' and remember that a relation is a spatio-temporal fact which may, as in the examples given, itself turn into a thing ; and it is seen at once to be untrue that a relation exists somewhere from whence it descends upon its terms like a bed-cover upon the sleepers in a common lodging-house. For instance, the cognitive relation is distinguishable both from the act of knowing and the object known, but if it existed without them it would have nothing to do.

On the other hand, if to be internal means that a relation is a quality of its terms, or belongs to them as a quality does, then a relation is not internal to its terms. Inherence is itself a relation, as between the quality which inheres and the rest of the qualities. But a relation does not inhere in its terms taken singly. On the contrary, inherence we shall see means to be included spatially in a thing ; and relation from the nature of the case, as being the situation which unites things, is outside each of them spatially (or rather spatio-temporally). Thus the act of cognition or the cognitive capacity is inherent in the knower, but the cognitive relation to the object is outside that act, is its compresence with the object. Indeed, it is clear that if relation were inherent like a quality in a term, then since the relation implies the correlative term, the correlative would in some sense be internal to the other term. Thus the child would be internal to the father and the object known internal to the knower, as has in fact been sometimes held. No one would, of course, pretend that a relation can be a quality of *both* its terms taken together. We must therefore say that no relation is internal to its terms in this sense of inherence. But if internality of relation means only that it cannot exist without its terms, relations are in this sense internal ; that is, if the things between which they exist are really terms of the relation. For a thing may be outside the relation in other respects. Thus paternity is external to a man before he is a father ; but when he is a father he is a term in the paternal relation, which as it relates him to the child is internal in this sense to both. It is a further question and, as we shall see, the only question of real importance whether things can be considered outside certain relations, and which are such relations, as *e.g.* this one of paternity.

Thus neither of the alternatives, relations are external, relations are internal, is true without qualification or in a valuable sense. If we separate the world into terms *and* their relations we are making an abstraction. The things are conceived as if they did nothing to each other (which is impossible in Space-Time) or were unrelated ; and the relations as if they did not relate. The world consists of things *in* their relations. Since this is the notion which is most obviously denied by the alleged externality of relations (let us call it the crude externality of relations), we may reject crude externality. It implies an original or crude discontinuity in Space-Time ; and, as we have seen, without a primordial or crude continuity of Space-Time we could never understand its constitution out of its parts. In truth we form this notion only because we first dissect the things from the original continuum and then build it up again. We hew our stones from the quarry and then restore the quarry from the stones.

But though the question whether relations are external or internal ceases thus to be of great importance, there are distinctions to be drawn amongst relations themselves ; according as they are categorial or empirical, and according as they are intrinsic or extrinsic to their terms ; which raise a different question but one connected with the other question. For relations are clearly enough not external to their terms as terms. The idea of their externality only arises because things before they become terms in a relation are not necessarily the same as when they have entered it. Categorial characters and the relations founded on them belong to everything. Anything stands

Intrinsic and extrinsic relations

in some relation of space and time to other things ; it has quantity and is greater or less than something else and the like. Its size may alter but some size it retains. It has attributes and is causally related with other things, though it may change its colour or affect a different substance. Strictly, categorial relations are not altered by entry into a relation, it is only the empirical determinations of them that may be altered.

Empirical characters of things are those which they have from the grouping of Space-Time elements into complexes, and empirical relations are the non-categorial relations of things which they have in virtue of their being parts of Space-Time. But under the designation empirical I include two sets of characters. One set are variations of Space-Time itself or of the categories. For example, triangularity is an empirical determination of shape, for not every finite is triangular. It is what is commonly known as a primary quality. Again 'and' and 'but' are empirical variations of the category of relation, as 'like' is of the category universal. The other set are in a stricter or more special sense empirical, for they carry with them variation of what is called quality, secondary quality like colour or higher quality like life or consciousness.

Now, amongst these empirical relations some are intrinsic to the things and some are extrinsic. Thus a man as man stands in human relations to other human beings ; for instance, he must be the son of somebody or possess sociality. But he need not be a king or a father or a servant. His intrinsic qualities are expressed in his intrinsic relations, which therefore are in a manner internal to him. But his extrinsic relations depend on circumstances, such as juxta-position or the environment, and when he enters into these relations they are in a manner external to him. This distinction corresponds to the logical distinction of what is essential to a thing and what is accidental to it. What is most intrinsic to a thing is its typical character, manhood for instance to man ; but the intrinsic qualities and relations expressing them include what is specific to the individual and all the so-called 'properties' which follow from them, as well as those truly inseparable accidents which are only properties awaiting the disclosure of their connection with the essential characters. Thus a man's relation to his kind is intrinsic or essential ; but to have a son or a wife is an accident, and, thanks to death or the law-courts, it is what the logicians call a separable accident. It is plain that categorial relations are intrinsic also, but they are absolutely intrinsic, for nothing can be which does not carry into all its relations its categorial characters. What varies with the relation is the empirical character of the relation arising out of the category. A thing may now be above and now under another ; it may be far off or near another thing, five feet or two inches longer than another. Extrinsic empirical relations may therefore be pure variations of categorial relations, or these variations may themselves be attended by qualities, as for example in the paternal relation.

Thus there are in fact three kinds of relations, the strictly categorial, the essential, and the extrinsic. The first two classes are both called intrinsic. Empirically intrinsic relations are relatively unalterable. So long as the things retain their individuality their intrinsic relations are not changed by entering into extrinsic ones. A man remains a man though he becomes a king or a father or a slave. But just because its qualities are empirical and not categorial, the extrinsic relation may alter the qualities of the thing. Thus a man may be brutalised by the possession of power, or become egotistic or parochialised by the concentration of his affections on his child to the neglect of society. Misfortune may turn him from a genial to a sour man, he may become a disappointed man. The qualities intrinsic to the individual suffer first, but extrinsic relations may affect even the typical characters. For example, in the stages of intoxication, where a man may be said to enter into an extrinsic situation, first his voice loses its individual character, then he loses the more typical capacity of rational speech, and finally the most typical of characters, the capacity of co-ordinated movement and locomotion.

A man may become subhuman by degradation or isolation, or monstrous by insanity, or he may by natural death
or violence cease to be a man at all. No wonder that
such extrinsic relations which alter the parties to it, seem
to be external and indifferent to the real nature of the
thing.

The
ultimate
question
raised.

It is the contrast of the categorial and empirical characters and relations which is of the greater importance
for metaphysics. For it sheds light upon the question
whether the partial character of existents affects their
claim to be considered real or true, whether, that is, we
must allow reality to the parts or deny it to anything
but the whole. The categorial characters of things
remain, whatever extrinsic relations they may enter into,
and hence their reality in these regards is unaffected.
It is only the empirical modifications of these categorial
characters and relations which are affected. Now partiality
can only vitiate the reality of anything so far as entering
into a whole changes the thing. Therefore the categorial
determinations of things are perfectly and absolutely
real or true. For, assuming them all to be fundamental
determinations of Space-Time, we can recognise no higher
standard of their reality. But empirical characters
(whether modifications of the categories or qualitative)
may be affected by extrinsic relations. Hence it follows
that we cannot be sure that we have the intrinsic nature
of a thing or a relation unless we have satisfied ourselves
that no extrinsic relations will affect them, and universal
propositions are therefore only possible under this proviso.
This is the first limitation on empirical truth. There is
a further question which the time has not yet arrived
to discuss, for it belongs to the problem of the ' one and
the many ' : whether the liability of all finites to suffer
in their non-categorial intrinsic characters destroys their
reality or only affects the difficulty of discovering it.
But it will already be apparent that subject though they
are to change, to conversion into things of different
nature, this does not destroy their claim to be real so
far as they are what they are. For they are of the same

stuff as the Space-Time which connects them and in which those relations arise which may alter or destroy them. They only become in changing, as for example by death, other variations of the same matrix, and they remain relatively real.

The difficulties which Mr. Bradley has found in the notion of qualities and relations[1] are due in the first place to the inversion of the natural order of things. Begin with the primordial fact of the parts of Space-Time in organic connection with one another; qualities and relations are then mutually implied without contradiction, because, as we have seen, the very notion of contradiction is a birth of Space-Time itself, which is the ultimate standard of reference. I return to this below. But put aside this consideration. The difficulties then arise from treating relations in the abstract as if they did not relate; the opposite error to that committed by those who, maintaining relations to be external, treat them as if there were nothing for them to relate.

In the first place, relations are said to depend on qualities, and qualities on their relations, and this is thought to be contradictory. It could only be self-contradictory if the dependence were identical in the two cases. But Mr. Stout has pointed out that while relations depend on the qualities for their very being, qualities depend on their relations only for the fact that they are related, not for the qualities themselves. Thus the distance of Glasgow and Manchester arises from, depends on, is the manifestation of, the positions of those towns. But they do not owe their position to their distance, they only owe to it their distance. The towns must be there to be so many miles distant, but their distance is not something by itself which steps down and connects the town, but is the fact of their connection in space. Or, again, a man is a father because he is a male, whose functions have been realised; he does not owe his being a father to the paternal relation, but that relation implies his being a father.

[1] *Appearance and Reality*, ch. iii.

Mr. Stout has endeavoured[1] to simplify the discussion by adding to the notion of quality and relation that of "relatedness." Relations then depend on qualities for being what they are, but qualities depend on relations only for their relatedness. It is difficult to see, convincing as the argument is, that relatedness adds anything to enlighten the matter. It in fact suggests that relations can be relations without relatedness, that is without relating ; otherwise the distinction would not be drawn. This is the very proposition which is contested. We have the conception of qualities independent of relation and relation independent of relatedness. The last is not a fact. Nor is it true that qualities can exist outside some relation or other, though there may be a quality, *e.g.* maleness, which may exist outside the relation of paternity. But then the male quality is in certain relations of its own, of likeness and difference, to the female.

Qualities, terms, and relations are alleged to be "infected" with the evil of the so-called infinite regress. But this allegation appears once more to depend on the abstraction of relation from its business of relating, so that we have the ironical result that relations whose externality Mr. Bradley strenuously denies are treated in effect as if they were external. The relation it is urged is itself related to the qualities. The paternal relation is related to the father. Thus for a relation to be applied a new relation is required, not of course the same as the original relation or necessarily so ; and this intercalation of relations can plainly go on to infinity. But is it not clear that if a relation is itself in relation to its term, it is not doing its work of relating ? If it really relates, it relates ; by itself and without the interposition of a fresh relation. If A is the father of B, his paternity is continuous with, being the situation which connects, A and B. Similar considerations apply to a subtler form of the same supposition, that a relation can be one without relating. Consider

---

[1] *Proc. Arist. Soc.* N.S. vol. ii., 1901–2, 'Alleged self-contradictions,' etc., pp. 1 ff.

A as he is in the relation, say B, and as he is in himself,
say C. There is then a new relation between B and C
breaking out within A. But if B stands for a quality
outside the relation, like maleness outside paternity, it
is irrelevant, for this is not the quality which enters into
the relation. If it does not, and the quality in itself is
different from the quality in relation, the relation is being
regarded as external to the quality, in other words, as
not relating it to its correlative.

These reflections are, as it seems to me, sufficient to Space and
T me-
their alleged
inconsist-
ency.
show that relations between terms and qualities though
they present difficulties do not present inherent contradiction. But I am very ready to admit that in the form
in which I have presented them, in the insistence that a
relation must relate, there is an undercurrent which bears
us back continually to the real and given fact of continuity
contained in Space-Time, without which such a postulate
that a relation must relate loses concreteness. Now for
Mr. Bradley himself Space and Time are but special cases
of the difficulties of relation ; and he would repel the
assumption of an original continuity, because continuity
in its conceptual description is so patently a relation
between terms. For us the criterion of contradiction is a
derivative of Space-Time. For Mr. Bradley, Space and
Time are to be judged in respect of reality or appearance
by the human or reflective criterion of contradiction,
which draws its authority from our thought. We are
bound therefore to examine the alleged contradiction of
Space and Time independently, and our answer must be
that they seem contradictory because neither the Space
nor the Time which is examined is real Space or real
Time, I mean that it is not even the real appearance
which it is alleged to be. For each of them is supposed
really, and not merely as in mathematics provisionally, to
be distinct from the other. When this error of fact is
corrected, the arguments against their ultimate reality
are seen to be fragile.
Suppose then (what is not the case) that relations and
terms are only apparent characters of things, not ulti-

mately real ; and consider Space by itself. We may
plausibly maintain two propositions which seem to
contradict each other : first, Space consists of extended
substances (shall we say ?) ; and second, it is a mere
relation. It cannot be substances, or spaces, alone, for
these themselves contain parts and involve relation among
them ; and every term we choose for the relations
breaks up into relations without end. " Space is
essentially a relation of what vanishes into relations,
which seek in vain for their terms. It is lengths of
lengths of— nothing that we can find. On the other
hand it cannot be a mere relation. For every such
relation is a relation between terms which are themselves
Spaces." [1] Space is thus neither a relation nor anything
else, and the contradiction, even verbally, seems hopeless.
But the spaces are supposed to be resting and the
relations to be distinct from what they relate. Now
there is no such thing as resting Space. It is essentially
temporal. Spaces, if we could conceive them at all as
existing by themselves, might be stationary, and the
relation between two spaces might be a kind of mechanical
bond, a relation which does not relate. It might be
supposed even to be the connecting or intermediate space,
but there would be no cohesion, and hence the contradiction. But Space is spatio-temporal. Now Time is
of its essence fluid, is succession. The Time which
is in Space drives on any space into connection
with some other space, and secures to it continuity.
Thus spatial relation is of the very being of any two
spaces, for it is their connecting situation into which
they are compelled by their time. The terms and
the relations are distinguishable elements in one and
the same empirical fact which is spatio-temporal. For
the same reason any space breaks up into parts without end because the time which is in it distinguishes
it into parts within the original piece of space ; and
the infinity of this process being vital to space is not
the bad infinity which is the counterpart of our human
helplessness, but the good infinity which is implied

---

[1] *Appearance and Reality*, ch. iv. pp. 36-7 (ed. 1).

in the real nature of the thing[1] and is self-repre-
sentativeness.

Let us now turn to Time. If Time be taken apart
from Space it is, as we have so often seen, a mere 'now'
and can admit no before or after. The argument starts
by affirming, what is true, that the now of Time implies
before and after ; but it takes a somewhat different form
from the argument about Space. For there the parts of
Space are presented together. But when they are taken
apart from Space we cannot have present and past or
future presented together. "Presented time is time
present." But if the now involves before and after,
there is a relation between before and after, and the
puzzles of relation and its terms reappear. Either the
now is a duration and breaks up into parts or nows without end ; or if it is not a duration it becomes a relation
between terms which are in themselves timeless, for these
terms not containing a before or after are not time.
Duration is either substantive and breaks up into parts,
or a relation, or rather a number of relations, connecting
timeless elements and therefore not having the unity
necessary to time.

Now all this maze of difficulties (which I hope I have
rendered the spirit of) comes from neglecting the intrinsic
spatiality of Time. You may indeed admit that Time is
represented by a line. The mere pictorial representation
of Time by Space does not however help, for you are
then faced with the difficulties alleged against Space.
But if Space is of the very being of Time, Space sustains
Time as it fades into the past or dawns into the future.
It is then not true as an empirical fact that "presented
time is the present time." The now and the then are
presented as now and then, and are presented together
but not in the present of the enjoying consciousness but,
as befits them, the one in the present, the other in the
past.[2] The then is never a part or aspect of the now.
The now is continuous with the then which was and the

---

[1] For the distinction of the two sorts of infinite regress, see B.
Russell, *Principles of Mathematics*, ch. iv. pp. 50-1, § 55.

[2] Above, Bk. I. ch. iii.

then which is to be. Space gives to Time its continuity as Time gives to Space its continuity. Space enables Time to be Time, that is a duration of succession. Any relation between moments of time is then a piece of Time itself, and duration is not a relation of the timeless but of the timeful ; and while duration is made of the instants it connects, these instants are connected by duration. For the relation and the terms are of the same stuff. This possibility is overlooked by the antagonist view, just because Time is treated as unspatial, and consequently before and after have no attachment but are degraded into aspects of the so-called present. Just as Time drives the pieces of Space into connection, Space compels the moments of Time to remain attached, and not vanish into nothingness.

What Mr. Bradley has done then is to take a fictitious or abstract Space and Time and demonstrate that they are abstractions. The effort to show up abstractions can never be praised too much. But it is misdirected when it seeks to prove that realities, mis-described so as to be abstractions, are abstract. And now mark the revenge which the universe takes upon those who do not accept it upon its own conditions. Thought which sets up its canon of satisfactoriness to itself loses its contact with the world of Space and Time which it declares to be appearance. The "what" of things is severed from their "that" ; and thought moves in a world of its own. Thought which repudiates the Space-Time of which it is an element cannot be truly concrete.

Once more we return to the truth that the difficulties of continuity and infinity, of which these embarrassments as to Space and Time are examples, arise from neglecting the initial or crude continuity and infinity, positive characteristics, of Space - Time itself. The conceptual notions of continuity and infinity build up again the original which they have begun by dissecting. But it remains true that Space - Time itself in its empirical character is the basis of continuity and infinity, of order and series, and of all the categorial characters of things

which a thinking resting on human standards, not spatio-
temporal ones, seeks to degrade into realities which in
comparison with the ultimate are only appearances.[1]

[1] In a later chapter (*A. and R.* ch. xviii.), Mr. Bradley completes
his assault on Space and Time by suggesting that there may be more
than one Space or Time, and that in different Times the order may
be reversed. This raises questions which belong to a later stage, when
we are considering ideas in their relation to reality. I much regret
that my criticism of Mr. Bradley should be thus divided, but I cannot
discuss everything at once. (See Bk. III. ch. viii. Suppl. Note.)

CHAPTER V

ORDER

The category. IF order is a category it might seem eminently to be due to the interference of mind. The mind, it might be thought, compares things in respect of certain characters, *e.g.* magnitude or shades of colour, and arranges them in a scale in which any one thing precedes another and is in general between that other and some term which precedes itself.[1] But a moment's consideration is enough to show that such comparison depends on the characters and relations of the terms themselves, and, what is more pertinent, the acts which the mind performs in arranging terms in an order are themselves in order, only that the order is enjoyed instead of being contemplated. Thus if lines are ordered according to their increasing magnitude, the successive apprehensions of the lines are also ordered in magnitude.

We have order when there are at least three terms of which one is between the other two, that is, when B is between A and C. Order is a category of things because of betweenness of position in Space-Time. This betweenness is, as we have seen, a fundamental feature

[1] Compare B. Russell, *Principles of Mathematics*, § 231, p. 242, for the independence of order of any psychological element. "People speak of a series as consisting of certain terms *taken* in a certain order, and in this idea there is commonly a psychological element. All sets of terms have, apart from psychological considerations, all orders of which they are capable; that is there are serial relations, whose fields are a given set of terms, which arrange those terms in any possible order. . . . Omnipotence itself cannot give terms an order which they do not possess already : all that is psychological is the consideration of such and such an order."

in Time, and points in Space are between each other in virtue of the Time in which they are generated. What applies to positions in Space-Time applies equally to complexes in Space-Time. We may indeed have things or points which are contemporaneous. But they are between each other in space in virtue of the time in which their positions in space are generated. 'Between' is therefore a crude or elementary feature of Space-Time and attaches to the elements of Space-Time themselves and to complexes of those elements.

Betweenness which is the characteristic of order communicates with relation, and order may be resolved into relations. Thus, as Mr. Russell shows, terms x, y, z are in an order when there is a relation R such that x is in the relation R to y and y in the relation R to z, in other words, when there is a transitive relation between the terms, and it is asymmetrical. Thus if the relation is of magnitude, x is greater than y and y than z and x than z, and the relations of y to x and z have a different sense. If the terms are points of time y is before z and after x. This simplest of all orders is at the basis of all order. But though in this way order may be expressed in terms of relation, order is not a mere combination of relations. For the introduction of asymmetry into the transitive relation already implies betweenness. The transitive relation of equality of magnitude would not be sufficient for betweenness of magnitude. Such betweenness can only be generated by a relation which being transitive has direction and is therefore asymmetrical. Betweenness is a crude datum to which the conception of a transitive asymmetrical relation is due. Between is therefore as much a specific datum, though resoluble into two relations of different sense, as a motion along the diagonal is a specific motion though resoluble into components along the sides of the parallelogram. There, too, the mere components are not equivalent to the resultant unless they are really *components*, that is unless, in the language adopted by Mill, their collocation is also given. Betweenness being thus primordial, order is a category distinct from relation, just as existence is distinct from relation though existence is always in relation to other existence.

Order involves at least three terms, and any three terms may constitute an order, under the conditions in which order is expressed relationally. Each term in the order is ordered according to the nature of that order. But not each term is necessarily between other terms. This is only the case when the series has neither beginning nor end ; as in the case of instants or the real numbers. In the order of colours, in the order of precedence of nobility, in the order of species in a genus, and the like, there may be first or last terms or both which are not between in respect of that order ; though they will always be between in the fundamental order of Time or Space. Further it is clear that when two terms are said to be in a certain order, as *e.g.* cause and effect in the order of priority, or two colours in respect of the order of hue or brightness ; they are so described in so far as they are selected members from a real order : *e.g.* in causality the order of time.

A universal character of things.

Order is a difficult conception which I am unequal to the task of treating adequately.[1] What has concerned us here has been to indicate that like other categories it is a character of things which is a crude, primordial feature of Space-Time, and can only be indicated as such, or, if described, order is being described like continuity in terms of what is derived from it. It is difficult to discuss the conception at greater length at this stage, for the assurance that all order is in the end spatio-temporal can only be got from considering order in its more special determinations, like the order of numbers or of quantity, which we cannot yet assume to be spatio-temporal. Order has not usually been reckoned among categories at all, and does not form one of the Kantian categories. Yet that all things have order of some sort can readily be seen,

---

[1] Mr. Russell has treated it with great fulness, *Principles of Mathematics*, Pt. IV.

if it is only order of position in Time or Space, or quantitative or numerical order.

But the varieties of order are not only these categorial special orders but empirical ones ; and some of these may be enumerated. Most important of all, perhaps, is the order of the qualities of a given kind or modality of sensation ; for example, that of pitches of sound or hues of colour. Such order has of course no reference to the position of notes on a musical instrument like the piano, or of colours in the solar spectrum. It belongs to sounds or colours as experienced, that is as sounds or colours, which for us are sensa. It is an expression of their ultimate spatio-temporal character. Sounds form an order of pitches, ultimately because their wavelengths are a series in which each is spatio-temporally between two others, and could be known (not heard) as such if the sounds were produced from the one place. Mr. H. J. Watt has even maintained that pitches of sound and hues of colour are not differences of quality, but that there is only one quality, sound, or colour, and pitches and hues are merely terms in an order, determined by the one quality.[1] Whether the modalities or classes of sensible qualities themselves, sound, colour, taste, etc., constitute an order, cannot in the present state of our knowledge be asserted.

Besides this important example of empirical order we have such order as that of descent from father to child—the genealogical order, and we have the larger order of descent in animal types determined by distance from a common ancestor ; there is the order of great-

---

[1] 'The elements of experience and their integration : or modalism,' *Brit. Journ. of Psych.* vol. iv., 1911. See also further papers in vols. vi., 1913 ; vii., 1914 ; and his later work, *The Psychology of Sound* (Cambridge, 1917). I do not feel inclined to accept his statement that sound is a quality and pitches merely their order (see below, p. 267), but should regard them as intrinsically qualities forming an order of qualities. On the other hand, when we are dealing not with the sensa but with the sensing of them, we shall see that the corresponding sensings are merely spatio-temporal patterns of response which have no pitch-quality (nor sound quality either), and in respect of them Mr. Watt's doctrine is true.

ness from the merest weakling up to the superman, or in moral matters the order of merit which belongs to actions not in virtue of their goodness (for "all goodness ranks the same with God") but in respect of their largeness or splendour. And the list might be extended to some length. Order is therefore far from being confined to purely categorial orders with which the term is so closely associated in the mind. But it depends ultimately in every case on spatio-temporal betweenness.

Order and the other categories

Order communicates with existence, as being itself an existent, and as internally constituted of existents. It is relational in itself, and at the same time there may be relation between different orders, as for example in correlation of the order of general intelligence to order of sensibility in some department of sense. Lastly, it communicates with universality ; it is a plan. And not only is order universal with regard to its categorial special determinations, like the order of number, but all these categorial orders are universal in respect of their empirical examples ; thus we may arrange things in weight or brightness, or even numerical order may assume such particular forms as the order of even or odd or square numbers.

While order thus communicates with universality, its distinctness from universality is a more important matter, and at the same time more difficult to make clear. When points are considered in their order of position, the transitive relation is that of greater (or less) distance from a fixed member of the series (whether distance is taken as equivalent to interval or distance proper, that is unlikeness of position). The relation, distance from a given point, is universal to any of the distances of the points from the fixed point. But then it is not this distance which is the order itself ; that order can be resolved into those relations, but is not identical with them. The order is rather that of position in the ordered series, and this is not the universal of the different positions in the series, but is the collective name of all the positions. There is no true universal or plan of construction, to be called position in the series, of which the members of the series are modifications as different dogs are modifications of the plan or law of dog-construction. For position in the series or order implies the order as a whole. To hold that belief would be an instance of the concrete universal over again, like regarding the parabola as the universal of its points, or the State as the universal of its citizens, or the self as the universal of its activities. For a less elementary illustration let us turn to Mr. Watt's conception of pitches as the order of the one quality sound, or colours as the order of colour. It does indeed seem unnatural to hold that there is only one quality sound or colour ; rather it would seem that, according to common usage, the pitches and hues are qualities which are ordered in respect of sound or colour. But what is of value in the doctrine is that it recognises order as an intrinsic (I should say categorial) character of the pitches and hues, and sound as such and colour as such are then orders named from the qualities of their members. Now neither sound nor colour is a true universal. There is no quality colour of which the various hues are instances, nor, though this is more difficult to verify, is there probably for experience any universal, sound, of which the various pitches are modifications, certainly no true universal, pitch. In both cases we are considering the colour or sound psychologically as experienced, that is as sound or colour, and not as physical complexes which follow a certain law, in which case both sound and colour are universals. This difference between the relation of colour to the colours, and that of a universal like dog to individual dogs, has long been observed. Mr. Watt's conception enables us to say that colour is the order of colours, and is, I should say, not itself a quality ; and the like is probably true of sounds. Thus the order of individuals is not their universal ; and individuals regarded as instances of a universal are not considered as ordered in respect of that universal.

Thus order is a characteristic of every existent, distinct

from other such pervasive characteristics, and communicating with them ; and it appears undoubtedly to be a category and on the same level of rank [1] with existence, relation, and universality.

[1] For rank among the categories see later, chap. ix. pp. 322 ff.

CHAPTER VI

SUBSTANCE, CAUSALITY, RECIPROCITY

A. SUBSTANCE [1]

ALL existents, being complexes of space - time, are The category. substances, because any portion of Space is temporal or is the theatre of succession ; or what is the same thing because all succession is spread out in space. In other words, spaces and durations are not themselves substances as if substance were a notion anterior to them and applied to them ; but because Space-Time is what it is, and every space is a duration and every duration an extension in space, substance is a determination of all things which occupy Space and Time. We are introduced here to a category which arises not so much out of the character of spatio-temporality taken as a whole given entity as out of the 'relation' (if we may misapply a word strictly applicable only to pieces of Space-Time [2]) between the spatial and the temporal elements in any space - time. For simplicity and brevity it will be enough to speak of substance as a piece of Space which is the scene of succession without stating the same thing in terms of Time, in the reverse order. Any existent is a substance in this account of the matter. Even a simple motion in

---

[1] For the subjects of this chapter, especially Substance, I have found much profit in Mr. C. D. Broad's *Perception, Physics, and Reality* (Cambridge, 1914), ch. ii. 'On Causation.' For substance, see especially pp. 94-6, which confirmed and helped me in views which were already in formation in my own mind. I have borrowed some of his language and illustrations.

[2] On the use of the word relation as between the space and time elements themselves, see some further remarks later, ch. ix. p. 324.

a straight line is an extreme instance of the life of a substance, though the motion be not repeated and the substance endures or remains identical only for the duration of the single motion.

But it will be easier to deal first with what are ordinarily called things which possess many qualities connected together, and to consider simpler substances in the light of the more complex ones. Qualities it is assumed are correlated with certain motions ; and it is indifferent for our purpose whether the quality belongs, as will be here maintained, to the motion itself ; or belongs to mind and is the mental correlate of the motion, as is the belief of those who distinguish primary from secondary qualities, but recognise a primary correlate of the secondary quality. A thing or complex substance is then a contour of space (*i.e.* a volume with a contour) within which take place the motions correlated to the qualities of the thing ; and the complex substance or thing is the persistence in time of this spatial contour with its defining motions. Thus movements correlated with the quality yellow and others correlated with the quality hard are contained within the contour of the atom or molecule of gold. Within the contour the qualities are grouped according to the law of the construction of the substance. The various movements which constitute what has been before called that 'configuration' of space-time which the thing is, define a certain outline of space, that is, a certain volume of space with its outline. As Time moves on the substance may change in its characters or in the relation of them one to the other but always within the limits set by the law of its construction. Our most easily understood example of substance is found in our own mind. There the activities of mind change from one moment to another according to the objects which engage it. Sometimes indeed the consciousness located in one portion of the extended mind lapses into unconsciousness. But always we have under the various changes in the distribution of our attention in Time the same relative configuration of movements within the total outline occupied by our minds. It is the persistence of this including space throughout a lapse of time, a persistence which means, as we have seen in our original account of Space-Time, a ceaseless redistribution (in the form of motions) of instants of time amongst points of space, which makes our minds a substance and a substantial identity. Or we may take as another instance an organism with different activities in different parts of the structure, all these activities constituting a configuration of space - time bounded within the space of the organism. Or we may, as on previous occasions, consider the organism as a substance from the point of view of the changing distribution in the maturity of its cells.

The persistence of a piece of Space in Time which results from the retention of the configuration of its movements according to its law of construction does not of course imply that the piece of Space is stationary as a whole. On the contrary, no substance occupies the same place continuously, if only because of the movement of the earth or other heavenly body, and it may change its place also by locomotion or transference. But the contour and internal configuration remain within limits the same, though not the position of the whole thing.

The movements underlying qualities may be complex and the configurations of a thing with qualities is undoubtedly very complex. In a simpler substance such as a vibratory movement which has the quality sound, the excursion of the vibration fills and defines a certain contour of space and a comparatively simple one. When we come to the simplest substance of all, the life of which is movement in a straight line, what we have is the occupation of the most elementary contour in space, viz. a point by an instant in time. To understand such simplicity we had first to understand the nature of more complex substances. It might be thought that the whole excursion of the point was the contour of the substance. But in fact the sweep of the movement is comparable to the translation of our mind (or say our body) as we move ; only that in the simpler case the translation is the very essence of the life of the point whereas the essence of the life of the mind as mind is in the movements which take place within the mind's spatial contour. For the point-instant is of itself motion, it is the element of motion. A point is not a stable or fixed thing but in virtue of its time is connected with some other point-instant. The meaning of motion is, as was noted before, not that the point of space itself moves as if it were a material body shifting its place, but that the time of a point ceases to be present, and the present is transferred to another point continuous with it. That is to say, the contour of the substance remains the same as the original point. The simplest substance is consequently a movement. When we take this movement in its limiting form we have the point-instant, which may thus be called a momentary substance. For a point-instant is by its very nature a movement, not something statical. It is an ideal, not an actual movement ; and just for this reason it is the actual elementary existent, and is real just in virtue of its ideal character.[1] The conception of substance at this limit, at which it becomes momentary, is hardest to grasp, and I may add rewards most when it is grasped.

Identity of substance. The identity of a substance is individual identity as persisting through a duration of time. Numerical identity was occupation of a point-instant or complex of them. Generic identity or identity of sort was the preservation of a plan of construction throughout repetition at different times or places. When the repetition of a plan is found in its varying phases in the duration of an individual we had individual identity. We see now that substantial identity is equivalent to individual identity. Before, under individual identity we were thinking of the universality of the plan of a particular in respect of the moments of its life. The notion of substantial identity represents these moments as woven together through the constant changes of its internal motions in accordance with a plan of construction. Individuality regards the repeated plan ; substantial identity the persistence of the particularised universal or individual through a period of time. In practice substantial identity and individuality

[1] See on this subject later, ch. ix. p. 325.

are the same conception ; and by the individuality of a thing is meant in general its identity of substance. This combines then the two elements of repetition of a plan with persistence of the contour of space within which the motions take place which obey the plan. Personal identity is a special instance of substantial identity. It means the coherence of our mental life within an extension which is occupied variously through the changing moments of our life. Only since the enjoyed spatial extension of our mind is overlooked we are apt to think of it as merely coherence in time, as if there could be such coherence except for the space which establishes it. In all cases it is the spatial contour which provides the unity of substance, that spatial extent being itself meaningless without motions to occupy it, that is without persistence in time.[1]

What changes are compatible with the retention of substantial identity is an empirical question which can only be decided by reference to each case or kind of cases. In the first place, it does not follow that qualities are always localised in the same part of the volume of the space or substance, though this appears to be the case with minds where the kinds of consciousness corresponding to certain objects are more or less definitely restricted in locality. Even organic bodies may change colour in different places as when we blush, or as in the crustaceans before mentioned which change their colour with the time of day. Under this head would come the famous question of Sir John Cutler's stockings which had been so darned with green silk that not a thread of the original black silk was left. Were the stockings the same or not ? It would seem to be the case that though the stockings were not in the end of the same material the configuration of the motions within the substance had been preserved. In the all-important matter the substance had not ceased to be a stocking and retained its empirical identity.

In the second place, the contour itself may vary within limits without destroying the constructive plan, and so far

---

[1] For the problems raised by the lapse of intervals of mental life from our consciousness see later, Bk. III. chs. i. A and vi.

as this is the case the identity of substance remains. The main distinction of aggregates and organised beings lies in this, that an aggregate may be diminished without essential alteration, except naturally of those characters which depend on the aggregation as such, *e.g.* magnitude of the substance or strength of the material. This is because the components of such secondary substances are alike. Even here if a block of marble is chipped it is difficult, if the process of chipping continues long enough, to call the remainder the same marble ; there is only a piece of it, the substance remains the same only generically. Organisms grow, and parts may be removed, it is found in experience, without destroying the identity of the substance, though the contour may be much altered, as by the loss of a limb. Everything depends on the importance of what is lost for the plan of the whole. We can only note these limits as they occur in experience. A man may lose a leg and not be much altered, while an atom may lose two alpha particles and become a different chemical body.

The empirical questions as to the preservation of the identity of mind and how, when it is ruptured, it may be revived, questions which have already been hinted at, will meet us again at a later stage of the inquiry. Another question belongs entirely to a later stage, and that is the relation of a thing or substance to its appearances ; which of its appearances belong to the thing itself, which are mere appearances and imply something else in addition. This question, as indicated by the word appearance, concerns the connection of a thing with the mind or other ' percipient ' and belongs to the empirical relations of things.[1] Here we have considered substance, as a union of qualities, as it is in itself.

That unity then is supplied by the space (that is the space-time) within which the qualities are disposed. Each quality inheres in the substance because it is included in the space which unifies the substance. Thus the proposition, this sugar is sweet, means that the universal sweet in an individualised shape, that is as a definite and

---

[1] Book III. chs. vii., viii.

particular motion, is found within the volume of the sugar. There is a complete difference between such a proposition and one in which the predicate is the class-concept of the thing, *e.g.* this is sugar, where the predicate is the total plan of configuration which determines the contour of the space of the substance.

A conclusion of some importance seems to be implied in this conception of substance. Not only is the inherence of the sweetness and the whiteness merely the fact that the motions correspondent to these qualities occur within the contour of the substance, but these motions occur in different places. The qualities of a substance do not interpenetrate. It can only be supposed that they do, if qualities are treated as mental creations or ideas and, because they are such, are somehow regarded as not being in space or time. But the motions at any rate which correspond to the qualities are separate from one another and differently located. They seem to interpenetrate only because not distinguished in our apprehension. The motion of whiteness (which for us is white) may to our coarse apprehension be in the same place as the sweetness ; and we may say the sugar is white and sweet all over. But two different motions, when not com-pounded into a single-resultant motion, do not occupy precisely the same place. One may take place in the interstices of the other, as it were, and be indistinguish-able for us in locality. When a body is sweet and white all over, the motions of whiteness and sweetness are repeated in various places and intermixed, as blue and red points of colour may be dotted over a page one set among the other. The motions of white are spread over the volume like stippled points in an engraving and the sweetness motions among them. Just as blood is seen uniformly red though only the red corpuscles in it are red, so the sweet and white stippling gives the impression (through different senses) of a uniformly sweet white thing.[1]

> [1] The above applies, at any rate directly, only to qualities (*a*) of different modality, (*b*) on the same level ; *e.g.* the different secondary qualities of matter, of which I am mainly thinking. As to (*a*), the mole-

Qualities d penetrate

Thus a substance in respect of its qualities may be described as a space of a certain contour stippled over with qualities. There is no pretence of any mysterious support of qualities, such as Berkeley shrunk from and thought to be a "brute senseless somewhat." The support of qualities is nothing more nor less than the space-time within whose spatial contour they are united, they themselves being parts of the space, whose contour their configuration defines. For though we have spoken mainly for convenience of the space-contour, yet remembering that substance is persistence of this spatial contour through time, each moment of the substance being a particular of which the law of configuration is the universal (the singular universal), we must think of substance as a specially defined volume of space-time. The substance may be material or mental or living. But ultimately the substantiality of it is its defined volume of space-time.

Connection of qualities.

Within this volume the motions to which qualities belong are, primarily speaking, juxtaposed. But their relation is more than is expressed by the somewhat depreciatory name of juxtaposition. One of the great difficulties that have been felt as to the reality of substance is that it appears to be a mere aggregate of qualities. Sugar is sweet and white and hard and the like. But Space and Time are continuous, and to be within a volume of space-time is to be connected by a space-time. And in saying this we need take no account of the

---

cules of a tuning-fork vibrate with a single vibration compounded of those of the fundamental tone and the overtones. Is there here a single quality, or several separate qualities heard confusedly ? (*b*) A higher quality, life, is a movement (see Book III. ch. ii. B) of living substance which carries with it movements, say of colour, in the material parts. I do not discuss these difficulties.

For the question under (*a*), see F. Brentano's *Untersuchungen zur Sinnespsychologie* (Leipzig, 1907), an extraordinarily stimulating book, to which I shall have to refer hereafter (Bk. III. ch. v., on the intensity of sensations). He speaks, however, of psychological sensory contents and the space of sensation (*Empfindungsraum*), not as I do of external qualities in an external Space.

purely empirical fact that within a substance which is compound there may be empty space-times or pores not included in the substance itself. How far the empty space-time, empty that is of qualities, belongs to the substance or not is an empirical affair. The space-time within which the electrons of the atom are supposed to circle about their nucleus, is perhaps not a pore in the substance but part of it, just as are the interstellar spaces of the solar system. On the other hand, the pores in a sponge do not belong to the substance of the sponge.

Now the space-time within which the motions are found which have their qualities (if they have any) makes these qualities into a continuum. Such an answer is sufficient. But more exact and explicit description of their connection is desirable. To supply this is a difficult matter, but it must be attempted. We have first to refer back to the general account of Space-Time. Structure we saw was provided for by the fact that any instant is repeated in Space, and there is therefore intrinsic simultaneity of certain points. Now given this fundamental connection as a basis, different lines of advance from it will leave us with events in the substance which are simultaneous with one another though of different qualities. Thus at least a whiteness and a sweetness condition of the substance may co-exist, not in virtue of a direct connection between whiteness and sweetness but as the joint outcome of processes beginning with the primordial connection. Qualities would on this showing be connected together by a remoter relation. This corresponds to the familiar (Lockeian) notion that the various qualities of a substance are traceable to the nature of the primary qualities of their primitive constituents. The correspondence is of course not exact but on the contrary very inexact. But it consists in this, that the multiplicity of properties of a substance is not haphazard but rooted in some simple state of affairs which enables many qualities to belong together within one contour and to be in part simultaneous. For though any substance is, like the universe as a whole, doing its work at different times in its different parts when considered with reference to some point-instant of it, there must be structure and simultaneity for it to be a substance at all. (This statement includes at the limiting case a simple movement.) A body, for instance, could not be dying all at once in every cell if it is to be a continuous structure. It was only the gradual darning of the black silk stockings with green silk which prevented them from being another pair of stockings. It is of course empirical what original movements are provided for in the substance. But an empirical connection is not the same thing as a purely haphazard one of mere juxtaposition.

But besides the remoter connection of organised movements, with their qualities, there is also the direct interconnection of qualities or movements such as is illustrated for us in the mutual support of the functions of an organic body by one another, the sustainment of nervous action, for instance, by nutrition, and the regulation of nutrition by nervous action. Here we have reciprocal action of different substances within the whole substance. This reciprocity means causal relation within the substance and is only possible through the connecting space-time. Reciprocity we propose to discuss presently. Now reciprocal actions are at a certain instant of time simultaneous ; and so far as there is mutual interaction between movements within a substance there is a more special simultaneity of events within it.

On both grounds we are able to understand, though I confess the matter is difficult and the account given of it inadequate, how a substance can have many qualities at the same time. The connection in whatever form is a spatio-temporal one.

B. Causality

Space-Time or the system of motion is a continuous The category. system, and any motion within it is continuous with some other motion. This relation of continuity between two different motions is causality, the motion which precedes that into which it is continued in the order of time being the cause and the other the effect. Motion, like murder, will out, and no motion is indifferent to other motions within the universe. Thus the contraction of certain muscles in a boy's hand and arm is transformed into or continued into or replaced by certain intramolecular movements in a stone which constitute a translation of the stone at a certain velocity ; this motion is transformed into the shattering of the window which the stone strikes. A blow from a bullet on a target is transformed into motions in the target which constitute a dent in it. An electric stimulation of a nerve ending is transformed into a movement up the nerve (I will not attempt to characterise the intimate nature of the movement, which is of a highly complicated sort) which ends ultimately in a sensation, which is itself a movement (or is correlated with one). A dose of digitalis so affects the pneumogastric nerve as to end in a cessation of the heart's action, which is equivalent to a new set of intramolecular movements in the heart and is not a bare negative, but only a negative of its previous actions. The motion of light, that is a motion of a complex sort in the supposed ether, at any rate the motion belonging to that substance which is light, is transformed into certain motions in a photographic plate, of a chemical order.[1]

It is immaterial, with our metaphysical conception of Causality a substance, whether we describe a cause in popular a Substance

[1] I have been helped in this chapter by Mr. Broad's discussion of causality (*Perception*, etc., ch. ii.).

language as a thing or substance affecting some other thing or substance and producing an effect in it, or in the stricter language of the logicians call the cause an event or process which precedes another event or process and without which the second event or process, the effect, does not exist. I say 'does not exist' in place of the common phrase 'would not exist,' for our only means of knowing what would or would not, or can or cannot, exist is to discover what does or does not exist. The popular notion of a cause as a thing is inadequate, for a thing can only be a cause in respect of the events in which it is concerned. On the other hand, the logical notion of causality as a connection of events is inadequate so long as an event is regarded as an isolated occurrence and not as a process which if the event is a cause is continued into the event which is its effect. With such static or statuesque isolation of its events the causal relation is a piece of philosophical mythology. But a substance is a system of motions and whether the cause is a substance or a motion is all one. A cause is the motion of a substance, or a substance in respect of its motion. Thus the cause of the breaking of the window-pane is the motion of the stone or the stone in motion. There need not be for the causal relation any other substance than the motion itself. A thing in motion is only a very complex substance in motion. We have no difficulty in conceiving the substance of light as causing a chemical effect, even without introducing the notion of an etherial substance in which that motion is conveyed. The real reason why it is preferable to describe a cause wholly in terms of motion is that a thing is causal of its effect only in respect of the motion which is concerned. Thus a heavy stone breaks the window-pane in virtue of its velocity and mass. A grain of sand propelled with the same velocity might not have the same effect. We introduce the stone in order to note the mass which is engaged. But a thing may contain many qualities which are unessential to the effect. Thus, for example, a blow with a bat on the head or a blow with equal force of impact from an iron billet will produce the same effect. It is the business of science to disengage in the action of substances what is the part essential to the effect. The rest admits of variation. The thing may be in this sense only the vehicle of the cause, in Bacon's phrase. The real cause is the motions which are continued into the motion which is the effect.

Causality is thus the relation of continuity between one substance and another, whether those substances be things or merely motions which we are not in the habit of calling things (*e.g.* light). The causal relation is the obverse side of the existence of a substance. For the category of substance communicates with that of existence. Every substance occupies a space-time. Now existence is other than and continuous with other existence, or it is in relation to other existence. Hence a substance, having existence, is at once different from another substance and continuous with some other substance. But all continuity is continuity of space-time; it is not merely stationary continuity but a moving one. Causality is thus the spatio-temporal continuity of one substance with another; and the cause is the motion which precedes that into which, let us say, it passes or is transformed. For we can find no words to describe something so elementary as this primitive crude relation except we borrow from particular instances of it, such as are implied by 'transformation' or 'passing into' or other such language. Substances share in the relational element of existence and that character of them is their causality in respect of some other substance.

One matter of importance should be noted before we proceed. A substance or motion or group of motions is causal only if it is continued into a different motion. Thus there is no causality in the continuance without change of the same motion. A body perseveres according to the first law of motion in its state of uniform motion in a straight line unless subjected to the action of an impressed force. But we cannot say that the earlier part of the motion is the cause of the later

Causality and uniform motion.

into which it is continued. For the later part of the unchanged motion is the original motion or substance. The bare continuance of a motion signifies no causal action from something else. Indeed the first law, if I may venture on the statement, does little more than say this. It declares that any motion is as such a uniform motion, and that its path should be a straight line hardly adds to our knowledge, for it is probably true that the very definition of a straight line is that it is the path of a uniform motion ; the fact of uniform, that is unaccelerated and unaltered, motion being anterior to the notion of a straight line. It is only when motion suffers some change of acceleration or direction that it postulates a·cause, and we then ask what motion it was preceding this result which was continued into the change. For the continuity of a cause with its effect means not that the cause is as it were lost in the substance which it affects, but that it is added to the motions already existing there. Hence the very different effect produced by one and the same cause in different substances. The stone which breaks a window-pane may only bury itself in a soft window-cushion or a mound of earth.

Thus the continuance of a motion requires no cause but that motion of which the uniform motion is the effect and this is different from it. A motion does not cause its own continuance, is not as it were the cause of itself, but is itself. Self-causality, so far as that notion is legitimate, requires a different interpretation.

The purpose of this observation is to guard against a mistaken doctrine that the cause of an event is the immediately preceding state of the thing in which the event occurs. For this would allow the position of a body in uniform motion to be due to its preceding position. Causality would become an insignificant notion if it could be applied with this looseness. There is an additional objection to the doctrine. It implies that a causal process can be treated as a succession of states, the proviso being that they shall be in immediate sequence. But there is no such thing as immediate sequence in a continuous series, the very nature of which that there is no next term to any term. A cause is not an event followed by another event, as if the events were states of a substance. For out of such events neither continuity nor substance could be constructed. A state which is the cause of another state of the same thing can only be an ideal section of a process or motion. And thus interpreted, the proposition that any state of a thing is the effect of a preceding state can only mean, if it is to be true to Space-Time, that motions at any instant are continued into different motions by what is called immanent causality.

All causality being the continuous passage of one motion or set of motions into a different one is transeunt. Immanent causality is nothing but transeunt causality between the substances which are contained within a substance. Thus, for instance, the passage of the thought of an action within our minds into the realisation of that thought in actual fact is (in part) immanent causality. A better example would be the internal repression of a wish where the whole action seems to go on within the mind, though undoubtedly it requires the presence of the body. The intramolecular actions of a body, or the interactions between the parts of an organic system, or the interconnection of movements within the system of an atom are other cases of immanent causality. The distinction is clearly a relative one, and merely a matter of convenience in description. A case of transeunt causality between two independent substances like the cricket-ball and the bat is immanent causality, if the ball and the bat and the intervening space are taken to be a single substance, as they may with perfect legitimacy be taken to be.

Moreover, the distinction is relative in another and more important sense. No substance is self-contained as being disconnected from the rest of Space-Time, and therefore from other substances. The immanent causality of an organism is sustained by the environment. Nervous action is affected immanently by nutrition,

Transeunt and immanent causality.

but nutrition is an effect of external substances, and nervous action contains essentially motor-response to the surroundings. When a thought brings about its own realisation in an act of will the immanent process is the transition of the thought into a perception and that is purely mental, but it implies the action of the body on its surroundings so as to produce the physical conditions, *e.g.* the lifted weight, which are perceived in the act of perception. To suppose an absolutely self-contained substance is in fact to omit the fact that it belongs to Space-Time, or rather perhaps it is to suppose that the Space in which it exists is stagnant instead of being essentially temporal. Even an atom is but a substance precipitated within the matrix in which all substance grows. The only self-contained reality in which all causality is immanent is the universe itself, and its immanent causality is but the transeunt causality of the existents it contains. But the infinite whole itself is not a cause, for the categories are only determinations of finites or other beings within Space-Time which these parts of the whole owe to the properties of any space-time. Thus when the universe is spoken of as self-causing, this is either an illegitimate phrase, used metaphorically of the whole ; or, when it is used with a clear apprehension of its meaning, it signifies only that the various movements within the world are the outcome of other movements in a different distribution. In other words, the immanent causality of the universe is, to repeat ourselves, only another way of expressing that every existent in the world is in causal relation with other existents. Only in this sense is the world *causa sui*. All other self-causality is relative, it merely omits the dependence of the substance on the rest of Space-Time.

Summary. Causation is thus a perfectly definite character of things ; it is the continuity of existents within continuous Space-Time as subsisting between substances, which are themselves motions or groups of motions. Like all the categories it is pervasive and no substance escapes it. Causality is nothing less than this fundamental relation between substances. But it is also nothing more. No conception has been so persistently riddled with criticism. It has been declared from the point of view of logic to be either useless or superficial ; from that of metaphysics to be self-contradictory. All these complaints seem to me to depend on taking it either to be more than it is and to have a meaning other than that which it has in the usage of science and especially of physics ; or else to take it for less than it is, and to omit its characteristic features. To consider these criticisms in detail would be a task of much time, and all that I can hope to do is to touch upon them and in the main to let the exposition speak for itself. But before doing so it will be better to complete the positive exposition of causality, though there will necessarily be a latent reference to destructive criticism.

In the first place, then, the cause is a different motion or set of motions from the effect. The mere continuance of the same uniform motion is as we have seen not a causal connection. The only identity between cause and effect is to be found in their continuity. We are not even to suppose that the moment at which the cause takes effect or the effect begins to be caused is as it were a meeting-point of the two motions ; as if there were some single point in which the two processes overlapped. The continuity of the causal relation would be destroyed by the supposition. It would be a revival in a new form of the ancient puzzles of motion and the paradox of Achilles : the causal motion and the effect motion being broken up into steps of a progression. If this were the case the cause would not produce its effect, nor the effect begin, the point in question being the limit which the cause would tend to but never reach.

It might be urged that the cause is actually carried over into the effect ; as when, to take a very simple case, a shove on a moving body accelerates its motion. But this is no mere persistence of the original motion ; that motion is replaced by the acceleration of another motion. When the stone shatters the window there is not even the semblance of its continuance. The cause is

Cause and effect different

only continued in the resultant of itself and the original motion of the patient. Now a resultant is what it is and different from the components. Other cases of a qualitative sort may mislead similarly, like Hegel's example of the rain, which is the same water in the air and in the ground which it wets. Really, the effect is something quite dissimilar : the falling water is distributed differently from the resting water. In the action of digitalis on the heart, not even such accidental simplicity is to be found. The effect need not be like the cause and rarely is. And it never is identical with the cause. That would be uniform motion and the universe would be a blank.

Cause prior to effect.   Causality is essentially a temporally continuous relation and the cause is prior to the effect. Movements, and substances generally, may be simultaneous with each other but the relation is not one of causality. It is either, first, that of reciprocity where action and reaction are simultaneous ; but a reaction is not the effect of the action but is the answering causality of the patient on the agent. This covers the simultaneous existence of qualities in the one substance where the qualities affect each other mutually. Or, second, the simultaneity may be the persistence of the same effect owing to the persistence of the cause ; so that the effect of one dose of the cause is simultaneous with the next dose of the cause. In this way things, as bearers or vehicles of cause, and effect are simultaneous but not the cause simultaneous with its effect, not the particular dose of the cause simultaneous with its own effect. Or we may have simultaneity of motions which arise from points inherently contemporaneous. Otherwise simultaneity of cause and effect does not exist and would imply that the relation was merely a spatial one.

As it has been urged that cause and effect are identical with one another, so likewise it has been urged that cause, as it takes effect, occurs at the same instant with the effect as that effect begins. But this is either a tautology, or is untrue. The cause is the process in so far as it precedes the effect and the desire to find an identity of time between the two arises again, it is probable, from supposing the moments of the process to be contiguous instead of continuous.

It is essential therefore to causality that causation proceeds from before to after. Consequently it is only in a logical sense that the effect can be held to determine the cause as much as the cause the effect. We can only mean by this that when the cause and the effect are precisely stated they are reciprocal : when the cause, that is, is purged of what may indeed occur in a particular case but is accidental to it, and when the effect is stated in terms so precise as to presuppose one cause only and not a choice of several ; when, to take the familiar example, the death from drowning is distinguished from the death by hanging, and the two not lumped together under the general designation of death. The reciprocity of cause and effect means then that unless there were the precise effect there would not be the precise cause. But such determination is logical and not real determination, and the effect cannot be interchanged with cause except as a basis of inference. We cannot in any real sense therefore say that the future determines the present, for the future is not yet and a future event introduces the order of Time. In that order the future does not determine but is determined. The present would not be what it is unless it causes the future which it actually does cause, but to regard it as dependent, except in the above logical sense, on the future is to take Time half as an accidental feature of the universe and to contemplate the world as spatial instead of spatio-temporal. Thus it is in no sense true that the future drags the present into its future condition as if it operated *a fronte*. All causality is *a tergo*.

This might seem to contradict what was said in an earlier chapter [1] of the experience of the future in enjoyment. We anticipate something in our minds and this anticipation was described as the enjoyment of the future, not as present but as future. Now such anticipation leads on to performance, and hence it would seem that in this case

[1] Book I. ch. iv.

at any rate the future is causal. Why not therefore extend this consideration and explain teleological action as action which is determined by the future end to be attained ; so that animals and men are dragged to their issues from the future ? The answer to this is to distinguish between the future event as it will be when it is actual, in which case it becomes not future but present ; and the future as it is enjoyed, before it is realised. Such enjoyment is the future in idea, and this is the only way in which the future as future can be enjoyed. This future enjoyment is causal to its own realisation as a present. But this enjoyment drives us not *a fronte* but *a tergo* like all other causality. The transition is still from the before to the after. For the future as future precedes the future as it is when it has become a present and precedes it in the order of my enjoyment. In the same way my enjoyment of the past as past precedes in my enjoyment, as it should, the real present, for it is only by dragging the past up from the depths of memory, "the dark backward of time," that I enjoy it as past. When, on the other hand, the future is said in any other than a purely logical sense to determine the present (just as much as the past obviously does), the future is taken to mean the actual distant event, and then the statement is untrue and falsifies the significance of Time. If Time be taken seriously all causality proceeds from actual present to actual future, and is never determined by the actual future. It may be determined by the future as future but this forms no exception to the proposition.

Causality
11
relation.

Finally, the causal relation is a relation of existents. One substance is the agent and the other its patient which suffers its effect. Agent and patient together form a relatively closed system and, as we have seen, within that system the causality is immanent. There is no causal relation between the infinite whole and any one of its parts. There is only such relation between one part and another. The whole system of things does not descend into the arena and contend with one of its creatures. The business of science in its search for causes (and it is not asserted that this constitutes the whole business of

science) is to discover what precise events are connected
as causes with what other precise events as effects.   The
task may be one of infinite difficulty and may at best lead
only to probable propositions.   The rules of the logic of
discovery are rules of procedure in this quest.   Where
the causal connection can be established, it is done by an
elaborate machinery of negative instances, by which the
cause is narrowed down so as to contain only so much
as is relevant to the effect.[1]   Where experiment is not
possible other devices of approximation have to be used
which supply the place of experiment.   In the amusing
prelude of the *Sophist*, Plato attempting to get a definition
of the sophist employs his method of division in order
to "hunt the sophist down to his lair."   What science
does is to hunt down the cause of an effect to its lair.   It
may not establish exact connection but only a remote
one.   Yet it seeks, in the phrase of Mr. Venn, to screw
the causal circumstances up closer and closer to the effect.
This procedure is not open to the objection that the only
satisfactory statement of a cause is the whole universe.
If this were true the idea of cause would indeed retain a
certain usefulness in practice, but as a theoretical basis of
procedure in science it would be useless.   But the
objection rests on a misconception.   It assumes that the
operation of the stars is a motion which interferes with
the causal act by which a man knocks another down ; and
does so because there is direct or indirect connection
between all parts of the universe, throughout Space-Time.
The question rather is whether the intimate causal relation
mentioned is interfered with by the rest of the universe
which undoubtedly sustains it.   The question is the same
as when we ask whether the properties of a triangle which
undoubtedly imply the Space from which the triangle is
delimited are affected by the sustaining and surrounding
space.   What science has to do is just to discover these
limited, intimate, relations of existents which are called
causal ones.   Everything which it finds by inquiry
relevant has to be included and becomes part of the
substances involved.   Everything which, though its

[1] Bosanquet's *Logic*, vol. ii. ch. iv. pp. 115 ff. (eds. 1 and 2).

presence is assumed, does not interfere so as to control or vitiate, lapses for the special causal relation into the position of an immaterial condition. So much at least follows from the fact that the world itself is not a category and cannot be a cause.

Causality, no power, nor force.

We can now ask how far the modest but pervasive category of causality is open to the objections raised against it, which have grown into a formidable revolt against its authority. Hume's great service to this topic was that he purified the notion of causality of anthropomorphism ; he denied or rather he failed to find in experience any power in the cause to produce the effect or any necessity in their conjunction. It is true he read experience amiss. For though no cause exhibits mysterious power, it possesses a relation of connection which Hume with his inherited conception of an atomic experience made up of single and isolated pieces was unable to detect. Subsequent philosophy has been engaged in restoring the connection which he overlooked. But the spectre of power and necessity which Hume laid has been busy with men's minds and is accountable for the discredit upon which causality has fallen.

No notion of power or necessity is contained in the conception of causality as a category. Still less is the connection an anthropomorphic one. The experience we have in our own persons of causality is so far from giving us a notion of mysterious and unexplained efficacy or power, that it is but an example of the same relation as we find outside ourselves in external events. Rather we must say that power is the continuous connection which we observe in ourselves and can more easily and directly observe in ourselves in enjoyment than outside us in contemplated events. Our power is an instance of causality ; causality is not the work of power. But since the idea of a power in the cause to produce its effect suggests that the relation is presided over by something akin to spirit,[1] some entity behind the relation which

---

[1] In the sequel (Bk. III. ch. ii. B) it will be maintained that ultimately there is in all things something which corresponds to spirit in ourselves.

brings it into existence, we are perhaps well rid of the conception which is harmless if it were once " defecated " in Coleridge's famous phrase, " to a pure transparency." Defecated conceptions still retain their body and colour in the general mind.

We need therefore shed no tear over power ; and we may view with equal equanimity the discredit of force which has followed power or is in course of following it to the place where those notions are preserved, which are not so much false in themselves as such that the mind cannot safely be trusted to use. With power in the cause to produce the effect may go necessity of connection. The only necessity which philosophy can recognise is that of inference. But there is no necessity in things except fact. Nothing is added to causal relation by the adjective necessary. Every fact carries with it necessity, the necessity at least for the human mind of accepting it. There is no other necessity even in mathematics, which is often regarded as the special domain of that goddess. It is a fact that a triangle's angles are equal to two right angles, a fact which is discovered by inspection as all facts are discovered. It is only the extreme simplicity of the triangle, that it has none but empirical spatio-temporal character, which induces us to think that the connection of its form with the property named is necessary. For mathematics is no exception to the rule that science is empirical, and that its discoveries are won by attention to the nature of its subject-matter. Not even metaphysics is exempt, though its experienced material is non-empirical in nature. ' Must,' if I may repeat myself, was made for human beings in the relation

---

But the point of that doctrine is not so much that things are spirits, as that spirit is only an advanced form of something which is found lower down in all things. Our awareness of power is but our consciousness of the causal relation between our will and our acts. The mischief of the conception that a cause has power to produce its effect is that it introduces some mysterious element of connection other than that of simple continuity. Hume went too far in the opposite direction. For us causality is not so much an example of power as power is an example of causality.

of superior to subject.   It has no part in science ; though the science of man takes account of ' must.'

Objections
ca   ty.
(1) from
logical
atomism.
Stripped of these dangerous anthropomorphisms the principle or law of causality that any event has a cause means nothing more nor less than the proposition that a motion is continuous with some precedent motion.   Such a principle is not necessary but *is* non-empirical as following from the nature of Space-Time and not from the nature of the particular events that happen to be connected in space and time.   It is difficult to under-stand how in this sense it can be dispensed with, unless science is to avow itself a mere tabulation of isolated facts reduced to generalisations.   It is worth while glancing at some of the reasons which seem to make the idea of cause dispensable.   One of them is that causes and effects regarded as substances or things are in the first instance qualitative, and it is only in the initial stages of science that we are concerned with such relations of qualities.   Fire expands bodies, digitalis stops the heart ; propositions like these are merely the first steps beyond empirical descriptions.   The further science goes the more it concerns itself not with connections of qualities but with measurement and with processes or motions ; how much heat is related to how much elongation, what processes there are set up by digitalis which are connected with the heart's cessation.   Moreover, it is not only relations between independent substances which demand investigation but in an eminent degree the constitution of things in terms of primary qualities ; not what heat does but what heat is ; what are the primary processes which underlie the world of qualities, or, in the technical phrase, which are the ground of qualities.

Thus the higher stages of science become to a large extent attempts to formulate in quantitative terms the processes which occur in nature.   What we seek is not causes but formulae, expressible in equations.   What place is here for cause?   What is there in the law of gravitation which involves cause ?   Did not Newton himself in declining to make hypotheses as to the cause of attraction limit himself to the formulation of the facts compendiously stated in that law ? What else is science but such a set of compendious formulae ? "In the motions of mutually gravitating bodies," says Mr. Russell,[1] "there is nothing that can be called a cause and nothing that can be called an effect ; there is merely a formula." But apart from the fact that the deeper reasons for such formulae remain a subject of inquiry (the cause of gravitation is an actual problem of physics), a formula such as that of gravitation involves two elements. One is that of quantitative description of the motions that take place. On its other side, the formula asserts the reciprocal determination of two motions by one another, and this implies causality on the reasonable conception of what is meant by the causal relation. Qualitative causal laws are replaced by quantitative formulae, but so far as science aims at connecting together motions it is observing the law of causality, only in a less undeveloped form. I am bound to pass by the more explicit doctrine of Mach and his followers, that cause is but a useful means for shortening the work of description, for this doctrine implies a conception of thought which is inconsistent with our hypothesis of the relation of mind to things. Concepts are for us either realities or they are nothing. They may indeed be erroneous, but even then they are objective. That science is made by inventing concepts which are verified by experience is a perfectly true account of how we come to know. That our concepts are nothing more, are not (if we could but get the right ones) actual constituents of the objective world and not merely inventions of ours, this is at least not the principle on which we are conducting our inquiry.

Another reason for the discredit of causation is the sheer misconception of it for which philosophers are themselves in part responsible, that it means not a relation of connection but a frequency of conjoint occurrence. Two events apparently presumed to be disconnected may be taken to be cause and effect when if one is repeated

---

[1] 'On the notion of Cause,' *Proc. Arist. Soc.* N.S. vol. xiii., 1912–1913, p. 14. Reprinted in *Mysticism and Logic* (p. 194).

the other is repeated—'the same cause, the same effect.' Attention has been diverted from the nature of causality itself to the nature of the conditions under which we can succeed in discovering causal laws ; and the notion of the causality of a cause has been confused with the universality of the connection. An easy triumph is thus prepared for those suspect causes. There is no event which is repeated, and a conception of causality which is nothing but the repetition of a brace of events would indeed be useless. Now we have seen already that repetition, not bare identical repetition but under variations, is essential to the existence of a law, but is distinguishable from the contents of the law. The causal relation of two events is the relation between the events whereby they become immanent action in a single substance composed of the two events and of what is needed to unite them. The causal relation is not the repetition of the pair of similar events. The truth is that without the repetition we should not discover laws, and that at best owing to the great complexity of things and the great distance of actual repetition from mere repetition we can only hope for approximations to certainty. The practice of the logicians has been enough to show that the causal relation is not equivalent to the criterion 'same cause same effect.' For it is vital to the discovery of causal relations that in the absence of a cause the effect is absent. This criterion it is which gives meaning to the negative instance. It is no doubt a legacy from Hume that the world should be broken up into disconnected events which are found together or in succession in experience. But Hume, to do him justice, did not attribute any causal relation to the events themselves, as his successors did, but to the expecting mind. I can only account for causality's still being held by those who profess adherence to Hume to be a relation, by supposing that relation is understood to be something that can be said about things and not a concrete set of transactions into which they enter.

The extreme of atomism is reached when causality, supposed to be equivalent to necessity and based on

identical repetition, is considered to be an ideal limit
constructed by the mind which is at the opposite extreme
to complete independence of two things on one another.
What science then has to discover is not causal connections, which are mental, but real correlations.   No one
would undervalue the formulae of correlation proposed
with this end in view.   But it is surely plain that this
view is inspired by the fear of the bogey of necessity, and
that unless we are to regard the world as made up of
discontinuous units, against the spirit of our hypothesis,
there is no meaning in correlation except as a first
approximation towards the more intimate relation of
direct or indirect causality ; that we proceed statistically
by establishing correlations where direct experimentation
on causes is not open to us.   The quest for correlation
implies that events are determined, and determined in
reality and not merely logically, by one another in a
certain order.[1]   To discover such determination, the
weighing of numbers may at one stage of a science be
our only means.   We aim at the plan of things by
numbers where the plan is not immediately or directly
accessible.

It is from an entirely different point of view, in fact (2) from
on the very ground of the systematic interconnection of l g ca
things, that a different school of thought depreciates the idea sm
relation of cause and effect in comparison with that of
ground and consequent.   We have followed them in
maintaining that what matters in science is the connections
of things.   For us therefore the discovery of the cause
of an event or motion or thing with qualities is the
detection of what precise motion or group of motions or
things or events is continuously connected with the
effect.   The cause and effect make a system involving
process.   But it is urged by the writers in question that
a cause as a mere event in time contains something

[1] Compare chapter v. on 'Contingency and Correlation — the
insufficiency of Causation' in Mr. Karl Pearson's *Grammar of Science*,
Part I. (London, 1911, ed. 3), with Mr. A. Wolf's remarks in *Proc.
Arist. Soc.* vol. xiii. N.S., 'The Philosophy of Probability,' §§ 3-5.

irrelevant to the characters of the system. Time has for them the taint of relative unreality and it infects the cause. And they point to systems like those in geometry where no Time, as they allege, is involved. Cause as an event in time is an incomplete ground, and the scientific ideal would be rather that of a system or the pattern of geometrical ones.[1]

It was this ideal which Spinoza employed, and the inadequacy of his effort to make causal connection satisfactory might have served as a warning. In truth it would rather seem that whereas, according to these writers, the relation of ground and consequent is fundamental and that cause and effect adds something irrelevant, the relation of ground and consequent eviscerates the causal relation of its essential element of Time : implication is a notion posterior to causation. Time is indeed supposed to be mere 'time,' mere succession, and it is such 'time' which is suspect. But there is only one sort of Time and a sensible event in time possesses that time-reality. If we mean mere time, a cause is not an event in mere time. If we mean real Time, Time is itself part of the ground. The ground of any consequent is fundamentally process and is spatio-temporal. Either therefore process is essential to the ground or else the cause or event in time which is irrelevant to the ground or which is the ground in an imperfect form is not the real event which is intended by cause. The preference of ground and consequent to that of cause and effect is in fact an attempt to translate what is essentially temporal, where Time is taken as real, into something stationary. To do so we must reintroduce process into the stationary contents of the ground, as when our subject-matter is itself historical, e.g. in psychology or physics. The example of a geometrical system is misleading. For stationary Space is but Space - Time with the Time omitted, and the omission is legitimate if it is only supposed to be provisional. The preference in question depends on the confusion of what is timeless with

[1] For the topic of this section see Bosanquet, *Logic*, vol. i. pp. 264 ff. ed. 1 (252 ff. ed. 2).

what is independent of any particular time, as all universals are.

Real grounds are to be distinguished from logical grounds, though they may coincide. The real ground of any event or character, when it is not merely the so-called formal cause, which is equivalent to the fact explained, as when vibrations of the ether are called the cause of light, being in fact identical with them, is a complex of motions of which the event or fact to be explained is the causal outcome. But logic, if we may anticipate a later chapter,[1] is the science of truth, or of how our beliefs, as expressed in propositions, are to be systematised into a coherent whole at the guidance of reality. For it therefore the reason why or 'because' is not always the cause; whereas in reality the reason is the "moving why" of which Burns speaks. When A is equal to B, and C also, neither B nor the equality of A and C to B is the cause of the equality of A to C. All manner of good reasons for a conclusion are different from the cause of the fact stated in the conclusion. The cause is always a reason, but a reason need not be the cause. But we are not therefore free to regard the logical ground because it is the more general in logic as superior to the relation of cause and effect in the reality. Truth is like a work of art and has its own prescriptions, always dictated by reality. We go about to arrive at reality by methods proper to truth, and we are able to dispense in certain cases with direct reference to causal interrelation. But the ideals of logic cannot be used to depreciate the causal relation.

These are difficulties which affect the use of causation (3) from in science and logic. Metaphysically it has been main- physics. tained that causation is not reality but appearance. For us since the universe of Space-Time divides itself into motions and yet retains its continuity, the continuous connection of motion with motion is as much ultimately real as the Space-Time of which it is the history. But the charges brought against it on metaphysical grounds

[1] Bk. III. ch. ix. B.

may be lightly touched on here, for either they imply that causality is a relation which does not relate or they depend on misinterpretation of continuity. Thus when causation appears to be obnoxious to the infinite regress, for that A should cause B there must be some third thing C which moves A to its work, it is assumed that a cause is not itself causative. It is waiting for an inducement. Something, as Mr. Broad so well puts the point, is wanted to stir it into activity. But its real activity consists in passing over into its effect.

In the next place it is urged, by Mr. Bradley, that causation can neither be discontinuous nor continuous, or that it must be both, and is therefore contradictory. It cannot be discontinuous and must be continuous, for if it were discontinuous the cause would persist unchanged for a time and then suddenly change. Again, it is apparently assumed that for a cause to work it must have an inducement. But the cause does its work not by a change in itself but in leading on into something else. A cause might well remain unaltered for a time and then finding its patient produce its effect. The proposition that causation is not discontinuous is indeed true but not for the reason stated. Equally it is said causation cannot be continuous for the cause would then be without duration. "The cause must be a real event, and yet there is no fragment of time in which it is real."[1] This appears to mean that a cause must occupy a finite time in order to act ; which is the assumption already rejected ; and it appears also to assume that a continuum is put together out of adjacent points (in the likeness of spatial points), whereas the essence of a continuum is that being neither space-positions only nor time-positions only, all its points are instants and all its instants points. A continuum is a process and causation is a process. If the cause is something stationary, causation is indeed inexplicable. But it is in fact not stationary, and its continuity does not mean that at any one instant the cause is succeeded by something else which begins at the next instant but that any instant is the point of passage of a

---

[1] *Appearance and Reality*, ch. vi. p. 61 (ed. 1).

motion. To repeat an often-stated proposition, continuity is the conceptual formulation of motion itself, and, hard as it may be to say where cause ends and effect begins, yet if cause is itself a process and effect another and different one, the relation between the two is the transition of the one which is earlier into the later motion, or group of motions.

C. Reciprocity

Causality is a relation between substances in virtue of which a motion or group of motions in the one is continued into a motion or group of motions in the second and thus alters the pre-existing motion of the second substance. Now the second substance, or the patient, is already a motion or group of motions, and the effect which the cause produces is determined by the second substance as well. The transaction into which the two substances enter, so far as they constitute a closed system, is a two-sided and not a one-sided transaction. It is one in which each partner is cause and effect in turn. The situation which is the relation of the two substances is from the point of view of the first an effect on the second, but from the point of view of the second an effect on the first. The action of A on B is *ipso facto* an action of B upon A. In the transaction each partner exercises its own causality ; the effect on B is a continuation of motions in A, and the effect in A is a continuation of motions in B. There is thus only one total situation arising from the relation of the two and it appears as an effect in B of A and an effect in A of B. Thus the pull of the horse, in Newton's example, on the rope attached to a heavy stone is a pull of the rope on the horse ; the push which I give the earth by the intramolecular movement which follows my will to jump is the push of the earth upon me which actually is the jump that I am said to make. When a ball strikes another moving in the opposite direction, the motion imparted to the second in one direction is precisely the same transaction as consists in the rebound of the first ball. When a moving ball overtakes another moving ball the acceleration imparted to the one is a deceleration of the other, and the one ball loses its motion to the other, which it accelerates, just because of the internal movements of the second. One motion

evokes an alteration in another motion into which it is
thus continued, but it does not act upon the void, and
the pre-existing motion which it accelerates is continued as
an element in the same transaction into the acceleration
in a contrary direction of the overtaking ball. In other
and more familiar words, an effect is produced only in
what resists. Every action is at the same time a reaction.
But this does not do away with causality. The action of
A on B is the causality of A. The effect on B is
posterior to the motions in A. The reaction of B is its
causality exercised upon A, and is posterior to the
previous motions of B. Reciprocity between A and B
is therefore reciprocal causality. Moreover, the reaction
begins at the same moment as the action and two bodies
in reciprocal action are simultaneous so far as concerns
this moment. Thus the reciprocal attraction of the earth
and the falling stone is a single transaction which is the
beginning of the two opposite movements of the earth to
the stone and the stone to the earth. It is this kind of
case where the transaction is so obviously a single event,
viz. the diminution of the distance of earth and stone,
which has induced some to omit the element of causality,
the earth on the one side and the stone on the other, and
attend only to the mutual accelerations, inversely propor-
tional to the masses of the parties engaged.

The simultaneity of two interrelated substances in Corollaries.
respect of their action on each other is irrespective of the
continued existence of the substances, such as we find in
what Mill calls permanent causes, like the earth or other
heavenly bodies. The substances might act on each
other in virtue of their life and the life expire in the
interaction. It would still remain true that the action
and reaction would begin simultaneously in the dead
substances left. Where we have permanent causes the
two sides of the transaction are being constantly renewed
and the two interacting processes persist beside each
other.
Two interacting substances form a system or single
substance. What is true of them is true also therefore of

the substances within a substance, such as the qualities of a single substance or the parts of an organic whole. There is simultaneity between such actions and reactions within the substance, and here we have such account as I am able to give of the structural character of things apart from its intrinsic simultaneousness. The various parts of a substance sustain each other by reciprocity and so far there is simultaneity. But it is the result of causal process and therefore of succession.[1]

The same thing holds true of independent substances. When they come into relation they are in reciprocal action and simultaneous in respect of certain processes. This simultaneity is thus an outcome of the successive character of Space-Time. Once more both in respect of single things and in respect of the world as a whole, we come back to the truth that apart from the intrinsic necessity of some simultaneity of points, the fact that at any one moment Space is filled with some event or other is derivative from the successiveness of Space. A purely simultaneous Space would be a Space which perished with its perishing moment. A Space which is occupied by Time at various stages in the intrinsic succession of Time allows both for the persistence of Space and for its complete occupation at any moment.

Mechanical and reaction.

Action and reaction are conceptions drawn from mechanics and founded as now we see in the nature of Space-Time itself. The question may be raised whether organic reaction falls under the same head. In particular it might be asked, if a luminous body is the cause of our visual sensations, do we in vision react on the luminous object ? It causes vision in us, but do we alter it ? The answer will illustrate the real nature of action and reaction. For the character of the reaction depends on the nature of the body affected, and so does the effect produced by the cause. Now owing to the complexity of an organic body the characteristic effect of the cause may be only a remote effect. Thus the immediate mechanical effect of light is pressure on the eye, and

[1] Above, ch. vi. A, p. 276.

there is mechanical reaction to this. But the psychological effect is remote and arrived at through a long
chain of action, whether chemical or not I need not
inquire. It takes time for the mental effect of light to
be produced, but when it is produced there is at the
same time an action on the part of the organism of motion
which is commonly spoken of as the motor reaction.
This motor reaction is an integral part of the whole
situation in which the action of the light ultimately takes
effect. For it is a short-sighted insight which supposes
that the sensation of light is something which occurs first
and then releases the motor action which ultimately leads
to turning the eyes to the source of light. We may
rather see reason to believe with Mr. C. S. Myers[1] that
the actual sensation depends on the type of the motor
response and that the sensation emerges with the motor
process. Thus when the light produces its effect on the
centres of vision the organism with its preformed
structure is reacting towards the external world.

We must thus note first that the reaction of the
organism may be remote as compared with the first
effect of the stimulus. And again it will be very complex
in the end if the whole substance directly or indirectly
affected is complex. Hence, to quote a famous argument
to which we shall recur later in another connection, a
telegram may leave me cold which owing to its contents
may throw another person into profound agitation of
mind and of response. In the next place the essential
character of the reaction may be masked by the difference
of the conditions here and in a simple mechanical response.
For the reaction may take effect not so much on the
source of stimulation as on other objects. In general
and as a matter of fact organic reactions are in their outcome directed towards the stimulus. The organism
performs motions which are designed to secure more of a
pleasant and less of an unpleasant stimulus, by what Mr.
Baldwin has called a circular process, or a process of
imitation, which repeats itself. The sight of a tasty

[1] *British Journal of Psychology*, vol. vi., 1912: 'Are the intensity
differences of sensation quantitative?' I. § 1. See later, Bk. III. ch. v.

thing reacts in the seizing of it to eat. Our reactions are in the first instance practical and do tend to return upon the object. But the object being only remotely the cause of the visual reaction, the reaction to it may be directed on some different object. Thus in purely intellectual apprehension of the fruit the reaction may take the form, in the end, of speech. Or an insult may be avenged not on the person of the culprit but on some one else, or a man may recoup himself in the circle of his home for the vexations he has suffered from his business. These are complexities arising from the complexity of the situation and of the organism. What concerns us to observe is that any action on the organism issues upon the external world sooner or later in some part of it, whether directly connected with the original source of the stimulation or not. The organic reaction considered in its complexity is the issue of the organism's affections in effects upon the external world. And they are not without grounds who look upon an organism as an apparatus whereby actions received from outside are converted into effects upon the outside world again. The simplicity of mechanical action and reaction is not to be expected in these cases where we compare the ultimate source of action and the ultimate shape and locality of reaction. The equivalence of action and reaction may however be traced at every stage of these highly complex transactions.

CHAPTER VII

QUANTITY AND INTENSITY

THE category of substance was as we saw a feature of any space-time which arose from the relation between the elements of Space and Time in it to one another. Existence was the occupation of a space-time. Substance was the persistence of a space in its time or the occupation of a space by a duration. Causality and reciprocity were relations of substances. The categories to which we now come, quantity and intensity, or, to follow Kant's terms, extensive and intensive quantity, also arise from various essential relations within Space-Time of Space and Time to one another. As regards nomenclature, I shall follow Mr. Russell in using quantity as the concrete term and magnitude as its corresponding abstract term. Magnitude is to quantity as universality is to universal or causality to the concrete relation of cause and effect. Thus quantities may be equal to one another but their magnitudes are not equal but identical. In ordinary practice the term intensity is used indifferently, I think, for intensive quantity and its magnitude. So too magnitude and extensive quantity are commonly used convertibly. But while any magnitude may be greater or less than another magnitude, it is convenient to be able to describe equality of quantity by a distinguishing phrase, identity of magnitude. Moreover when in what follows quantity is used by itself, it stands for extensive quantity.

As before, quantity and intensity are not concepts which can be applied to spaces and times, but they are features of things which are complexes of space-time because of certain characters belonging to any space-time. Extensive quantity is the occupation of any space by its time or rather the occurrence of any space in its time, or what is the same thing, the occupation of any time by its space. Space as so occupied is a length or area or volume. Time as so occupied is a duration. Of two spaces generated by the same motion the greater space occurs in the greater time, and the greater time occupies the greater space. More or less of a motion is more or less extension in space or time, the space traced out being in correspondence with the time in which it is traced ; and this is extensive quantity — that is the crude or initial character which the thought of quantity represents. Quantity is thus equivalent to the bare fact that Space is swept out in Time, or that Time is occupation of Space.

Intensity or intensive quantity, on the other hand, is the occurrence of various spaces in the same time, or what is the same thing, the occupation of the same space by different times. The simplest case is the velocity of a simple motion. The same time occupies a greater or less space according as the motion is fast or slow ; or the same space occurs in a greater or less time, according as the motion is slow or fast. A less simple but still simple case is the intensive quantity of a sound. If the pitch remains unaltered the louder sound has the greater amplitude of vibration ; more space being contained in the same time of vibration. Thus while extensive quantity is the fact that a space is occupied by its time, whatever that time is, intensive quantity is the fact that Time may be filled by Space and Space by Time un-equally.

The ground of this distinction is that a space (or a time) is both a whole and also a continuum of parts. Considered as a whole, a space is traced out by its time and more time means more space, by what we are accustomed to call, with the use of numerical notions, the addition of space to space. That is to say, when two spaces are compared, for instance two lengths, the one space covers the extent of the other and something more.

But a space is also a continuum and infinitely divisible. Now two spaces, say two lengths, may be traversed in the same time, for owing to the continuity of Space and of Time there is a one-to-one correspondence between the points of the two unequal lengths of space and between them and the time which is also a continuum. Thus intensity is a relation of Space to Time in virtue of the continuity or infinite divisibility of each, which secures that the time being the same it may be filled with any extension of space ; and the space being the same it may be filled with any extension of time. Extensive quantity is an affair of addition ; intensive quantity is an affair of concentration, or in numerical language of division.[1]

Thus extensive quantity belongs to existents so far as the space and time of their space-time vary together ; they have intensive quantity so far as one or other remaining constant the other varies. In Kant's language, in extensive quantity the idea of the parts makes that of the whole possible ; in intensive quantity the idea of the

Measure-ment of intensity.

---

[1] An excellent illustration of the difference between extensive and intensive quantity is provided by a problem which arises in psychology or psychophysics in connection with the estimate of just perceivable differences of length of lines as measured by the eye. With lines of moderate length, the just perceivable difference follows Weber's law and is approximately a constant fraction of the length. But when the differences of length are larger we tend to equate not fractional but absolute differences, *e.g.* the difference of 5 and 7 inches seems equal to that of 10 and 12 inches, not to that of 10 to 14 inches, as it should if Weber's law held. H. Ebbinghaus, from whom I borrow this account (*Psychologie*, vol. i. § 45, pp. 504-5, ed. 1, Leipzig, 1902) explains the reason very clearly. When the difference of length is very small we compare the two lengths taken altogether, measuring by the movement sensations of the eye; and we compare two impressions which have different strength or intensity. But when the differences are larger, we tend to superpose one line on the other and find out the actual difference by subtraction. Thus in the second case we compare the lines as extensive quantities ; in the first, we are as it were considering the lengths intensively. There is an apparent contradiction here with the statement of the text that extensive quantity arises out of the relation of the time to the space in spaces taken as wholes ; whereas here we say that in taking the lines intensively we take them as wholes ; but a little reflection shows that the contradiction is only apparent.

whole makes the parts possible. It follows from this that one quantity may be added to or subtracted from another; it is but a matter of the shorter or longer generation of the two quantities. But an intensity cannot be subtracted from another nor added to it. All that we can do is to have a series of intensities which can (again in Kant's language) decrease from any given intensity downwards to zero; or increase from zero upwards to a given intensity; as when hot water cools and its temperature decreases in intensity continually, or as when the note of a tuning-fork dies away in loudness. An intensity is not increased by adding to it a fresh intensity; but only the additional stimulus, increased by a measurable extensive dose, brings about a condition of intensity which is unitary and has more of intensive quantity than the intensity with which it is compared. Psychologists have often urged this point in respect of the intensity of sensations, that the sensational intensity (for we are not concerned with whether sensations are extensive) is something complete and single and that it is unmeaning to add or subtract the intensities of sensations. Hence extensive quantity is directly measurable, for extensities may be correlated directly with numbers and this constitutes measurement.[1] But intensities are not measurable directly but only indirectly. That is, we can make a scale of intensities beginning with some one arbitrary intensity as a standard, and arranging the others at various distances from this standard, and we can measure in this way the distances of intensities from one another. Thus the intensity of temperature is measured by the numbers on the scale of a thermometer. In dealing with sensations we may arrange intensities in a scale where each sensation appears to sense to be equally removed from its predecessor on the scale. So stars are arranged in order of their magnitude, when the star of the first magnitude is as much brighter than one of the second as that in turn is brighter than one of the third.[2]

---

[1] B. Russell, *Principles of Mathematics*, p. 176.

[2] The measurement of intensities as an arrangement of unitary intensities according to their intervals is admirably explained by H.

Intensities are thus indirectly measurable by correlation with what is directly measurable. It is therefore incorrect to maintain that because intensities are unitary, they are not measurable at all. For measure depends on correlation with the series of numbers and this correlation is possible even in the case of intensities. What is true is that 'more or less' means different things in the case of extensive and intensive quantity. Intensities are more or less as being further or nearer from a standard intensity. They constitute therefore a class whose members are primarily ordinal and are a series. The class of extensive quantities may be arranged ordinally, but the ordinal arrangement is secondary, for extensities differ not merely by unlikeness but by actual distance in space or time. Intensities are intrinsically ordinal and are secondarily correlated with numbers, whether with the arbitrary divisions on a thermometer, or, as in the case of sensations, in the experiments which attest the law of Weber, with the extensive measures of their stimuli.

The intensity of sensations, that is of processes of sensing, is a particular case of the categorial character, intensity, at a highly developed stage of empirical existence. We have been concerned with the category itself as applicable to finite existence at every stage, and have tried to trace it to its root in the relation of Space and Time within Space-Time. This account of the matter is so closely allied to Kant's difficult but famous doctrine of the 'Anticipations of Perception,' that it may be worth while to pause for a moment for a word of comparison. Kant established once for all the difference between intensive and extensive quantity, and the debt which psychology in particular owes him in this matter has been too little acknowledged. But his purpose was not psychological. Since there is in sensation, which is empirical, a filling of the moment of time with an intensity

Comparison with Kant's doctrine.

Ebbinghaus, *Psychologie*, ed. 1, vol. i. Bk. I. § 6, pp. 60 ff. Cf. also Introduction to E. B. Titchener's *Exp. Psych.*, Quantitative (Instructors' Manual), New York, 1905.

which cannot be regarded as made up of parts by successive addition, Kant urged that there must be in the object intensive quantity or degree. For since Time cannot be perceived by itself, that is without something which occurs in it ; and much less therefore the filling of a Time with various intensities of sensation ; there must be in experience itself something to account for this awareness of the filling of time. This 'degree' in the quality of an experience is not itself empirical, that is, in our phrase, it is not one of those characters which vary from bit to bit of experience but is pervasive. It must therefore be referred to the mind itself ; it is one of those elements of objective experience whose non-empirical character Kant recognises by such reference. In this way the mind 'anticipates experience' by the axiom that any perception must have some degree (or intensive quantity) or other. From our point of view, the non-empirical element in experience is not referable to the mind but to Space-Time itself and it has nothing to do with anticipation at all and nothing specially to do with perception. But in essentials I have been following him. Only, Kant seems unable to give a satisfactory account of the reason of intensive quantity. He contrasts with extensive quantity the intensive filling of Time by sensation, but he can only explain this by reference to the empirical fact that a given intensity of sensation can decrease to zero in time. It is true that the sound falls away in loudness in a lapse of time, but this is only the empirical consequence of the filling of the moment of time from which the fall of intensity began ; and there is no definite connection established, if any can be, between the lapse of time needed for the vanishing of the sound and the intensity of the sensation. As we have seen, that intensity is to be explained by the connection of Time with Space.

Just as intensive quantity depends upon Space-Time itself and not upon mind, so and more obviously does extensive quantity. Quantity for Kant arises in the process whereby the mind traverses in time an extension in space, so that we apprehend quantity in the act of adding homogeneous parts to one another. Quantity is in this sense the work of the mind. For us Space-Time is sufficient of itself. For Space-Time containing a moving principle, Time, generates quantity. No mind is needed for the "composition" of Space, nor could Time, as Kant himself so often urges, help mind to the composition of Time without Space. Space-Time therefore does the work of itself without making an appeal to mind.

CHAPTER VIII

WHOLE AND PARTS : AND NUMBER

Whole and
parts as
categorial. EVERY existent is a whole of parts, because Space and
Time, in different senses, disintegrate each other. Time
breaks up Space into spaces, and Space enables Time
to consist of times. Each of them, as we have seen,
secures the continuity of the other ; Space by supplying
connection to the fleeting instants of Time, Time by
providing elements within the blank identity of Space.
It is but repeating the same thing in other words, when
we say that, besides sustaining each other's continuity,
they break each other up. Time disintegrates Space
directly by distinguishing it into successive spaces ; Space
disintegrates Time indirectly by making it a whole of
times, without which whole there would be no separate
times either. Considered by themselves they have no
parts ; they owe their partition to one another in their
mutual involvement, and they divide each other in
correspondence. In this division Time plays the directer
role and takes the lead.

What applies to Space and Time as such applies to
any space or time as they exist in any empirical being.
Everything is in the end, in its simplest terms, a piece
of Space-Time and breaks up therefore into *parts*, of which
it is the *whole*. It is purely an empirical matter, that is
a matter arising not from the fundamental character of
Space-Time but from the empirical grouping of parts
within it, what the whole may be. It may be a line or a
volume in which parts are united continuously. It may
be an aggregate of things with definite qualities, a pile
of shot or a company of soldiers, or a library of books,

or a collection of quite heterogeneous things, like the contents of an antiquarian shop or the different members of our bodies.   The *things* thus aggregated are not themselves continuous but discontinuous ; but they are continuously related by the space and time which intervenes between them.   There would not be aggregate wholes composed of individuals but for the connecting space-time.   But the individuals, owing to their specific qualities, form an isolated object of interest apart from their connection within Space-Time, and it is the space-time which they themselves occupy which is resolved by their separation from one another into parts.   Moreover it is these aggregates of 'qualited' individuals which being nearer to our senses are our first experience of wholes ; and it is later and by some effort of reflection that we first dissect individual aggregates like bodies into their constituent parts and later still observe that a bare extension is itself composed of parts.   But it remains that the intrinsic resolution of Space-Time through the internal relation of Space and Time is the basis of all distinction of parts, no matter how loosely the whole is united of them.

Number is the constitution of a whole in relation to its Number. parts ; and it is generated in the concurrent or correspondent distinction of parts in space and time within a spatio-temporal whole.   It may be described indifferently as a plan of resolution of a whole into parts or of composition of parts into a whole.   All existents are numerable or possess number, because in occupying a space-time they occupy parts of space in correspondence with parts of time.   It matters not whether the parts be equal or unequal, homogeneous or heterogeneous in their qualities ; or whether the wholes are of the same extent of space-time or not.   A group consisting of a man and a dog is as much a two as a group of two men or two shillings ; though its parts are unequal in quantity and different in quality ; and as much two as a group of two elephants or mice which occupy as wholes very different quantities of space-time.   To arrive at the number of a whole of

individuals we have to abstract from the quality or
magnitude of the individuals. Their number concerns
only the constitution of the whole out of its parts or
resolution of the whole into them. In itself number is
the correspondence of the space and time parts which is
involved in this resolution ; but it is a consequence of
this that the number of a group establishes a correspondence between the members of the group and those
of any other group which has the same number-constitu-
tion. All twos correspond to one another in virtue of
their twoness, that is of the plan of constitution of the
whole from its parts. Number is therefore the plan of
a whole of parts.

Number is a different category from extensive
quantity, though closely connected with it : quantity
communicates with number. They are different because
it is a different relation of Space to Time which lies at
the basis of them. Quantity expresses the fact that Space
is a duration, or that Time sweeps out Space in its flight.
Number is the concurrent resolution of either into parts.
But since this is so, quantity is directly numerable, for in
the generation of a quantity there is the making of a
whole of parts by successive addition of the parts. Kant
in making number the ' schema ' of quantity noted the
connection of the two, but mistakenly overlooked the
more important difference. The category whose schema
is number, if any such distinction of schema and category
could possibly be recognised, as it cannot, would be not
quantity but that of part and whole. Intensive quantity
does not communicate directly with number, for it is not
a whole of parts. The connection is only possible
indirectly through correlation of intensities with extensive
quantities.

Number a
universal.

Being a plan of constitution of a whole of parts,
number is universal or communicates with universality.
It is a non-empirical or *a priori* universal, arising out of
Space-Time as such. The various cardinal numbers,
2, 4, 7, etc., are empirical universals which are special
plans of whole and parts and are species of the category

number.   These special numbers have for their particulars
the groups of things (or even of parts of areas or lines
or hours) which are apprehended empirical embodiments
of these universals.   Thus the number two is embodied
in two pebbles, or two men, or two inches, but is never
to be identified with them.   The King's gift to mothers
with triplets is given for the triplets, not for the number
three.   Nor is the number two a mere abstraction from
concrete groups of two things but is the plan (itself
something concrete) on which this group is constructed.
Hence however much the observation of collections of
things may provoke us to attend to numbers and their
combinations, we no more derive arithmetical truths from
the things in which they are embodied than we derive
geometrical truths, such as that the two sides of the
triangle are greater than the third side, from actual
measurement of brass triangles or three-cornered fields.
These are not the foundations of arithmetic or geometry
but only the devices by which kind nature or our teachers
cajole us into the exercise of our attention to or reflection
upon numbers and figures themselves.   Figures in
geometry and numbers in arithmetic are the empirical
objects so described which we observe for themselves ;
and numbers are empirical universals in the same way as
triangle and sphere and dog are empirical universals.
Thus the special numbers are the variable and shifting
material in which number as such, the category number,
is embodied.   This rarefied, but still concrete, material is
what Plato described under the name of the "indeterminate dyad," indicating by the name dyad its capacity
of multiform realisation of number as such, and pointing by
this superb conception to the way in which we are to understand the real relation between a universal and its sensible
particulars.[1]   It is therefore by no accident but in virtue
of the intrinsic character of number and numbers that
universality was represented by him as number and the
particular universals or forms as particular numbers.   It
is only elaborating still further the appositeness of this

[1] See J. Burnet: *Greek Philosophy from Thales to Plato*, ch. xvi.
pp. 320 ff.

conception when we try, as I have tried before to do, to explain all universals as spatio-temporal plans that are realised in the sensible particulars, which are in themselves spatio-temporal existents constructed on those plans.

Unity.   Arithmetic then is the empirical science whose object is the special or particular numbers (themselves universals) and the relations of them. One conception remains difficult, that of the number 1, itself.[1] It has sometimes been thought that 1 or unity depends on the act of thought (*e.g.* in counting) which constitutes an object one. But clearly this could only be true if the act of thought were itself enjoyed as one, and thus the explanation would be circular. Now it is safe to say that unity is a notion posterior in development to multiplicity. That 2 is equal to 1 + 1 is not the definition of 2 but something we learn about it, and Kant was perfectly justified in calling such a proposition synthetic. Probably the greatest step ever made in arithmetic was the elementary discovery that the numbers could be obtained from one another by addition of units, or before that stage was reached, that 6 could be got by adding 2 to 4. The numbers are to begin with distinctive individuals, as distinct from one another as a triangle from a square.[2] Enumeration was a reduction of this distinctive difference in the empirical material to a comprehensive law of genesis. Bearing this in mind, that numbers have different numerical quality, we may see that unity is the whole which is the same as its parts ; or to put the matter otherwise, any object compared with a whole of two parts or of three parts, could be arranged in a series with it, in so far as in the single object the whole and every part coincided. That is, unity is a limiting case of the distinction of whole into parts in which the distinction has vanished, or it is a piece of Space-Time before its division into parts. Thus unity is rather that which is

---

[1] I do not attempt the difficult problem of the number zero.

[2] Compare on this matter F. H. Bradley, *Logic*, pp. 370, 371 ; and below, p. 319.

left when 2 is removed from 3 than what is added to
2 in order to make 3.   In any case it is a discovery that
given a series of numbers, 2, 3, 4, etc., there is a number, unity, belonging to the series and based on the same
concurrence of Space and Time as the numbers, from which
the other numbers may be derived by addition, when
addition is suitably defined.   I say, suitably defined ; for it
is clear that though we may add together things, we do not
add together numbers in the same sense ; but the sum of
two numbers is the plan of a whole whose parts correspond
to the parts of each of the two numbers when they are
taken together.   We discover in this way empirically that
12 is 7 + 5 and 1 + 1 is 2.

Unity it may be observed in passing is different from
a unit.   It has sometimes been thought that a number is
a multiplicity of equal units ;   but, as we have seen,
number has nothing whatever to do with equality of parts
in a whole.   A unit is in fact a thing (or even a piece of
Space or Time) which is used for purposes of measurement.   Measurement is effected by securing correspondence with the series of numbers.   The simplest and most
convenient method of doing this in dealing with things
is the adoption of a unit of the same stuff as the thing
and taking wholes whose parts are each the unit thing.

Finally, the reference of number to the corresponding
parts of space and time within any space - time may
serve to explain why as a matter of history the extension
of the idea of number from integers to fractions, irrationals and other numbers has been accomplished in connection with geometrical facts and has arisen out of them.

In this account of number I have ventured to differ   Number in
from Messrs. Frege and Russell's often-cited definition   extension.
of cardinal number as the class of classes similar to a
given class ; though it is clear that so far as my version
of the matter may be taken to be correct it is arrived at
by reflection on their doctrine and is suggested by it, and
is merely a translation of it into metaphysical language.
In fact they define number in extensional terms, which
is proper to mathematics, while the account here given is

the intensional side of the same subject-matter.[1] Moreover, it has been indicated that if number is the constitutive correspondence of Space and Time whereby a whole is a whole of parts, it would follow from this that there is correspondence between the members of all classes which have the same constitutive number. From the side of extension then a cardinal number may be described as a class of such classes. But this description starts with entities belonging to classes ; that is it begins with finites, at the very lowest finite spaces or durations, and number is defined by reference to them. Just for that reason the definition tells us something which is true about number, but does not tell us what number is, any more than to describe man as the class of men tells us what man is. It gives us a description of number and not acquaintance with it. It is thus not a metaphysical account of number but something which follows from number ; and it would not therefore, so far as I can see, explain why any existent is numerable. Before, it has been suggested that this method of defining number makes it amenable to mathematical treatment, and that it offers a notable instance of the difference between mathematical and metaphysical treatment of the same thing. Consequently it is not in the least pretended that the account here given could be used for making arithmetical discoveries ; while on the other hand the extensive definition of number is. It is not the business of metaphysics to make discoveries in arithmetic, which employs such concepts as are most suitable to its own purposes. The metaphysical definition may be useless for mathematical purposes. It is enough that it should be useful for metaphysical purposes. The two accounts refer to the same reality ; but while the one, the metaphysical one, points to it with the finger, the other describes it.

Number is apprehended through counting, but the act of counting does not explain number. Number is a category which belongs to all existents as wholes of parts

Number and counting.

---

[1] Hence it will be observed this account applies directly to all numbers, while the definition by classes applies directly only to integers.

in Space-Time, and it applies to mind and mental acts in the same sense as to external things. The whole of enjoyment experienced in counting five is a whole of mental acts and has number like the external thing that is counted. Hence we learn number in counting groups of material things, as in exchanging sheep and oxen for cowrie shells or dollars, or in measuring lengths by our feet, or estimating the height of a horse by our hands. But the counting itself is only compresent with number and is itself numerable.

Since number is constitutive of a whole of parts, we do not count unless we experience a whole as made of parts. Hence it is that as a matter of fact we may find processes performed which simulate counting, but where objects are taken in, we say, as a whole, but not as a whole of parts. A thing may have parts without having its parts recognised as parts and without therefore being in the strict sense a whole. We take in a crowd by its individual look of magnitude or extension. A boy may identify a card used in a musical-box, pierced with a vast number of holes in an intricately complex arrangement, and name its tune ; but he clearly is not counting or discriminating parts. Many of the performances of animals which seem like counting may, as Mr. Bradley has pointed out, be explained without reference to counting. Apart from any indications that may be given by human beings to the animal, a group of three things looks or feels different from one of two ; and this may be sufficient for the purpose. It cannot be said that the arithmetical powers of the lower animals have been established, and scepticism is not unbecoming in respect of horses and dogs, no less than of pigs. If such capacity of real counting were established our estimate of animals or ourselves would undergo some modification. But it would at most be a chapter added to the story of when and how the mind comes to apprehend number. Metaphysically the interest of counting does not lie here but in the fact which may be verified in all the categories that when the mind is aware of number it also enjoys itself as number.[1]

[1] See later Bk. III. ch. vi.

CHAPTER IX

MOTION ; AND THE CATEGORIES IN GENERAL

THE last in our list of categories is Motion itself, along with Space and Time which are in fact always equivalent to motion, though they may be taken provisionally in separation. The question may reasonably be raised whether motion is a category at all and not rather the lowest form of empirical existence, for all such existents are motions and complexes of motions. But in fact, though every empirical existent is some sort of motion or other, it is the sort of motion which it is that makes it empirical : whether a straight line or a triangle or a wave-motion such as that of sound or light or the neural movement that corresponds to a sensation as enjoyed. That it is a motion or a space or a time is *a priori* or non-empirical ; and in fact the category of motion is but another expression of the fact that every existent is a piece of Space-Time. But the category is not Motion, taken as equivalent to Space-Time as a whole, nor are Space or Time as wholes either of them a category, as it will be the office of the succeeding chapter to explain at such length as may now seem necessary. Space-Time is the one stuff of which all things are made and is not itself a category but a singular, to which terms applicable to things are applied only through the necessities of speech. Accordingly the category we are now dealing with is more properly described as a motion or a space or a time, or by their abstract terms—motion, spatiality, temporality. Everything is a motion, a space-time.

It might be objected that a motion or a bit of Space-

Time is a really existent concrete thing and therefore cannot be a category. Such an objection would imply a complete misunderstanding of the nature of categories. They are not expressing mere adjectives of things, but concrete determinations of every space-time. Existence is the occupation of any space-time. Universality for all its abstract name is a concrete plan of arrangement of space-time, relations are connections which are themselves space-times. Abstract characters are separations made by us from concrete things ; but what we are referring to are concrete determinations of things. There is therefore no difficulty from this point of view in treating motion or a motion as categorial. A more serious objection would be this : we must recognise that a motion has a character allied to and of the same kind as quality. There is a motion-quality as there is redness or sweetness. Motion is not a succession of point-instants, but rather a point-instant is the limiting case of a motion. So far we have seen Mr. Bergson to be right in his protest. But while all other, empirical, qualities are correlated with motions, the 'quality' motion is purely spatio-temporal, that of being a space-time. There is nothing but the spatio-temporal fact ; there is nothing superinduced upon it. The quality of motion which a motion possesses in its indivisible character is, if I may repeat a phrase, a limiting case of empirical quality. It might be called a categorial quality were it not that, as will presently be stated, quality, that is empirical quality, is not categorial at all. Once more the exigencies of language constrain us into using such terms as best we can find for describing the indescribable. For motion is elementary and there is nothing simpler.

I follow therefore the guidance of Plato in reckoning motion as a category. For Plato it is one of his " greatest kinds of beings," which are what we call categories. Unfortunately he combines it in a pair with rest, which is not an independent category but only means, as we have seen, the absence of comparative motion in reference to some given motion, and is in fact a relative term. For Plato indeed the doubt we have raised as to whether motion is a category at all, but only the first form of empirical existent, could not arise. Even if we are entitled to consider the *Timaeus* as much as the *Sophist* as representing his own view and not merely that of his Pythagorean friends, motion must still be for him a category. For the matrix of becoming, the matter of things, is not for him as for us Space-Time but only Space, and movement requires to account for it a category of motion.

Thus a motion in so far as it is a particular sort of motion is an empirical existent. In so far as it has the character of motion, that character is categorial. According to the sense in which the phrase 'a motion' is taken, it means a category or an empirical existent. Motion is thus the border-line between the categorial and the empirical region. Our discussion serves to point the truth that categories and empirical characters are not separated by a hard-and-fast distinction as Kant supposed. It is rather the distinction between what is pervasive in experience and what is variable and not pervasive. For empirical things are complexes of that very Space-Time of which the categories are the fundamental characters. Accordingly the categories can be and have been studied by the same so-called empirical or experiential method as empirical things are. To this point I shall return again.

Grades of the categories.

At the same time the discussion leads us further to a matter of great importance as well as difficulty, namely the relation of the categories to one another. There are grades of rank within them. Motion is more complex than all the rest and includes them. It communicates with all the others. A motion is a substance and exists and is in relation to other motions. We seem to have three grades within the categories. The major categories are the first four—existence, universality, relation, and order. These communicate with each other as has been seen. Existence is different from other existence. As universal a thing is of the same sort as other particulars and different from another sort of particulars. Relation exists and has in turn universality, in the same sense as a thing is universal. The next group of categories—substance, quantity, number, etc.—communicate with each other and with the major group, but the major group do not communicate with them. Thus a substance is in a relation of causality with other substance, and it exists. But existence is not a substance, nor is relation necessarily causal, it may be a relation of number. Perhaps it might be urged that an existent is also a substance. Yes, but its bare existence, its mere occupation of Space and Time, is not equivalent to substantial occupation. A substance is universal, but a universal as such is not a substance. In fact that it is a substance is the error which underlies the notion of the 'concrete universal': when we treat a universal as a singular existent we are going beyond universality to substance.

Motion forms the last or third group of the categories. It presupposes the other categories and communicates with them. But they do not communicate with it. Even substance is not itself motion, though every *thing* besides being substance is motion. Substance represents motion only in respect of its persistent occupation of space through a lapse of time; but it does not include quantity, nor intensity, nor number. Whereas in motion the full tale of the fundamental determinations of Space-Time is told and motion is consequently the totality of what can be affirmed of every space-time.

Perhaps the above description may serve as a gloss upon Plato's conception of the communion of the greatest forms with one another; how vastly more important such intrinsic communication is than the mere overlapping of different universals in a thing which is say both man and black; and how distinct it is from the parti-cipation of a particular in its universal; while at the same time, when the universal is taken to be the plan of the particular spatio-temporal configuration which its particular is, we can see how the participation of the particular in the universal is illuminated by the intercommunion within the world of forms—as indeed is implied in Plato's own doctrine of the forms as the union of the form of number with the indeterminate dyad.[1]

Besides these categories proper, we shall find that there is yet another group of characters belonging to empirical existents. They are relations arising out of the nature of Space-Time which subsist between existents, but they differ from the categories proper, in presuming that there are empirical things in existence. They concern the connection of empirical things with one another; and may perhaps be spoken of as derived or even empirical categories. These form the subject-matter of the following Book.

It should be added that in speaking of the minor categories of substance, number, etc., that is of the second order of categories as depending on 'relation' of their two elements of Space and Time to one another, I have used the term relation from the poverty of language. There is strictly speaking no relation between a time and a space, for relations subsist only between existents, and Space and Time are only provisionally separated features in Space-Time. But 'relation' having been used of existents is extended so as to cover any connection. The connection is not a relation but a given feature of any space-time and is only called a relation by analogy. Similarly though the qualities of a substance are related to each other in the strict sense, it is only by an extension of the term that substance is said to be 'related' to its qualities, or again, as we have seen before, a universal is said to be related to its particulars, as if the universal could exist by itself, whereas it is the particulars which are related to one another by the relation of identity of sort arising out of their plan.

Point-stants and infinites.

The categories apply obviously to all finites in the ordinary sense of that term; but they apply also to everything empirical, everything which is not the whole of Space-Time but a part of it. Thus they apply to what I have called empirical infinites, like the infinite numbers, or as we shall see later to the infinite deity, because these

[1] See before, ch. viii. p. 315.

are not the whole of Space-Time. However much an infinite number is conceptual, it is rooted in Space-Time like all numbers, and to that radical connection with the common matrix of becoming owes the reality which it possesses. But the empirical infinites offer less difficulty than the point-instants themselves. The categories have been illustrated from point-instants as well as from ordinary things or complexes of pure events. They exist, have universality, and substance, and the like. Even the categories of quantity and number belong to them and that of whole and parts, when point-instants are considered as limiting cases. They are empirical like the infinites, for each point-instant has its own individual character, is a 'this.' Yet since they are the elements of Space-Time which is the source of all categories, they illustrate that intimate connection of the non-empirical and the empirical which will be touched on less briefly in the following chapter. But they cannot be treated as finites, regarded as having a separate existence like ordinary finites. That would be to introduce the notion of the real self-subsistent infinitesimal ; which is inadmissible. Point-instants are real but their separateness from one another is conceptual. They are in fact the elements of motion and in their reality are inseparable from the universe of motion ; they are elements in a continuum. So far from being finites, they are the constituents which are arrived at as the result of infinite division and belong to the same order as the infinites. Consequently they must be regarded not as physical elements like the electrons, but as metaphysical elements, as being the elementary constituents of Space-Time or Motion. Real they are, but if the apparent contradiction may be pardoned, they are ideal realities. In any case they are not apprehended by us purely through sense, but with the aid of conception and by some other mental function yet to be discussed. I do not attempt to minimise the difficulties of this statement, which may I trust be removed or lessened as we proceed. My object here is only to point out that they and the empirical infinites alike are contained within the one original matrix and share the characters which every portion of it possesses. There are empirical elements and empirical infinites, and both are empirical and both in their degree real and yet ideal. Thought if it is correct does not deprive its objects of reality. But reality makes room for ideal objects supposing them to be always in touch with Space-Time ; and this both sets of exceptional cases are, the point-instants as constituents of Space-Time, the infinites as a special class of complexes within it.[1]

Quality not a category.

Our list of categories omits two notions which have pretensions to be accounted categories, quality and change, and the omission must be justified. I will begin with quality, for convenience, though change is so closely related to motion, that it would seem to have prior right. Quality is not a category but an empirical generalisation of the various specific qualities of things, or a collective name for them all. It is not open to me to say that there is no discoverable determination of Space-Time as such which is called quality, as there is one which is called quantity ; for this would be begging the question. But it is open to me to ask, is there any pervasive determination of things on the strength of which we can say the thing has quality ? for otherwise quality would not be a category of things. Now to this question the answer is that there is none. We know from experience that there are qualities—red, hard, fragrant, sweet, life— corresponding to certain sorts of spatio-temporal complex. But experience does not acquaint us with quality as such ; as it does make us acquainted with quantity or substance as such. It is not relevant to point to what we have ourselves called the quality of motion, for this quality, empirical as it is, is the limit between the non-empirical and the empirical, where the two are indistinguishable. Were there no empirical qualities we should not need to speak of the motion-quality at all. Quality is to specific qualities as colour is to red, green, and blue. It is a collective name for them but not their universal. It

---

[1] The subject is returned to in Bk. IV. ch. i. *a propos* of the infinite qualitied entity God.

may gravely be doubted whether there is any plan of colours which may be called colour, which is modified and specified in red, green, and blue as the plan of man is modified in European and Mongolian man. But even if this could be maintained in the case of colour, it cannot be held that there is any plan underlying red and hard and life which is modified into these specific qualities.

Contrast quality with quantity. Quantity as such is a real determination of things of which definite quantities are modifications or copies, which participate in the universal or plan. The same thing is true of the other categories. But it is not true of quality. It may be answered that everything possesses some quality or other, and therefore quality is categorial ; everything is a complex of Space-Time and to complexity corresponds quality, it will be said, upon our own showing. But the objection does not hit the mark. Complexity in Space-Time makes everything a complex, but not a quality. It is specific sorts of complexes which are hard or sweet. Complexity as such is not a qualitative but a quantitative or purely spatio-temporal determination. Let us for the sake of definiteness revert to colours. The quality of the colour varies with the wave-length of the vibration. Now every colour has some wave-length or other. This is its universal determination as a complex of motion. But length of wave is a quantity and not a quality. When the length is definite there is colour. But length of wave as such has no colour as such. Or to revert to the general question irrespective of the illustration from colour : all portions of Space-Time are empirical complexes. But we may not therefore say that 'empirical complex' is a category. For being empirical is only a collective designation of empirical things. In so far as everything is empirical it is not categorial. There is no category of empiricity which pervades all empirical things. There are only empirical things. In the same way there are red and green and hard and sweet and life and mind ; and these are qualities. But there is no universal, quality. Quality is therefore not categorial but empirical. Kant himself though he regarded quality as a category could only use it in experience, could only schematise it, in the form of intensive quantity, which is as good as saying that as quality it was useless as a category. The truth is, it is not a category at all.

Change not a category.   There are two reasons why change cannot be regarded as a category. The first is that it is not pervasive for there may be persistence without change, as in the persistence of a quality, or, if the possibility of this be doubted, in the case of a uniform motion. But the more important reason is that change always involves empirical elements. It is a transition from one empirical determination to another. Primarily change is change of quality, and quality is always empirical. We may, it is true, also have change in quantity as in the velocity of a motion ; or a change in direction. But even here it is a transition from one empirical determination of quantity to another. Now a category implies no empirical determination in the finites to which it applies. For instance, relation is a category and an empirical relation is between empirical existents, e.g. father and son. But the category relation does not depend on the empirical character of its terms but on their categorial character of existents. Change on the other hand implies in its nature that that from which the change takes place and that to which it proceeds are empirical.

Change is not mere difference ; but the passage from something to something different. A change of quality is more than a difference of quality it is a process from the old quality to the new. A change of mind, a mere change in my sensation, is experienced by me, or is felt, not as the possession of a different decision or a different sensation, but as the passage from the one mental state to the other. Remembering that all existents, no matter what qualities they possess, are in the end complexes of motion, we may describe change as a species of motion which replaces one set of motions by another ; it is grounded in motion and may be described as a motion from one motion to another. The nature of the transitional motion may be different in different cases. Thus one thought may lead on to another and the motion is experienced as a direct transition between the two thoughts. The first thought leads on to the different thought. But the motion of change may not be of this simple and direct kind. Causes at work in my mind may end in displacing one thought from its prominence or activity in my mind. When the pale skin blushes and changes in quality from white to red, there is no direct transition from the motions correlative to whiteness to the new set, but some cause is at work, some motion, which ends in the displacement of the white motions by the red. Where a motion changes in velocity or direction, it is at the instance of some cause or motion. In every case we have not a mere difference but a motion which ends in the substitution of one empirical condition for another.

Change is then not categorial but empirical, and it is an empirical variety of motion, which is still categorial. Accordingly I am unable to accept the doctrine of Mr. Bergson that change is the stuff of things. It can only be so regarded if change is a loose expression for motion. Thus Mr. Bergson writes : " there are changes but there are not things which change ; change needs no support. There are movements, but not necessarily invariable objects which move ; movement does not imply something which moves." [1] The second proposition is I think true, but not the first. But their juxtaposition as if they were saying the same thing appears to imply that change and movement are identified. This cannot, however, be maintained. Change is change of something else, though it is not necessarily change of anything that can be called a thing, like a material body. Movement is anterior to things which are complexes of movements, and it is quite true that that movement is a stuff of which things are made and is not a mere relation between things which already exist and are said to move. But while the same may be said of change with

[1] H. Bergson, *La Perception du changement* (Oxford, 1911), p. 24.

respect to certain things, change always implies movement and is movement from one movement to another. Change is an alteration in something else, viz. in movement. For Heraclitus, of whom Mr. Bergson is the modern representative, as for the other Ionians there was a stuff in which change occurred or which embodied change and it was fire. But bare change cannot take the place of fire. On the other hand bare motion or Space-Time can, and change is an empirical form of that stuff.[1]

The categories have no origin.

The categories then being the fundamental determinations of Space-Time are the pervasive features of the experienced world. According to our hypothesis things are complexes of Space-Time, and we have seen relations are spatio-temporal connections between them. Nothing therefore but exhibits categorial features ; nothing therefore but obeys the principles in which these features reappear in the form of judgments. Everything has being and is a substance, every event has a cause, everything is related to something else, by way of quantity or causality or difference or otherwise. To the question whether there are privileged or *a priori* parts of experience, the answer therefore is that there are. To the question whether these privileged elements are due to mind or are in any peculiar way the contribution of mind, or imposed by mind on the objects of experience, the answer is that they are not. On the contrary the categories enter into mind as they enter into the constitution of everything else. The mind being a highly developed spatio-temporal complex, that is to say being in its simplest and ultimate expression such, is an existent, a substance, a cause, numerable, and its acts have intensity, and affect each other causally and reciprocally. To the question whether the *a priori* characters of the world are derived in some manner from experience of things or are primordial and ultimate, the answer is that they are primordial ; they do

---

[1] Plato distinguishes motion into two sorts, translation or movement from place to place ($\pi\epsilon\rho\iota\phi\rho\rho\dot\alpha$) ; and change or alteration, motion from state to state ($\alpha\lambda\lambda\upsilon\dot\iota\omega\sigma\iota\varsigma$). *Theaet.* p. 181b. See Burnet, *Gk. Phil.* Pt. i. p. 245. I am following Plato, though with differences.

not come into being otherwise than as all things come into being and because things come into being. All things come into being endowed with the categories and with all of them. They are the determinations of all things which arise within Space-Time, which is the matrix of things, " the nurse of becoming."

On this conception, the time-honoured controversy on the origin of *a priori* ideas and principles becomes superfluous, or, if that phrase may sound too harsh to be compatible with the reverence due to great names in philosophy and psychology, these ideas have their origin in Space-Time itself. The controversy owes its fascination to the intrusion of mind. The very use of the words, *a priori* ideas, suggests that these categories are not features of the world, the greatest kinds of beings as Plato called them, but mere mental objects, or perhaps devices or instruments for understanding experience. Accordingly, since the time of Kant, the debate has turned upon how we acquire these ideas, since there can hardly be a doubt that we have them. Kant is himself in some degree responsible for this result. We have seen that for him the categories are the binding cement of knowledge, whereby the mere empirical material of knowledge becomes in the proper sense experience. Not finding this binding substance in the empirical materials themselves he referred it to the mind, not to mind in its personal or empirical capacity as an experienced object, as something which is made up of psychical states or processes in the same way as a physical object is made up of physical material ; but in its impersonal capacity as the subject of knowledge, which knowledge is not merely like an idea of Locke and his followers the possession of an individual but open to all minds. This, as I have said, was his method of expressing, and perhaps the only method open to him of expressing, the impersonality of knowledge, of real experience as distinct from the objects which may occur to you or me and not to another. But though he rightly saw that the empirical or variable element in experience was distinct from the *a priori* element, he did not see that what was empirical was in fact in the same kind as the non-empirical, that it was in itself the modifications of the non-empirical. As he did not merely distinguish the two but separated them, the categories became an artificial tie between things in a different kind from them. No wonder that he seemed to think of the categories and of Space and Time as tools for working up empirical experience, a "machine-shop" in the trenchant but entirely misguided phrase of James. They were not so for him ; but since their connection with the empirical material was referred to mind, it remained miraculous that causality or Space should be a part of experience itself as he was all the time insisting.

Kant's solution of the problem was not psychological, though it simulated that form. The problem has since become almost entirely psychological ; have we *a priori* ideas, and how do we come by them ? The attempts that have been made to answer the question have been psychologically unsuccessful, and metaphysically they have attained the failure to which, if our hypothesis be correct, they were foredoomed. For these ideas have no history, but lie at the basis of all history, whether history of the mind or of other things. They could not be derived from the experience which the individual has of empirical things. For how could we gather number, for instance, from things, if things were not already numerable ? And if they are, our idea of number requires no history except possibly of how it comes to clearness in our minds.

Then biology came to the help of half-hearted empiricism. The individual could not within a life-time acquire from external things through co-ordinated experiences of touch (or sight) and movement the notion of Space. But the acquisitions of a life might be transmitted from father to child, and the accumulated experience of generations might suffice. Thus, while Space or number are *a posteriori* for the race, derived from the observation of empirical things, they would be *a priori* for the individual who inherits the results of centuries of past experience. The biology, legitimate at the time the theory was formulated, has since become more than suspect. But

even if it were correct, how could experiences which were
not themselves spatial or numerical, no matter through
how many generations they were inherited, come to feel
or look like space or number ?

To Spencer's experiment succeeded the brilliant
hypothesis of William James, contained in the concluding chapter of his *Psychology*. Some of our experiences come to us through the front-door, by way of
sense ; some through the back-door, by way of our
cerebral (and mental) disposition. We see yellow when
a field of buttercups is presented to our eyes ; but
we also see yellow when we are dosed with the drug
santonin. The categories and all *a priori* ideas come to
us by this back-door method. By a fortunate variation
a brain is born whose mind envisages the world causally
or numerically, and being successful in its reactions to a
world which is causal and numerical, its kind prevails and
peoples the earth. The biology is above reproach, but
the theory is as defective as Kant's and, ironically enough,
its defects are much of the same sort. Unnecessary as
psychology, it will not bear examination as metaphysics.
It is assumed that I do not see causality or number in the
empirical object. But if so the analogy of the yellow
which we get either from the buttercup or from the optic
centres dosed with the drug is unavailable. In the first
place there is, so far as I am aware, no evidence that a
person who had never seen yellow from the buttercup or
other yellow objects would see yellow at all from santonin.
If the brain had not already functioned so as to see what
we call a yellow thing, would the stimulation of the optic
centre from within suffice ? This is a very seasonable
doubt, which, however, is too much connected theoretically
with a particular view of sensation to be dwelt on further
at this stage. Let us, however, suppose it to be possible ;
how would it help ? Let there be a mind which, when
the optic centre is stimulated in a special way, whether
from within or from without, sees yellow, and let it, not
having seen a buttercup before, see a buttercup. It
would see the shape of the buttercup and feel and smell
the flower, and it would see yellow. But why should it

·see the buttercup yellow ? Why attach the yellowness it sees to the buttercup ? Now the same question arises precisely with the *a priori* ideas. My brain when stimulated in a certain way thinks number or causality. But why does it attach number to this pile of shot, or causality to this murderer, if there is no number or causality written on the face of the empirical object ? You will have front-door experience *and* back-door experience ; but the problem to be solved is how the front-door perceptions come to be interpreted by the back-door ideas. If there are clues to guide the mind then the back-door ideas are not wanted. If there are none they are useless. Kant is avenged ; the mind is a veritable machine-shop of *a priori* ideas with which it fashions outward experience ; the accuser commits the very fault with which he unjustly charged the accused. And, over and above, the question remains which must not be answered here ; could any habit of mental action, due to endowment of brain, give us apprehension of number or causality, apart from the causality it enjoys in itself, unless it has exercised that causal habit at the call of some external causality ? The reservation contained in the words apart from its enjoyment of itself was not needed in the case of the yellow. For there the mind does not enjoy itself as yellow when the optic centre is drugged, but sees yellow in the same way as it sees a buttercup yellow.

The truth is, that no fortunate variation is needed to account for our envisaging the external world as causal and numerical. The brain and the mind themselves enjoy causality both internally in the relations of their processes and in their relation to things outside the brain or mind, and things outside are already causal and are so apprehended by the mind. The fortunate variations of brain or mind are not those which apprehend cause or number, for these belong to brain or mind as they belong to all things in space-time. The fortunate variations are those empirical ones, those special twists of talent or genius or sensibility, by which an individual discovers the law of gravitation or produces *Hamlet* or the Choral Symphony. We no more need a special gift for number than we need a special gift for yellow. In the one case we need eyes ; in the other case what we need is consciousness. Indeed, as we shall see more clearly hereafter, just because number and cause are categorial we do not need a special organ like eyes to apprehend them. We shall see that in contemplating causality outside itself the mind is aware in enjoyment of its own causality.

CHAPTER X

THE ONE AND THE MANY

The
categories
indefinable.

SPACE-TIME is thus the source of the categories, the non-empirical characters of existent things, which those things possess because of certain fundamental features of any piece of Space-Time. These fundamental features cannot be defined. For to define is to explain the nature of something in terms of other and in general simpler things, themselves existents. But there is nothing simpler than Space - Time, and nothing beside it to which it might be compared by way of agreement or contrast. They cannot even be described completely. For description, like definition, is effected by reference to existent entities. Not only all our language but all our conceptions are derived from existents, including in existents those of mathematics, particular figures or numbers. The utmost that we can do is therefore to describe in terms of what is itself the creation of Space-Time with its various features, and however little our description borrows from metaphor, it cannot but be a circuitous way of describing what is prior to the terms we use in our description and can therefore in the end only be indicated and known by acquaintance. Space-Time itself and all its features are revealed to us direct as red or sweet are. We attempt to describe what is only to be accepted as something given, which we may feel or apprehend ; to describe, as has been said above, the indescribable. With each category in turn we have indicated the basis of it in Space-Time—the occupation of Space-Time, the continuity of it which lies at the base of relation, its uniformity or the constancy of its ' curvature ' and the like. But it is plain that these descriptions are merely the best means open to us of inducing the reader to look and accept what he sees. The descriptions do nothing more than take the place of pointing with the finger.

More than once this has been propounded with regard to continuity, or to the statement that Space-Time is a continuum. A series of existents, say real numbers, occurs under certain conditions and then becomes a continuum. But we are in stating these conditions approximating to the original and indescribable feature of Space-Time which makes continuity of things in series possible. This original continuity is known only by acquaintance. The same thing is true of the infinity of Space-Time, and the remarks made upon this topic in a previous chapter [1] need not be repeated. Of the categories the same thing is true. Our description of Space-Time itself and of the features which belong to any bit of it is but a means of reaching by thought to what is deeper and more fundamental than the products of thought. It is a method which redounds to the honour of Space-Time in the same sense as it redounded to the honour of Cornelia to be named as the mother of the Gracchi.

Kant was thus mistaken in the sharp distinction which he drew between the forms of Space and Time and the categories. If our hypothesis is correct, empirical things are in the end complexes within that pure manifold of intuition of which he sometimes speaks ; and the categories belong to them because they are the fundamental features of Space-Time stuff. But there is a well-worn proposition familiar to idealists, and derived from Kant, that the source of the categories is not itself subject to the categories. This proposition is true. The categories applied for Kant to objects of experience, not to the mind which contributes them to experience. They apply in our conception of the matter to the empirical things which are special configurations in Space-Time and because they are such ; but they do not apply to Space-Time itself. Space-Time does not exist but is itself the

Space-Time not subject to the categories.

---

[1] Bk. I. ch. i. p. 40.

totality of all that exists.   Existence belongs to that
which occupies a space-time.   There is a perennial
question which is stilled by no assertion of its futility,
how the world came to exist or what made the world?
We can see at once the answer to the question, and
how far it is futile.   The world which is Space-Time
never and nowhere came into existence, for the infinite
becoming cannot begin to become.   It could only do so
in a larger Space and Time and at the order of some
cause exterior to it.   Now all existence arises within Space-
Time, and there is no cause which is not itself a part of
it.   Nor can we say that it has some neutral kind of
being, some being for thought.   For thought or thinking,
on our hypothesis that mind and things may be treated
on the same footing with proper regard for their empirical
difference, is an existent within Space-Time, and to say
that anything has being for thought means only that it
can be the object of thinking.   The being of the world
if it had such neutral being cannot be being for its own
creature.   Space-Time therefore does not exist but it is
existence itself, taken in the whole.   The question is thus
not so much futile as it needs enlightenment.   Space-
Time exists only in the loose usage of words in virtue of
which we have to say it is in Space and Time rather than
out of them—a matter to which we shall recur.

Space-Time is not universal ; for there is no plan of
it distinct from the execution.   Its only plan is to be
Space-Time.   Were it universal it must be repeated or
at least capable of repetition.   But how should the whole
of Space-Time be repeated ?   For if it could be, it would
not be the whole.   It is not, as we have attempted to
show at length, a relation, nor even a system of relations,
but it is through and through relational in the sense that
in virtue of its continuity there are relations between its
parts and the relations are themselves spatio-temporal.
Perhaps it is not necessary to run through the whole list
of categories to be assured that the father of them is not
also their child.   But two of them seem to lay special
claim to be applicable to Space-Time, the category of
substance and that of whole and part with its related

category of number. Is not Space-Time a whole, and a
one which includes many, and a substance? In each
case we must answer, no.

It is not a whole of parts, for a whole of parts is Not a
constituted by its parts, and is relative to other wholes of whole of
parts. Whereas Space-Time breaks up into parts and
wholes of them as it lives and moves. It is true a rock
may disintegrate into powder and still remain an aggregate
or whole ; but the whole is given to begin with. If
Space-Time were such a whole it would be given all at
once. But being Time (or indeed Space, which is the
same thing) it is not, as Mr. Bergson rightly says, given
altogether. To suppose so is to ignore the reality of
Time, to fail to take Time seriously. At any one
moment the universe is the whole of its existent parts,
but at any one moment the universe is not the whole
universe of parts. For in the redistribution of dates
among places, new existents are generated within the one
Space-Time. It may indeed be called not a whole of
parts, but the whole or system of all existents. But this
designation does but help us, by reference to the category
of whole and parts, to feel towards the infinitude of Space-
Time. In like manner Space-Time is in no case a unity
of many things ; it is not a one. For that implies that
it can descend into the field of number, and be merely an
individual, and be compared as one with two or three.
The universe is neither one in this sense, nor many.
Accordingly it can only be described not as one and still
less as a one, but as *the* one ; and only then because the
quasi-numerical adjective serves once more to designate
not its number but its infinite singularity ; or, as is more
clearly still expressed by calling it substance, that it is not
so much an individual or a singular as the one and only
matrix of generation, to which no rival is possible because
rivalry itself is fashioned within the same matrix.

It is not a substance, and only by a metaphor or Not a
analogy can it be called the infinite substance. For substanc
substance is an existent configuration of space in so far

as it is the theatre of Time ; it is a space with definite contour occupied by time, that is, is a space enduring in time. But infinite Space has no contours and is thus no substance. We are tempted still to call it substance because a complex substance like man is a grouping within its contour of many different substances, and we imagine Space-Time to be an extension of such a complex substance. In doing so we are forgetting that a substance however complex is related (by causality) to other substances and no such relation is possible for Space-Time as a whole. It may still be urged, substance is the occurrence of a space in time or the extension of time over a space, and infinite Space and Time are in the same relation to one another. But it is really only when you cut a finite [1] space out of the whole, or a finite time out of the whole, that it is possible in strictness to speak of a relation between the space and time of a substance. You can think of them apart from one another just because the time of which you speak is that part of a larger Time which is appropriated to the space in question, or because that part of Space is appropriated to the time in question. Infinite Space and infinite Time are one and the same thing, and cannot in reality be considered apart from one another. This statement is wholly independent of the question whether a finite space may not be sustained in its configuration through infinite time ; whether there may not be substances which having come into existence endure for ever ; which is entirely an empirical question to be settled by evidence.

When we attempt to extend the notion of substance to infinite Space-Time, we are in fact once more merely helping ourselves towards a statement of its infinite character, and the whole value of the attempt lies therein, and not in the use of the conception of substance. We are describing the infinite Space-Time as the substance which includes all substances and is the system of them. But the idea of infinity is prior to that of an infinite system of existents, which is really derived from it. We approximate to infinity by the notion of an infinite

[1] Or any space less than the whole.

system of existents, like numbers or substances, which is our conceptual reconstruction, by means of the blocks, of the quarry from which the stones were hewn. The infinite Space-Time is the totality of all substances, but it is prior to the substances by whose composition it is described. Thus to call it the one or the whole or the infinite substance is no more than to aim at its infinitude, in terms of the finite creatures of it. Only in this sense is it legitimate therefore to speak of the infinite substance.

In truth, infinite Space-Time is not the substance of substances, but it is the stuff of substances. No word is more appropriate to it than the ancient one of *hyle* (ὑλη). Just as a roll of cloth is the stuff of which coats are made but is not itself a coat, so Space-Time is the stuff of which all things, whether as substances or under any category, are made. If I call it the stuff and not the material, it is to avoid confusion with the very much more specific idea of matter, as matter is commonly understood. Matter is a finite complex of space-time with the material quality, as we shall afterwards see. The substance of the great writers of the seventeenth century is different from this stuff. It is the highest expression of the universe and not like Space-Time the universe in its lowest expression. Substance so understood is not mere persistence of Space in Time but means that which is absolutely self-contained and is the cause of itself. The stuff of the world is indeed self-contained in that there is nothing not included in it. But it is not the supreme individual or person or spirit, but rather that in which supreme individuality or personality is engendered, as we shall have to note in the sequel. Nor can it intelligibly be called the cause of itself. For causation is the more intimate relation between existent substances. To think of the world as causing itself is to imagine the world at one moment generating itself at the next moment, and splits the life of the world into independent moments which can no more account for causal relation than a motion can be explained as the succession of separate point-instants.

Space-Time as the stuff of things.

Thus Space-Time, the universe in its primordial form, is the stuff out of which all existents are made. It is Space-Time with the characters which we have found it to reveal to experience. But it has no 'quality' save that of being spatio-temporal or motion. All the wealth of qualities which makes things precious to us belongs to existents which grow within it, and which are in the first instance characterised by the categories. It is greater than all existent finites or infinites because it is their parent. But it has not as Space-Time their wealth of qualities, and being elementary is so far less than they are. Hence it repels two possible kinds of misdescription. It is first something positive. Not being subject to the categories it might be supposed to be entirely negative, not relation nor substance nor quantity nor number, not in time nor in space. It is in fact something very positive to which these determinations and all the qualities which depend on them owe their being. The other misconception is far more serious. Because it is not describable by categories the universe might be supposed to have characters or qualities superior to them. Thus Space-Time is not in space or time as though there were some enveloping Space or Time. It is itself the whole of spaces and times, as it is all existence, and all substance. But it must not therefore be supposed to be spaceless or timeless, out of Space or Time and to possess spacelessness or timelessness (eternity) as some superior qualities which confer upon it a unique character. All its characters are reflected in its children. Call it by what name you will, universe or God or the One, it is not above Space or Time. It is truer to use the careless expression, the universe is in Space and Time, than to describe it as timeless. Space and Time are, in the words of Spinoza, though not with the significance which he attaches to the phrase, attributes of the universe or Space-Time. In what sense there is divinity in the universe, we shall not attempt to understand till much later in our inquiry. Nor are we free to call it timeless or spaceless in order to separate it from the Time which is measured by the clock or the Space which is measured by the footrule.

There is only one Space and one Time, and though the mathematicians may deal with it by methods different from those of philosophy and common sense, it is still the same Space and Time which they all investigate each in its different way. It is such a misconception which has given rise to the notion of eternity as something different from Time and superior to it. But the only eternity which can be construed in terms of experience is infinite Time. If it is different from this it is out of all relation to Time, and if attributed to the world requires justification on its merits, and not because it may be thought to derive its nature from contrast with the alleged defects of ordinary empirical and mathematical Time. Space-Time therefore is ǀ neither in Time nor in Space ; but it *is* Time and it *is* Space.

Two topics now claim discussion which arise out of the relation of the whole Space-Time to its existents, and the questions so raised are answered from the same consideration, that the existents are of the same stuff as the whole. One is the ancient subject of the relation of the One and the Many. The other, which I will take first, is the distinction of the categorial and the empirical, the use of which must have already been the source of some difficulty in the course of the exposition. The nature of the distinction has been explained, but it must have seemed at times a shifting or evanescent one. I do not so much propose to ask again what is the distinction as to recapitulate the cases in which categorial and empirical seem to grade into each other. The categorial is the pervasive, and the empirical is the variable or contingent. But since categories are the fundamental features of, and space-time and empirical existents are variable complexes within, Space-Time, the boundaries of the categorial and the empirical are from the nature of the case hard to draw, and may seem indistinct and fluid. The *a priori* and the empirical are distinguished within experience itself. Both are experiential or in a general sense empirical. The strictly empirical is only the non-pervasive parts of experience, all experience being ultimately expressible in terms of Space-Time.

[marginal note:] Categorial empirical.

Strictly speaking, the empirical coincides with that which has quality. But we are compelled to recognise mere spatio-temporality as, in a sense, a quality, though it is in itself categorial. It is the meeting-point of the categorial and the empirical. Motion is categorial and is allied with the other categories which it sums up. But it is allied, on the other hand, in virtue of its unitary character with the series of obviously empirical qualities, red, sweet, life, consciousness. Hence it is that the various special determinations of the categories, of number, quantity, motion, are described in common philosophical language as primary qualities. To call spatio-temporality quality is little more than a name, but it illustrates the essential identity of stuff between the categorial and the empirical.

Once more the various geometrical figures are described as empirical, and the various numbers of arithmetic, including not only the ordinary integers but infinite numbers and surds. Number itself is categorial and so is Space. But the numbers and different figures in space are not pervasive but empirical. And yet we might be seeming to deal with categorial matter in treating these subjects. The distinction here is not so difficult to draw. It becomes much more difficult when we call point-instants themselves empirical,[1] though they are the very constituents of Space-Time, which is *a priori*, and the source of all that is *a priori*.

Another symptom of the intimacy of categorial and empirical was the difficulty experienced in respect of certain notions in determining whether they were categorial or not. Change being a relation of empirical terms could be assigned to the empirical, without much hesitation. But likeness and such thoughts as 'and' and 'but' and 'if' might easily be taken for categories of a derived order. 'Like' we decided to be empirical because it implied the overlapping of different universals in the same thing, and such overlapping is empirical and does not follow from the nature of Space-Time itself, but only from the fact that it breaks up into

[1] See above, ch. ix. pp. 324 ff.

complexes, and these complexes may exhibit the over-lapping of empirical universals.[1] 'And' means combination and 'but 'disjunction or obstruction between empirical data, but they are empirical relations and arise from the empirical character of their terms, when they are not purely extrinsic. Such notions as these, however categorial they may appear, lack the note of pervasiveness, and the reason of this is that they are not fundamental to any space-time as such.

Such difficulties in the working out of the distinction of categorial and empirical serve only to accentuate the intrinsic solidarity of the two. The whole empirical world may be described as, in its simplest terms, a multi-form determination under various circumstances of categorial characters. If the variable and the pervasive are alike Space-Time, this conclusion is natural. Any empirical thing is a configuration of space-time, when the thing is expressed in its simplest terms. And all categories are configurations of space-time. The only difference is in pervasiveness of the categorial as distinct from the empirical determinations. I am a fairly definite configuration of space-time; but I possess universality in so far as, being a man, my pattern is repeated else-where. In that respect I possess a character which every-thing shares with me. My empirical universal, the pattern of man, is shared with me only by other men. But all my empirical characters are specifications under my empirical conditions of categorial ones.

We come finally to the relation of the One to the Many? We are not asking yet what the One is, nor asserting anything other than that it is Space-Time; nor whether the elementary point-instants are monads like those of Leibniz or whether the complexes of them are governed by a dominating monad. These topics are not yet in place. Our question is whether the existents within Space-Time, being only crystals within that matrix, are lost in the reality of Space-Time or conserve their own. This question too has been already answered in

The One and the Many.

---

[1] See above, ch. iv. pp. 247 ff.

part by anticipation under the head of relation. For it is clear that Space-Time takes for us the place of what is called the Absolute in idealistic systems. It is an experiential absolute. All finites being complexes of space-time are incomplete. They are not the sum of reality. But their absorption into the One does not destroy their relative reality.[1] That could happen only if the real in which they are absorbed were of a different stuff from themselves. But to be a complex of space-time is to be of the stuff of which the universe consists. Now a configuration of motion is not destroyed by its relation to the circumambient medium but is, on the contrary, sustained thereby. It is the surrounding space from which the triangle is cut off which secures it its existence as a triangle. The society or State which is composed of individual men as citizens does not destroy the reality of its members as citizens but sustains it. Thus things being reducible in the end to these complex groupings of motions have such reality as falls to their share. They may be brief as the lightning in the collied night. They may be annihilated in the shock of motions within the domain of Space-Time, they may enter into new complexes and take on fresh empirical qualities, there may be ceaseless variation from the interplay of things ; or a thing may persist through appreciable durations, undergoing redistribution of motions and changing its qualities in correlation therewith, waxing and waning in bulk, even varying in shape and texture and yet preserving its substantial individuality, as when a man is mutilated by war or disease ; or it may persist eternally except for violence as the germ-plasm is said to do. My body (for I say nothing at present of my mind) dies and is resolved, like the rock, into its elements. There is here but a replacement of one kind of empirical reality by another. All these empirical variations take place within Space-Time and are changing configurations of it, and each of

---

[1] In the general conception of the relation of the parts to the whole of experience (which here appears as part of a systematic doctrine) I have been chiefly stimulated by Mr. Stout's metaphysical writings (in the *Proceedings of the Aristotelian Society*).

them being of Space-Time shares in the reality which belongs to its matrix. The difficulty is therefore not to be sure that a thing or a state of a thing or an event which happens to it really is but to know what it truly is. To discover this is the object of science. And owing to the imperfection of our minds which makes exact qualitative observation unattainable and the difficulties to be studied hereafter which stand in the way of exact apprehension of spatio-temporal figures of things, this object may be one to which we can only approach, but not attain.

Consider Space-Time, or indeed the universe however conceived, as lifted above its parts (or appearances as they then are called), as something from which they represent a fall and degeneration ; and the parts are unreal ultimately because of their finitude. Let it be the stuff or medium in which things are cultivated, and things of all kinds suffer from their finitude only in their incompleteness. They are not the whole reality but they are real in themselves, and it is only our imperfection as finites which conceals from us partially their true nature ; how that is they are delimited against each other in Space-Time. Within this matrix there may then be progressive types not so much of reality as of merit or perfection, as a rose may be a more perfect thing than a stone. There is room for an ascending scale of such perfection. But everything that truly is is really. The One is the system of the Many in which they are conserved not the vortex in which they are engulfed.

END OF VOL. I

Printed by R. & R. Clark, Limited, Edinburgh.

NEW WORKS ON PHILOSOPHY

THE IDEA OF PROGRESS: An Inquiry into its Origin and Growth. By J. B. BURY, M.A., Regius Professor of Modern History in the University of Cambridge. 8vo.

MIND-ENERGY. By Professor HENRI BERGSON. Translated by Professor H. WILDON CARR, in collaboration with the Author. 8vo.

IMPLICATION AND LINEAR INFERENCE. By BERNARD BOSANQUET, LL.D., F.B.A. Crown 8vo. 7s. 6d. net.

THE REIGN OF RELIGION IN CONTEMPORARY PHILOSOPHY. By S. RADHAKRISHNAN, M.A., Professor of Philosophy in the University of Mysore, Author of "The Philosophy of Rabindranath Tagore." Extra Crown 8vo.

A CRITICAL HISTORY OF GREEK PHILOSOPHY. By W. T. STACE, B.A. Crown 8vo.

ESSAYS IN CRITICAL REALISM: A Co-operative Study of the Problem of Knowledge. By DURANT DRAKE, Professor of Philosophy in Vassar College; ARTHUR O. LOVEJOY, Professor of Philosophy in Johns Hopkins University; JAMES BISSETT PRATT, Professor of Philosophy in Williams College; ARTHUR K. ROGERS, Professor of Philosophy in Yale University; GEORGE SANTAYANA, Late Professor of Philosophy in Harvard University; ROY WOOD SELLARS, Associate Professor of Philosophy in the University of Michigan; C. A. STRONG, Late Professor of Psychology in Columbia University. 8vo.

LONDON : MACMILLAN AND CO., LTD.

OTHER WORKS ON PHILOSOPHY

THE PHILOSOPHY OF RABINDRANATH TAGORE.
By Professor S. RADHAKRISHNAN. 8vo. 8s. 6d. net.

PROBLEMS OF THE SELF. An Essay based on the
Shaw Lectures, 1914. By Professor JOHN LAIRD. 8vo.
12s. net.

THE INTUITIVE BASIS OF KNOWLEDGE. An
Epistemological Enquiry. By Professor N. O. LOSSKY. With
Preface by Professor G. DAWES HICKS. 8vo. 16s. net.

MENS CREATRIX: an Essay. By Rev. Canon W.
TEMPLE. 8vo. 7s. 6d. net.

DEVELOPMENT AND PURPOSE. An Essay towards
a Philosophy of Evolution. By Professor L. T. HOBHOUSE.
8vo. 12s. 6d. net.

DICTIONARY OF PHILOSOPHY AND PSYCHO-
LOGY. Edited by Dr. JAMES MARK BALDWIN. With
Illustrations and Extensive Bibliographies. Crown 4to.
Vol. I. New Edition. 60s. net. Vol. II. New Edition.
60s. net. Vol. III., in two parts. 70s. net.

ENCYCLOPAEDIA OF THE PHILOSOPHICAL
SCIENCES. Edited by WILHELM WINDELBAND and ARNOLD
RUGE. English Edition under the Editorship of Sir HENRY
JONES. 8vo.

> VOL. I. LOGIC. By ARNOLD RUGE, WILHELM WINDEL-
> BAND, JOSIAH ROYCE, LOUIS COUTURAT, BENEDETTO CROCE,
> FEDERIGO ENRIQUES, and NICOLAJ LOSSKIJ. 10s. net.

THE SCHOOLS OF PHILOSOPHY. A History of
the Evolution of Philosophical Thought. By Various Writers.
Edited by Sir HENRY JONES. 8vo.

> THE EVOLUTION OF EDUCATIONAL THEORY.
> By Professor JOHN ADAMS, LL.D. 12s. 6d. net.

> GREEK PHILOSOPHY. Part I. Thales to Plato. By
> Professor JOHN BURNET, LL.D. 12s. 6d. net.

> THE HISTORY OF MODERN PHILOSOPHY FROM
> HOBBES TO REID. By Professor G. F. STOUT.
> *[In preparation.*

LONDON: MACMILLAN AND CO., LTD.

2

Works by Prof. HENRI BERGSON

CREATIVE EVOLUTION. Translated by ARTHUR MITCHELL, Ph.D. 8vo. 12s. 6d. net.

LAUGHTER : An Essay on the Meaning of the Comic. Authorised Translation from the Sixth Edition by CLOUDESLEY BRERETON, L. es L. (Paris), M.A. (Cantab.) ; and FRED ROTHWELL, B.A. (London). Extra Crown 8vo. 4s. 6d. net.

AN INTRODUCTION TO METAPHYSICS. Translated by T. E. HULME. Crown 8vo. 2s. 6d. net.

MIND-ENERGY. Translated by Prof. H. WILDON CARR, in collaboration with the Author. 8vo. [In the Press.

A CRITICAL EXPOSITION OF BERGSON'S PHILOSOPHY. By J. M'KELLAR STEWART, B.A., D.Phil. Extra Crown 8vo. 6s. 6d. net.

HENRI BERGSON. An Account of his Life and Philosophy. By ALGOT RUHE and NANCY MARGARET PAUL. With Portrait. Extra Crown 8vo. 6s. 6d. net.

THE PHILOSOPHY OF CHANGE. A Study of the Fundamental Principle of the Philosophy of Bergson. By H. WILDON CARR. 8vo. 7s. 6d. net.

Works by Prof. HARALD HÖFFDING

A HISTORY OF MODERN PHILOSOPHY : A Sketch of the History of Philosophy from the Close of the Renaissance to our own Day. Translated by B. E. MEYER. Two vols. 8vo. 18s. net each.

THE PROBLEMS OF PHILOSOPHY. Translated by GALEN M. FISHER, and a Preface by WILLIAM JAMES. Globe 8vo. 5s. 6d. net.

THE PHILOSOPHY OF RELIGION. Translated by B. E. MEYER. 8vo. 15s. net.

A BRIEF HISTORY OF MODERN PHILOSOPHY. Translated by C. F. SANDERS. Crown 8vo. 9s. net.

MODERN PHILOSOPHERS : Lectures ; and Lectures on Bergson. Translated by ALFRED C. MASON, M.A. Crown 8vo. 6s. 6d. net.

OUTLINES OF PSYCHOLOGY. Translated by M. E. LOWNDES. Crown 8vo. 7s. net.

LONDON : MACMILLAN AND CO., LTD.

Works by BENEDETTO CROCE

PHILOSOPHY OF THE PRACTICAL. Economic and Ethic. Translated by DOUGLAS AINSLIE, B.A. 8vo. 14s. net.

ÆSTHETIC AS SCIENCE OF EXPRESSION AND GENERAL LINGUISTIC. Translated by DOUGLAS AINSLIE, B.A. 8vo. 12s. 6d. net.

LOGIC AS THE SCIENCE OF THE PURE CONCEPT. Translated by DOUGLAS AINSLIE, B.A. 8vo. 14s. net.

WHAT IS LIVING AND WHAT IS DEAD OF THE PHILO-SOPHY OF HEGEL. Translated by DOUGLAS AINSLIE, B.A. 8vo. 10s. net.

THE PHILOSOPHY OF BENEDETTO CROCE: The Problem of Art and History. By H. WILDON CARR, Hon.D.Litt. 8vo. 7s. 6d. net.

Works by Dr. BERNARD BOSANQUET

THE PRINCIPLE OF INDIVIDUALITY AND VALUE. Gifford Lectures for 1911. 8vo. 12s. 6d. net.

THE VALUE AND DESTINY OF THE INDIVIDUAL. Gifford Lectures for 1912. 8vo. 12s. 6d. net.

THREE LECTURES ON ÆSTHETIC. Ex. Cr. 8vo. 4s. 6d. net.

THE PHILOSOPHICAL THEORY OF THE STATE. 8vo. 12s. 6d. net.

THE ESSENTIALS OF LOGIC. Crown 8vo. 4s. net.

PSYCHOLOGY OF THE MORAL SELF. Cr. 8vo. 4s. 6d. net.

SOCIAL AND INTERNATIONAL IDEALS. Studies in Patriotism. Crown 8vo. 6s. net.

SOME SUGGESTIONS IN ETHICS. Crown 8vo. 6s. net.

IMPLICATION AND LINEAR INFERENCE. Cr. 8vo. 7s. 6d. net.

Works by Dr. F. C. S. SCHILLER

RIDDLES OF THE SPHINX. A Study in the Philosophy of Humanism. 8vo. 10s. net.

HUMANISM. Philosophical Essays. 8vo. 10s. net.

STUDIES IN HUMANISM. 8vo. 10s. net.

FORMAL LOGIC: A Scientific and Social Problem. 8vo. 10s. net.

Works by Prof. WILLIAM JAMES

THE PRINCIPLES OF PSYCHOLOGY. Two vols. 8vo. 31s. 6d. net.

TEXT-BOOK OF PSYCHOLOGY. Crown 8vo. 9s. net.

LONDON: MACMILLAN AND CO., LTD.